WEIRD FLORIDA II: IN A STATE OF SHOCK

ELIOT KLEINBERG

Weird Florida II: In a State of Shock

Eliot Kleinberg

ISBN 0-9771079-3-0

Published by
Chapin House Books
The Popular Book Division of
The Florida Historical Society Press
435 Brevard Avenue
Cocoa, FL 32922

Phone: (321) 690-1971
Email: wynne@flahistory.net

To Florida's journalists, especially my colleagues at the Palm Beach *Post*. If we hadn't seen all this with our own eyes, we wouldn't have believed it.

TODAY IN FLORIDA HISTORY

December 2, 1925: The Florida Cattle Tick Eradication Committee, founded in 1916, formally changed its name today to the Florida Chamber of Commerce.

—Florida Historical Society

WEIRD FLORIDA II: IN A STATE OF SHOCK

In 1998, *Weird Florida* made the bold statement that Florida "is the home of more nuttiness per square mile than any place on earth—and we dare the world to prove us wrong."

A few tried—California comes to mind—but no one came close.

And that was before:

The 2000 presidential election and the infamous "Butterfly Ballot."

Elian Gonzalez.

Most of the September 11 terrorists found to have lived and trained in South Florida.

The *National Enquirer* writing about being attacked by anthrax and not making it up.

The American Civil Liberties Union rising to the defense of a Palm Beach resident and confessed drug addict named Rush Limbaugh.

In fact, it seems the only crazy story lately that didn't have a Florida connection was O.J. Simpson. Oh. Wait. He lives here now.

So we figured the time was right for another round of stories -- some sad, some disturbing, but most pretty funny—from the land that seems to draw offbeat people like the Everglades draws mosquitoes.

The most remarkable aspect of Florida's weirdness is that few in Florida are surprised by it. They just shrug and put up with it.

In May 1999, a cow and her 3-week-old calf broke out of a South Florida pasture, walked through three miles of neighborhood streets to the Intracoastal Waterway, and jumped in. The next day, the local newspaper had a front-page photograph of a cow, ankle-deep in water, leaping to shake a lasso thrown from a police boat.

Later in the morning, calls came into the newsroom about that picture. It wasn't people calling to say, "Oh my God. There are cows in the Intracoastal." Instead, nonplussed readers were calling to say, "Ya know, you called that an Angus and I think ya got a Brahman there."

We even had trouble finishing this book. Things kept happening. For example: Miami-area police use a Taser on a 6-year-old. A goat and kangaroo found walking down a road in St. Lucie County turn out to belong to a former rapper. And a Hollywood woman claims her 10-year-old cheese sandwich bears an image of the Virgin Mary.

That all happened in *the same week*.

When *Weird Florida* came out, some people didn't get it. Famed radio commentator Paul Harvey called it "a cry for help." He described it not as a loving celebration of Florida's colorful aspects but rather an exposé on the order of *The Jungle*, Upton Sinclair's shocking look at Chicago's slaughterhouses.

And one reviewer on an on-line bookseller's web page wrote, "This shows just what a mosquito-filled muck hole, sand-flea infested, white-trash flooded, odd-ball inhabited place Florida really is. It made me glad I didn't live there."

At first such reactions hurt us deeply. Then, we thought: Florida's population has gone from two million at the start of World War II, to 17½ million now. If even one person reads this book and decides not to move to Florida after all, the public humiliation is worth it.

In that spirit, we bring you *Weird Florida II: In a State of Shock*.

WEIRD FLORIDA II: IN A STATE OF SHOCK
TABLE OF CONTENTS

SECTION I:

THE WEIRD FLORIDA HALL OF FAME
21ST CENTURY INDUCTEES

BUTTERFLIES OVER PALM BEACH:
THE 2000 PRESIDENTIAL ELECTION

REFLECTIONS BY AN EYEWITNESS

The 2000 Presidential election was the most dramatic political event in U.S. history. Some could suggest Watergate or the infamous 1876 election. But never before have the stakes been so high or, because of technology, the public's access to every single moment so widespread.

Waiting a month for a president in a time of street-corner newsboys and telegraphs and world isolationism is one thing. Waiting a month to pick the most powerful single political figure in the world amid live trucks and web pages is something different.

When the selection of president of the United States comes down to one county, and the number of voters deciding who will have his finger on the nuclear button, and who will be a regular on Sunday television talk shows, could fit in the ballroom of a hotel, that's serious business.

But the circumstances that led to this national crisis were so unusual, and events spiraled from that in such exponential degrees of weirdness, that you just have to laugh, whether your guy ended up winning or not.

All of those dumb Floridians who couldn't figure out the ballot? Three years earlier, they were dumb Long Islanders. Florida doesn't have a stupid ray.

And this all happened in Florida not because we're all stupid or can't do things right. This was one of those 10-car collisions in which many different factors had to all come into play.

You had the closest race in more than a century, the race coming down to one state, that state coming down to a few hundred votes, and the equivalent of one precinct spread among millions of voters. And a county with a demographic of elderly voters that spurred a well-meaning elections supervisor to

3

design a ballot she never realized would cause perhaps thousands of Jewish retirees to vote for...Pat Buchanan.

Oh, and by the way, the elections supervisor whose design might have cost Al Gore the White House was a Democrat. The Secretary of State, whose rulings might have given George W. Bush the White House, was one of Bush's state campaign chairmen. The Attorney General was Gore's state campaign chairman.

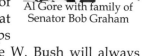

And the governor was George W. Bush's brother.

We will never know who really won the presidential election. The vote was so close and so many people intended to vote for one of these guys, but regardless of whose fault it was, their vote was not counted. And that means both of these men were victims. Al Gore perhaps

Al Gore with family of Senator Bob Graham

should be the president of the United States. George W. Bush will always have an asterisk next to an election that perhaps he won fair-and-square.

And the villain in this mess was not Bush, or Gore, or Katherine Harris, or either Supreme Court. It was a dinosaur of a voting system that was an absolute time bomb.

The tossing of numerous ballots in election after election had suggested this system was unreliable. But commissioners were not in a hurry to pick new voting machines over more cops, and voters weren't exactly flooding them with e-mails about it. Even the press dropped the ball. Reporters should have been asking tough questions when thousands of ballots were tossed

George W. Bush

out every year—some 10,000 in Palm Beach County alone in the 1996 race. But no one raised a voice because the races were never close.

A Brazilian journalist who covered Washington said on a Sunday talk show his countrymen back home couldn't understand how the world's great democracy and a technological leader could allow its most precious privilege to be victim to the whims of a cardboard card and a tiny punch.

Of course, everyone quickly lined up to get rid of the punch cards. One Palm Beach County commissioner said he'd supply his boat to take the machines out to sea and dump them overboard.

THE BUTTERFLY BALLOT

While the ballot seems simple enough spread out on a television screen, when it's shoved into that machine and you have to stick that little pin in and there's about a quarter-inch between the hole and the card, it's a different story.

And what appeared to be a circus on television, the painstaking recount, actually was the one part that wasn't circus. It was laborious work by people who didn't deserve the grief they got.

It isn't easy staring at a dimpled chad and thinking, "Well, this person obviously meant to vote for someone. But who?"

Chicago's Cook County, Illinois, threw out 100,000 ballots. You think it was a circus here? Could you imagine a recount in Chicago, which invented voting irregularities as an art form?

What made Palm Beach County the center of the world for a month was an intended good deed by elections supervisor Theresa LePore. Worried that retirees couldn't read the fine print, she put the ballot on two pages instead of one. Its alignment gave it a name: the "butterfly ballot."

But people said they feared their vote for Gore was registered as a vote for Pat Buchanan. In fact, Buchanan got more than 3,400 votes in Palm Beach County, a fifth of his total for Florida. Those 3,400 votes were one thing, but then Florida, the swing state in a razor-thin electoral race, went to George W. Bush by some 300 votes.

Three hundred.

That sparked recounts upon recounts and the national media swarmed into Palm Beach County.

After even Pat Buchanan conceded he couldn't possibly have received all those votes in Palm Beach County, U.S. Representative Mark Foley insisted that maybe all those Jewish retirees, Haitians, other blacks, Hispanics and retired union workers really intended to vote for Buchanan, not exactly a darling of those demographics.

On that first Saturday night, it started getting really weird. A former local TV news anchor and all-around toastmaster, Bob Nichols, had recently gotten out of the business he'd been in for 31 years. He'd left for a channel that then went belly-up when its executives were arrested. Nichols volunteered to be a spokesman for LePore that Saturday, November 11th. At a late night news conference, the eyes of the world were on Nichols and the world got a new buzzword: chad.

It's the tiny scrap of cardboard that's punched out of the ballot card when you vote. The manual recount focused on chads that didn't get punched all the way out. In a federal court hearing in Miami to stop the recount, the Bush campaign entered into evidence a videotape of Nichols' lecture, arguing it was evidence that the recount had become a fiasco.

Here's a quick chad glossary:

Pregnant chad or dimpled chad: still completely connected but has an indentation that suggested the voter wanted to punch it but just didn't press hard enough.

Hanging chad: one corner of the rectangle still attached to the ballot.

Swinging chad: two corners attached.

Tri-chad: three corners attached.

Garage door chad: attached only by the top and hanging like an overhead garage door.

Sunshine rule: light shines through the chad.

It didn't take long to find Chad Chad. He lived in San Leandro, Calif. and was an executive producer for a San Francisco-based television talk show. Turns out his real name is Chad Glen—actually he was born Glen Scillian— but he didn't want to mess with an unlisted number so he put "Chad Chad" in the phone book so people wouldn't bother him.

"I'm nothing more than a discarded hole," he groaned. "An anonymous paper slug."

"JERK"

Once the national television corps arrived, they wasted no time showing that they hadn't spent even 90 seconds learning basic information about the place they were presenting to the world.

They said "Palm Beach" when they meant "West Palm Beach." They said "Palm Beach" when they meant "Palm Beach County." They said "West Palm Beach County" or "Palm County" when they meant "Palm Beach County." They said "Condado del Oeste Palm Beach" when they meant "Condado del Palm Beach."

They said "Palm Beach community leader" when they meant "Boca Raton resident." They said "Boca ruh-TAHN" when they meant "Boca ruh-TONE." They said "Palm Springs" when they meant "West Palm Beach." They said "South Palm Beach" when they meant "Palm Beach County." They said "the county airport" when they meant "Palm Beach International Airport."

They said "interested citizen and lawsuit plaintiff, Andre Fladell" when they meant "longtime Democratic power broker, Andre Fladell." They said "commission chair Carol Roberts" when they meant "commissioner Carol Roberts."

They said, "We declare George W. Bush the winner at 2:23 a.m.," when they meant, "Well, maybe not."

Then, there were the lawyers.

Just hours after spokesmen for both sides insisted they didn't want to drag the close race into the courts, several lawsuits were filed in local and federal courts in West Palm Beach, Fort Lauderdale, and Tallahassee.

And Harvard constitutional scholar and former O.J. Simpson lawyer Alan Dershowitz, in town to represent people confused by the butterfly ballot, got into a shouting match November 16 with Fort Lauderdale attorney and law professor Bruce Rogow, who was representing elections supervisor Theresa LePore. Dershowitz called Rogow arrogant and a publicity hound. Rogow called Dershowitz "a jerk" who "never met a camera he didn't like."

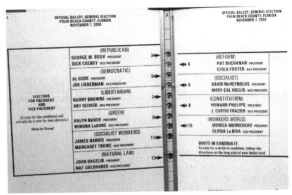

The infamous butterfly ballot in Palm Beach County

On November 14, no fewer than five judges recused themselves from hearing lawsuits about ballots and recounts. As he watched judge number five—Chief Judge Walter Colbath—on television, circuit judge Jorge Labarga said, "Thank God it's not me." Moments later, Colbath handed the case to Labarga.

And there were accusations of chads on the floor and even chads being eaten. On November 18, canvassing board judge Chuck Burton interrupted counting to remind counters to go outside if they wanted a soft drink. He said, "Heaven forbid we have something spill on a ballot. We'll be back in federal court."

Gore supporters march in Tallahassee.

In Florida, one thing's more important than picking the leader of the free world. As many as 300 national reporters who'd descended on Tallahassee for the continuing ballot squabble found themselves booted from their hotel rooms because of longstanding reservations for the November 18 Florida-Florida State college football game, which is a huge rivalry anyway, but this year featured the country's third-and fourth-ranked teams. Some found places 40 miles away; others rented rooms in fraternity houses. There was one report that among those booted was James Baker, the Tallahassee point man for George W. Bush.

Other countries had a field day with Florida's fiasco. Cuba denounced Florida as a "banana republic." In the Mexican daily *Reforma*, columnist René Delgado wrote, "If what had happened in the United States were to happen in Panama, the Marines would have already landed." And a group of Russian delegates offered to act as observers. Yeah. Russians.

"GOT CHAD?"

Of course, capitalism was at work.

Almost immediately, official samples of the infamous Palm Beach County ballot began selling on the eBay Internet auction site for as high as $127.50.

Two Lake Worth men were charged with trying to sell, also on eBay, an entire voting machine, complete with butterfly ballot. Later, the county decided to get into the business itself, to help pay the millions it would cost to replace the punch card machines with computer touch screens.

The Palm Beach County Tourist Development Council set up a booth in front of the Emergency Operations Center, where the ballots were being counted, and provided kits to out-of-town journalists.

"The reporters are looking for different angles and killing time," executive director J. Charles Lehmann said. "They can't leave, so we came to them."

A representative of Blopens, an Exton, Pennsylvania-based maker of magic markers that double as makeshift airbrushes, handed out free samples, flanked by mascot Billy Blopen, a woman dressed in a bright red, 6-foot-tall costume intended to resemble a marker. Billy Blopen carried a sign reading, "When will it finally 'blo' over?"

The best signs & T-shirts:

"Have lottery recount. My aunt punched wrong number."

(Flown behind a plane) "Surrender Gorethy."

"It's the count, stupid."

"Will flash for Gore."

"Got Chad?"

"The great thing about democracy is that it gives every voter a chance to do something stupid."

"We warned you. Signed: The Green Party"

Simon Goldfeder, 36, of Rochester, N.Y., had a sign that said "Lesbians against Cheney—we hate Bush" on one side and an obscenity playing off George W. Bush's last name on the other. He introduced himself as a "political terrorist" and then, after pondering the question for a moment, appeared to decide his career was a furniture maker. Answer to why he was there: "Because I'm a media whore."

Deborah Howell, in her 30s (she refused to give her age), a West Palm Beach paralegal, carried a Grinch doll with "Gore" marked in black across its chest and a poster that said, "How Gore stole the votes."

Street theatre was in full force.

Two California Republicans presented a take-off on Johnny Carson's "Amazing Carnac" skit. Doug MacKenzie wore a shimmering gold cape and turban and called himself "The Amazing Gorenac." Cohort John Durkin held a mock ballot to MacKenzie's forehead and asked him to divine which candidate it favored. MacKenzie incorrectly guessed that the ballot, marked for Bush, was meant for Gore.

Jesse Jackson, not satisfied with wall-to-wall coverage of his November 13 rally in downtown West Palm Beach, showed up the next day at the Emergency Operations Center, west of town, where he commandeered the county's stage and began a 20-minute tirade that the national press dutifully recorded. Inside the building, county officials seethed that Jackson had invited himself to use county property for a speech without asking first.

The Rev. Jesse Jackson speaks at a rally at the Capitol in Tallahassee.

Another time, as County Commissioner Carol Roberts stepped to the truck bed in front of the EOC that had served as a stage, a barricade fell over with a resounding bang that sounded just like a gunshot, causing the already exhausted and testy Roberts to jump.

State Representative Irving Slosberg, a Democrat from the Boca Raton area, went from reporter to reporter the week of the election demonstrating a "Votomatic" machine similar to the one used in the county to emphasize voting problems. After Commissioner Mary McCarty demanded to know how Slosberg got his hands on a piece of official county voting machinery, Slosberg said the machine had disappeared.

David Letterman stage hand Biff Henderson, sent down to "report" on the circus for the late night television show, used his professional acumen to guess that the November 13 rally led by Jesse Jackson drew 20,000 people. Most estimates placed it at 2,500.

Katherine Harris

On November 16, a representative of a comedy web page asked county judge Chuck Burton if he was having an affair with Carol Roberts. Burton, already at wit's end, suggested the man find a home on the Howard Stern radio show.

Here's the good that came out of all of this. Those cards are gone. People have finally realized that the corny mantra, "Every single vote counts," turned out to be right.

Palm Beach *Post*, November 8-December 14, 2004

POSTSCRIPT

Katherine Harris was elected to Congress in 2002.

In 2004, a real estate investor was charged with driving his silver Cadillac onto a Sarasota sidewalk and aiming it at Harris and about a dozen supporters before swerving at the last second. The former Florida Secretary of State was campaigning for reelection. Barry Seltzer was charged with aggravated assault. The registered Democrat told police the group had impeded traffic. "I intimidated them with my car. I was exercising my political expression. I did not run them down. I scared them a little."

Harris was reelected.

Associated Press/Palm Beach *Post*,
October 28, November 3, November 4, 2004

Palm Beach County Elections Supervisor Theresa LePore designed the butterfly ballot.

Theresa LePore was defeated for reelection in 2004.

In 2002, a 63-year-old suburban Lake Worth woman registered her poodle, Cocoa Fernandez, to vote. When the dog got its own card, LePore, already a national punching bag after the 2000 presidential election fracas, became the butt of jokes all over again. LePore later filed a criminal complaint against the woman. She also said the poodle would never have been able to vote since voters had to present their cards and photo identification.

Palm Beach *Post*, December 13, 2001

Two years after Democrats lost Florida in the presidential election, the state's Democratic party sold its Tallahassee headquarters to a West Palm Beach law firm. The party had been in the 2,900-square-foot antebellum mansion since 1976. Some say the building, known locally as the Towle House, is haunted. In 1994, several party workers complained to a reporter that they heard mysterious voices, slamming doors and furniture scraping the floor in the middle of the night. Simon Towle, who built the house in 1847, was a Whig Party leader

The Florida Democrat Party sold the-Towle house, supposedly haunted by a Whig.

who served as Tallahassee mayor, a legislator and state comptroller. The Whig Party disintegrated in 1855, and its followers went on to found, of all things, the Republican Party.

Palm Beach *Post*, July 2, 2002

ELIAN—A LITTLE BOY AND A LOT OF NOISE

During a visit to Cuba in late 2000, a South Florida reporter heard a joke that goes like this:

It's the year 2020, and there's a man with a sign protesting in front of the capitol building in Havana. He's shouting: "Free Elian! Free Elian!"

A woman walks by. "Free Elian?" she says. "But they returned him to our country 20 years ago."

"I know," replies the man. "I am Elian!"

For five months in 2000, the center of the universe was a small house in Miami's Little Havana section. There, a 6-year-old boy played on a swing set while hundreds surrounded him, willing to die to keep him in America.

His fate became the biggest international incident between America and Cuba since the Bay of Pigs and the Missile Crisis.

This famous photograph of federal agents seizing Elian Gonzalez earned a Pulitzer Prize. (Al Diaz, Associated Press)

It forced a national debate about whether a boy needs to be with his father, even if that means denying a mother's dying wish and returning him to the very dictatorship from which she lost her life trying to rescue him – and, in the process, giving a propaganda victory to South Florida Cubans' greatest villain.

The saga ended in one of the most dramatic police raids ever seen, ordered by no less an authority than the U.S. Attorney General. The photograph of a helmeted and rifle-toting agent confronting a terrified Elian, and the fisherman who had rescued him, in a bedroom closet won the photographer a Pulitzer Prize and became a lasting image.

Elian's mother and her boyfriend had decided to go the way of so many oppressed Cubans by slipping out of the Communist island nation in a motorboat for the ocean journey from Cuba to the Promised Land.

But the 16-foot boat, overcrowded with a dozen people, capsized two days later, on November 25, 1999. Everyone was thrown into the water. Everyone drowned—except one.

Some fishermen later found the boy, a month shy of his 6th birthday, clinging to an inner tube.

It was Thanksgiving Day.

Authorities turned Elian over to relatives in Miami and made plans to send him back to his father in Cuba. That's when the fireworks started.

The lawyer for Elian Gonzalez' father released this photograph of a smiling Elian hours after he was taken from his Miami relatives.

PROTECTED BY DOLPHINS

From the beginning, the Elian Gonzalez story had religious overtones for the passionate Cuban exiles who already see Fidel Castro as the embodiment of Satan and the fight to free their home island as the ultimate confrontation of good and evil.

One story said dolphins had circled the boy to protect him after the boat sank.

Some compared the rescue to the tale of drowning fishermen saved by the Virgin of Charity, the patron saint of Cuba.

Some saw Elian as Moses, put on the churning waters of the ocean by his mother and rescued so he could return to Cuba and lead his people to freedom.

Then there were those who noted his arrival just weeks before Christmas and the changing of the millennium.

There was the rumor that Castro needed the boy back to meet some condition of Santeria, the part-Christian, part-African religious following. Another said a Santeria priestess had warned Castro he would be overthrown by a child saved by dolphins at sea, and the leader needed the boy back in order to neutralize him.

It turned out later that Sister Jeanne O'Laughlin, president of Barry University and one of those negotiating for a peaceful settlement to the standoff, had been given a letter from one of Elian's Miami relatives which said he believed the Cuban leader planned to make a witchcraft sacrifice of Elian.

As the weeks dragged on, so did the debate.

The federal government said Elian was no different from all the others who came under a 1995 law that said all refugees intercepted at sea must be returned to Cuba.

One court after another agreed, all the way to the Supreme Court.

And many Americans chided their Cuban-American neighbors as ingrates and hypocrites. They said the Cubans were defying the very federal government that had taken them in and forgetting they had fled Cuba for a country that believed in the rule of law.

"Last time I checked, kidnapping and hostage taking were against the law in the United States," New York *Times* columnist Bob Herbert wrote.

And the Chicago *Tribune* said in an editorial, "The U.S. ought to endeavor to wrest our Cuba policy from the hands of Miami's lunatic fringes."

Exiles said the average American, born in freedom, had no idea from whence their ardor came. It wasn't the father the boy would be returned to, they said, but instead the state—and Fidel.

Even presidential candidate Al Gore broke somewhat with his boss, President Clinton, by suggesting Congress grant Elian permanent resident status.

But even some Cuban-Americans said those who wanted Elian to stay didn't speak for all of them.

Soon supporters of Elian were voting with their feet. Whether out of curiosity, as a show of support, or to form a human shield, hundreds began an around-the-clock vigil around the home.

The street had the look of a carnival, complete with vendors.

TV trucks paid to permanently park in swales and crews set up tables and tents for the long haul. Many times, reporters outnumbered protestors.

A man who showed up with a sign reading "Send Elian home" was pushed and shoved by the crowd before policed rescued him.

Every time a strange vehicle showed up, protestors locked arms and formed a chain to block the front of Casa Elian from anyone who might want to take the boy.

And in a scene more reminiscent of Alabama Governor George Wallace at the schoolhouse door, the two local mayors took a defiant stand.

Miami Mayor Joe Carollo, dubbed "Crazy Joe" years earlier by local columnists for his bombast and his communist-under-every-bed mentality, and Miami-Dade County Mayor Alex Penelas, who would be trashed in a 2004 U.S. Senate run, said they would not provide police assistance to any federal attempt to take Elian from the home. The federal government, they said, was on its own.

"ELIAN IS CHRIST"

In March 2000, an oily smudge appeared on a bank window near the Miami home. People gathered around it, some weeping and calling it an image of the Virgin Mary that had materialized in support of Elian and keeping him in

America. Later, a spot appeared on a mirror in the boy's very bedroom. It supposedly resembled the Virgin of Guadeloupe, said to have shown herself to a Mexican peasant more than four centuries ago.

One side outside the home read, "Do not deliver Elian to the Romans." Another said, "Elian is Christ. Reno is Lucifer. Castro is Satan."

On March 29, 2000, a crowd estimated at 10,000 formed a giant human cross in Little Havana during a prayer vigil for the boy. A bishop noted that Jesus was saved by his parents, who fled Herod's order to slay the male infants. In the same way, Elian's mother and stepfather spirited him away from Castro, the bishop said.

"In Cuba, some people have made Elian a symbol of the new Che (Guevara) so it is not so unusual that some people in Miami are seeing him as the new Christ," said the Rev. Gustavo Miyares of Immaculate Conception Church in Hialeah, who was one of the organizers of the prayer vigil.

Outside Little Havana, life went on in South Florida.

"Within Cuban exile Miami, this is a hugely important story. Outside that community, there are a lot of people who are sick of it, who are just saying, 'Send the kid home and get it over with," Miami *Herald* columnist Robert Steinback wrote.

The boy's grandmothers were flown to Miami, where they had a brief and harried meeting at a municipal airport. One later said she bit his tongue as a show of affection and inspected his penis to see how much he had grown.

The boy's father, a cashier at a resort hotel, was reportedly offered $2 million, a house and a job by his Miami relatives if he agreed to stay in America with Elian, but responded, "I have no price on my son." He flew from Cuba and waited for more than a week for his child. He said he would not meet with the relatives until the boy was back in his custody. The relatives filed an affidavit saying Elian's father had abused both his former wife and Elian.

When the family released a tape of Elian saying, "I don't want to go back to my father," opponents trashed them. They said the boy had been showered with gifts, worshipped by strangers and fed propaganda from relatives at an intensity and length that would make Castro himself proud. They called the tape a manipulation bordering on child abuse itself. And they suggested the well being of a little boy had been forgotten in the efforts to use him as a pawn in an international incident.

A pediatrician advising the federal government said later that the boy's Miami relatives were psychologically abusing him and he should be removed from them immediately.

When one court issued a temporary stay that delayed the transfer of the boy to his father, Little Havana erupted. Drivers blocked traffic, blasted salsa music, waved flags, and shouted, "Our miracle happened!"

But the stay ran out. Undaunted, the relatives defied the federal order.

The last thing Miami native and U.S. Attorney General Janet Reno wanted to do was have a show of federal force in her hometown, with the world watching. She even flew to Miami to meet with the family, but left without Elian.

The relatives insisted to the public that they would not betray the boy. Great Uncle Lazaro Gonzalez, leader of the Miami relatives, said, "Our position is we will not turn over the child—anywhere." He said the government "will have to take this child from me by force."

U.S. Attorney General Janet Reno wrestled with the Elian Gonzalez standoff. (Florida Photographic Collection)

"QUE PASA?"

At 5:15 a.m. on April 22, 2000, a van suddenly raced down the street and lurched to a stop outside the home. Border Patrol and INS commandos leaped out. In all, 131 agents would take part in the raid. The number of people outside the home had dwindled to about 30.

Agents fired tear gas in front of the home and behind barricades.

The agents used rams on the chain link fence and on the front door. As they rushed through the gate, 22 supporters got into the front yard and tried to form a human wall. Delfin Gonzalez, brother of Lazaro Gonzalez, shouted, "The world is watching."

One community leader was on the phone with Reno when the agents burst in.

Elian, who was on the couch with Lazaro Gonzalez, was swept up during the chaos and taken into a back bedroom by Donato Dalrymple, one of the fishermen who had rescued the boy.

Marisleysis Gonzalez, the cousin who had long ago adopted the role of the boy's surrogate mother, later described the scene as both horrific and unnecessary. She said the agents brandished automatic weapons and began screaming: "Give us the damn boy or we'll shoot you."

"I stood in this door and I stood like this (with arms outstretched) and I said, 'Don't shoot! We're not armed! I will give you Elian! Please! Please!'" said Marisleysis, who claimed the agents shoved the gun into her abdomen as she stood in front of her family and their attorneys.

It was in the bedroom, as Dalrymple held Elian in front of an open closet door, that Associated Press photographer Alan Diaz took the photo of the agent pointing his gun at Elian.

"They grabbed him! They ripped him from my arms," an emotional Dalrymple said later.

Immigration and Naturalization Service Special Agent Betty A. Mills then took Elian, who was wearing a T-shirt and checkered boxers, put a blanket over his head and walked out.

Kicking and screaming, Elian was carried through the house as family members burst into tears, some falling on their knees, helplessly held back by the agents.

Elian shouted, "Que pasa (What's happening)?" and, "Help me, help me!" as the agents hustled him out the door, loaded him into one of the white vans and drove away. As the vans tried to back down the street they were pelted with rocks, lawn chairs and milk crates, even a water cooler.

REWARD
ATTENTION!
MISSING CHILD!

http://www.impeachreno.org

Last seen 4/22/00 at 5:15 a.m. being removed forcibly by a woman and masked gunmen in a white utility vehicle with tinted windows. Abduction may be related to a conspiracy between the Clinton Administration and the only communist dictator in the Hemisphere.

Please contact: The Department of Justice or The Chief of Castro's Secret Police

Supporters still rail about the return of Elian Gonzalez to Cuba.

The whole thing lasted 57 seconds.

It was the day before Easter.

"NO REGRETS"

Within hours of the raid, the crowd had swelled to 300, and some 35 square blocks around the house had been blocked off. A spokesman for Miami police, who'd arrived to brief reporters, was pushed, punched, and spit on before six officers got him away. A crowd tore down a CNN tent. Police finally cleared the area. In other parts of town, protestors banged on police and fire-rescue cars. Others set tires and trash bins ablaze and threw newspaper racks into the street.

Furious Elian supporters staged a mass strike. Supermarkets, restaurants and other stores in the Little Havana area closed for the day. Several Hispanic members of the Florida Marlins baseball team sat out that day's game. There were worries that the civil disobedience would escalate, and include tactics used in previous protests, such as blocking roadways with dump trucks or placing rolling roadblocks on expressways and bridges during rush hours.

Janet Reno said she had "no regrets whatsoever" for the raid. Supporters said she had to uphold the law and return the boy to his father and that the show of force was necessary to prevent a riot.

England's *The Independent* opined, "Perhaps an unarmed constable should have dismounted his bicycle, knocked on the door and asked for the boy, sternly but politely... In retrospect, the guns up front were unnecessary. But this was America. Who was to say that not one of Elian's self-appointed custodians would be armed, and would not, in the emotional and ideological heat of the moment, start shooting?"

One college professor said the incident was a blow to Cubans' presumptions of the strength of their political clout.

The Miami relatives dismissed photographs of a smiling Elian reunited with his father in Washington hours after the raid, calling them fakes. Many newspapers had run them on their front pages the same day as the Elian-in-the-closet shot in an effort at balanced journalism. Relatives said the boy's hair was longer. Others said a missing lower tooth was not evident and the lighting appeared awkward. The lawyer for the father later tried to defuse suspicions by releasing more pictures.

Joe Carollo, the Miami mayor, was furious with Police Chief William O'Brien, who knew about the predawn raid about an hour before it happened and told only a few top assistants, citing security concerns.

As for the federal government, "What they did was a crime," the mayor said. "These are atheists. They don't believe in God. I feel I cannot trust this government."

Carollo later fired City Manager Donald Warshaw. Sixteen hours later, O'Brien announced he was retiring, saying, "I refuse to be chief of police when someone as divisive and destructive as Joe Carollo is mayor."

Soon, bananas started showing up at the front door of Miami City Hall. As in zoo. As in circus. As in banana republic.

HOLY ELIAN WATER

Soon, the street was quiet again. But in the months and years that followed:

"Casa Elian" became a shrine to the boy and the lost effort to keep him in America. It opened to visitors every Sunday. Inside, hundreds of news clips and photographs recounted the event. The race car-shaped bed where the boy slept was surrounded by many gifts, including a Spiderman suit, a dozen bicycles, numerous teddy bears and religious images.

A raft said to be the one used by Elian—who was on a boat, not a raft— fetched bids of $10 million on the eBay Internet auction service before eBay pulled the item. A website offered what it said was a lock of the boy's hair. Another sold bottles of Holy Elian Water.

The family tried, but failed, to sue Janet Reno.

Marisleysis eventually opened her own beauty salon.

Donato Dalrymple, the house cleaner and weekend fisherman who helped rescue Elian from the waves but could not save him from the federal agents, divorced his third wife and had a daughter by a relationship that later ended. He said in a July 2004 interview that he had removed the vanity license plate on his car that said "Elian" and was moving on with his life.

Miami Mayor Joe Carollo's wife sued him for divorce. Carollo was arrested for allegedly throwing a cardboard teapot container at her, but prosecutors dropped the charges. The mayor said the container hit her accidentally when he threw it at a wall. In November 2001, Carollo was ousted from office.

Former City Manager Donald Warshaw was convicted of mail fraud for stealing from a charity he helped found.

The U.S. House of Representatives voted for the most substantial easing ever of economic sanctions against the Castro regime. But the bill died in the Senate amid threats by President Bush that he would veto it.

And, of course, Elian. The boy would be seen in photographs in his school uniform, the all-white outfit and red neckerchief. The Cuban government opened a museum detailing his ordeal. A 2004 *People Magazine* article said that, 4-1/2 years after his return, Elian, now nearly 11, loved math, practiced karate three times a week, enjoyed swimming and sometimes liked to spike his hair. Observers said he was well-adjusted and enjoying life with his father and stepmother. But it also said he was a trophy of sorts for Fidel Castro, who has appeared at his birthday parties.

Perhaps years in the future, as the joke predicted, he would be found on a street corner, shouting, "Freedom for Elian!"

Chattanooga *Times Free Press*, February 13, 2000
Palm Beach *Post*, March 12, 2000
New York *Times*, March 29, April 3, 2000
Miami *Herald, South Florida Sun-Sentinel,* Palm Beach *Post*,
March 31, 2000-April 30, 2000
Miami *Herald*, November 7, 2001, June 7, 2004
USA Today, April 6, 2000
Chicago *Tribune*, April 15, 2000
Associated Press, April 14, April 19, 2000
Calgary *Herald*, April 25, 2000
Ottawa *Citizen*, April 26, 2000
Times Colonist, Victoria, British Columbia, April 30, 2000
The Times (London), May 1, 2000
Christian Science Monitor, June 29, 2000
Agence France Presse, July 2, 2002
People Magazine, November 29, 2004

SECTION ONE
CHAPTER
3

SEPTEMBER 11, 2001

On July 5, 2001, a police officer in Delray Beach pulled over a motorist for speeding. He let the man go with a warning. The pre-printed caution reads in part, "Take a minute and consider how your careless driving affects the people you share these streets with and try to help make our streets a safer place to be."

Nine weeks later, the motorist, Mohamed Atta, helped pilot American Airlines Flight 11 into the north tower of New York's World Trade Center.

It's human nature to try to find a little humor in even the most horrific things. The events of September 11, 2001, were so devastating that there's little place for that.

But a lot of creepy things happened in connection to what has become a simple, but universally known, acronym: "9/11."

And, of course, even as the dust was settling, those of us who follow such things were counting the minutes until the Florida connection surfaced. We didn't have to wait very long, and even we

Mohamad Atta, one of the ringleaders of the Sept. 11 terrorist attacks, lived in Palm Beach County. (FBI)

were surprised by the extent. It could be argued that, except for the actual locations of the attacks, no place played a larger role.

At least 14 of the 19 terrorists lived, at some point, in South Florida. They took flying lessons in at least six Florida cities. They enjoyed naked lap dancers, intimidated hotel maids, gave waitresses lousy tips, and argued with bar managers. They threw airplane manuals in dumpsters. They went on the Internet in a city library. They quizzed a pharmacist about how to relieve mysteriously irritated hands. They fooled a landlady, but not her dog, which never stopped barking at them.

The federal government knows a lot more about the movements of the terrorists in Florida for the months preceding the attacks. But the feds won't say. The U.S. Justice Department has rejected, out of hand, dozens of media requests for investigative documents, filed under the U.S. Freedom of Information Act. The feds argue that it's an ongoing investigation, and will be for a long time.

Meanwhile, a 15-year-old boy who loved to wave the American flag left a fan letter to Osama bin Laden and flew a small plane into the side of a Tampa high rise.

Just when it couldn't get weirder, the nation's first-ever serial bio-terrorism attack started in the same area where the terrorists had been hiding out. Connection or coincidence? Years later, there is still no answer.

"I'M A PILOT"

The Florida angle emerged even before one of the darkest days in U.S. history had ended. By the 11 p.m. news, reports were already surfacing that the FBI had checked out a South Florida airport in connection with the attacks.

The next day, more than 400 agents swarmed through Florida with search warrants, following multiple trails of clues. The FBI and police seized flight school records, surrounded houses and combed apartment complexes. They learned that in at least six cities, pilots learned how to fly in Florida aviation schools that advertise widely to recruit foreign students.

It didn't take long for one man to begin figuring prominently: Mohamed Atta.

Atta was identified as having taken flight training the previous year in Venice on the Gulf Coast. And three weeks before the attack, Atta spent at least four hours flying a four-seat Piper Archer plane he rented at the Palm Beach County Park Airport in Lantana. The owner said Atta presented a commercial pilot's license and demonstrated his piloting ability with a flight instructor who later described Atta as a capable pilot.

But Atta was also reported looking at crop dusters in Belle Glade, in the huge sugar growing area along Lake Okeechobee and west of West Palm Beach. That led to speculation he was planning to spray some kind of chemical or biological agent over the area. Within weeks of the attacks, the Federal Aviation Administration twice ordered nationwide groundings of crop-dusters because of what sources called a "serious, credible threat."

A man who loaded chemicals on crop-dusters at the Belle Glade airport said Atta visited the airport with two other Middle Eastern men the previous February. He asked a lot of questions and mentioned that he was a student pilot. The worker's supervisor said men came to the airport just about every weekend in July and August 2001, and most recently on September 8, three days before the hijackings. He said they asked questions about the flying capabilities of crop-dusters and the amount of chemicals they can hold.

The government was heavily criticized after the attacks for bureaucratic blundering. That became even more embarrassingly evident in March 2002, when a letter arrived at Huffman Aviation in Venice, saying the INS had extended student visas for Atta and Marwan Al-Shehhi, allowing them to continue their flying lessons. This came at a time when they had already been dead, and household names, for some six months.

An INS spokesman said the visas had been approved before the attacks and a paperwork backlog had delayed their mailing. That meant, of course, that at the time they committed the greatest act of terrorism in U.S. history, they were cleared to be in the country.

U.S. Representative Mark Foley, R-West Palm Beach, couldn't believe that Atta's name would not have jumped out to even a rank-and-file worker. He called the incident "a Keystone Cops operation."

At Shuckums Bar in Hollywood the night of the attacks, agents showed a manager pictures of the men. He and two bartenders positively identified them as Atta and Al-Shehhi.

Manager Tony Amos said the two and another man "got wasted" in his place, downing chicken wings; cranberry juice, Stolichnaya vodka and orange juice; and Captain Morgan's spiced rum and Coke.

Atta, who wore wire-rim glasses, sat at a front corner stool and talked with a third man while his companion furiously pumped dollar bills into a video poker game at the far end of the bar. Amos said the FBI did not show them a photo of the third man.

Atta argued with the manager over his $48 drink bill. When the manager asked whether he could pay, Atta got offended and said, "I'm a pilot for American Airlines, and I can pay my bill." He peeled out a hundred from a thick wad of currency in large denominations. He left a three dollar tip—about six percent.

FBI agents also swept through the North Perry Airport in Pembroke Pines, next to Hollywood, that first night. They got the owner of the private Broward Aviation operation out of bed to get them the tail numbers of planes at his maintenance and flight school. And they asked him not to tell anyone what they were after.

FBI agents spent at least an hour at a three-story condominium apartment complex in Coral Springs that Atta listed as his last address. He previously had a driver's license in Egypt. He had been issued a traffic ticket on April 26 for having no valid license. He had failed to appear for a June 4 hearing, and a judge had issued the warrant for his arrest when he was pulled over later in Delray Beach.

Charlie Voss, a former bookkeeper at Huffman Aviation in Venice, said two men stayed with him for about a week in 2000. They said they had just arrived from Germany and wanted to take flight training. He identified them as Atta and Marwan Al-Shehhi. Voss said he asked them to leave after Atta made an insulting remark to his wife.

And in North Florida, authorities at Embry-Riddle Aeronautical University in Daytona Beach said Waleed Alshehri, who graduated from the school, was an A and B student who lived nearby.

The owner of the Pink Pony Nude Theatre in Daytona Beach turned over to FBI Agents credit card receipts and a *Q'uran*, the Muslim holy book, left behind by bar patrons. The night before the attacks, the patrons had sat at the adjoining sports bar, racking up tabs of $40 to $80, and slipped back to watch the dancers writhing on the poles. One had boasted to employees that "America's going to see bloodshed."

Muslim scholars said knocking back hard liquor and cavorting with nude dancers don't exactly square with devout Islam. But then, neither does the murders of thousands of innocent people.

"I COULD HAVE TURNED THEM IN"

On June 21, Waleed Alshehri had checked into room B-308 of the Homing Inn, a modest hotel on a busy stretch of Federal Highway in Boynton Beach. He would check out on July 26. He gave an address that is the oceanfront Bimini Motel in Hollywood. Wail Alshehri and Satam al-Suqami used the hotel's address for Florida driver's licenses on July 3, and all three bought memberships at a World Gym in Boynton Beach.

The men in the room never used their telephone, although residents saw them on the pay phone. They appeared to be in their 30s, traveled in a red car and gave the impression they spoke little or no English.

Housekeeper Valrie Williams noted something else that was strange. Usually, she said, when she came to clean, longtime guests would do her the courtesy of making themselves scarce. They'd get their mail, or play tennis, or take a swim, or grab a coffee or a meal. But it was different with these guests, she said. She was never allowed to clean their room alone. A tall, slim man always sat in a chair partly in the walkway and partly in the threshold of the open front door in the doorway.

Michelle Laudenslager and her mother, Donna Cooper, both waitresses at the Denny's near the Homing Inn, recalled serving two Middle Eastern men who ordered little and said less, complained about their bills and left meager tips. The waitresses identified them as Mohamed Atta and Marwan Al-Shehhi.

At one visit, one ordered coffee. The other had orange juice and a vegetable omelet. One was tall and thin. The other wore wire-rim glasses. Both were polite. The men talked intently to each other but ceased their conversation when the waitress arrived. They left cash at the edge of the table for her to pick up and said "Thank you" when they left.

Laudenslager said Al-Shehhi and Atta were part of a group of five men who haunted the place for about four months, always during the graveyard shift, from 11 p.m. to 7 a.m. They usually ordered steak and coffee and lingered for hours. They were demanding, paid in cash and left a three dollar tip despite large amounts of cash in their wallets.

Marwan Al-Shehhi apparently was one of two men who rented apartment A-204 of the Hamlet Country Club condominium. The men said they were tourists and did computer work.

At the Delray Racquet Club. Ahmed Alnami and Saeed Alghamdi lived on the fifth floor of Building 1. Residents said they were reclusive, unfriendly and always carried gym bags or duffel bags wherever they went, even to the pool. At times there were as many as seven Middle Easterners at the apartment, and neighbors heard strange ping-ping-ping noises from the apartment all night. One said, "It was like they were chipping away at something."

Neighbor Stacy Warm said the men were "extraordinarily unfriendly. I rode the elevator with them 20 times and never ever did they say 'Hi,' even though I always did. There were at least four of them but my husband said he counted as many as seven. Sometimes an older guy would be seen with them. They wouldn't look at you in the eye. It was like you didn't even exist. I thought they were drug dealers. I thought about reporting them for that reason. When I heard about this, I thought, 'Oh my God, I could have turned them in.'"

A librarian at the Delray Beach Public library remembered the Alshehri brothers as having used the Internet. FBI agents scoured two computers.

In Broward County, the owner of a Deerfield Beach motel said he found aeronautical maps, books on how to fly 757 and 767 airplanes, food with Arabic labels and other items in the trash bin outside an apartment he had rented to two men who appeared to be Middle Eastern.

At a Walgreen's in suburban West Palm Beach, an employee found an envelope of photographs that had been left for developing by a man with the same last name as a hijacking suspect. One of the photos depicted an airplane.

Don Deck, a waiter at the Olive Garden in Greenacres, near West Palm Beach, remembered three men in silk shirts sharing a bottle of wine and veal parmigiana. One man ordered for all of them, but said little else to the waiter. Deck later said some of the men resembled photos of the hijackers released by authorities. He had first thought the men were in the Mafia, so he had looked at the name on the credit card slip. He later recalled that name was "A-T-T-A."

"ANTHRAX ATTACKS *ENQUIRER*"

AMI photo editor Bob Stevens died of anthrax, setting off a national panic. (AMI)

Within weeks of the terrorist attacks, the angst and paranoia around the country, and especially in South Florida, had everyone wound as tight as clock springs.

But there was more.

Bob Stevens, 63, worked as a part-time photo assistant for the *Sun*, one of several supermarket tabloids published by American Media International (AMI) in a huge complex in a northern Boca Raton industrial park.

Stevens had been visiting relatives in North Carolina and had awakened from a nap with flu-like symptoms. He and his wife had cut their trip short and returned home on Monday, October 1, 2001. At 2:30 the next morning, his wife took him to the emergency room at JFK Medical Center in Atlantis, near West Palm Beach, burning with fever and in a stupor. Soon he had fallen into a coma. Within four days, Stevens' kidneys would fail and he would die.

As Stevens sank deeper, his alarmed doctor pumped antibiotics into him and recoiled from what he saw under the lens of a microscope. At first he didn't want to even mention what he was thinking. He figured colleagues would just laugh.

Dr. Jean Malecki, head of the Palm Beach County Health Department (Palm Beach County Health Department)

It had been a quarter of a century since anyone had seen even an accidental case of inhaled anthrax poisoning. But that's what it was.

The doctor called local health director Dr. Jean Malecki. Health department workers contacted the Stevens family. In Atlanta, the Centers for Disease Control and Prevention chartered a jet and sent six investigators to West Palm Beach. Officials held a news conference.

Despite the proximity in both time and geography to the September 11 attacks and the local movements of the hijackers, U.S. Health and Human Services Secretary Tommy Thompson said in Washington, "It appears that this is just an isolated case. There is no evidence of terrorism."

At AMI headquarters, CEO David Pecker called all 300 or so employees together in the third-floor newsroom of the *National Enquirer*. Employees went home for the weekend, comfortable that whatever had taken their friend would not affect them. Everyone expected to return to work Monday.

But on Sunday, investigators found anthrax spores on the keyboard of Stevens' computer. And in the nasal cavity of Ernesto Blanco, a 73-year-old mailroom worker who was in a Miami hospital with pneumonia.

That night, the health department shut down the building. Employees were called at home and told not to come to work Monday. Instead, they were to go a nearby Health Department office to be screened. More than 700 people were tested.

The FBI took over, and U.S. Attorney General John Ashcroft announced that the search could become a "clear criminal investigation."

And the head of the CDC told Florida U.S. Senator Bob Graham there was no chance the two anthrax exposures could have occurred in the AMI building by accident.

On Monday morning, vehicles pulled up and people donned white protective suits and began vacuuming the building. Workers went to other locations and got the papers out.

Around the region, the panic was on. Doctor offices and pharmacies were inundated with calls for antibiotics.

Tri-Rail officials rode the trains to answer passengers' questions because Ernesto Blanco, the exposed mailroom employee, commuted from his home in North Miami.

Then, a third AMI employee was diagnosed.

That Monday was also the day tests showed the Boca Raton postal carrier facility had about 100 spores in it, the first confirmed link between anthrax and an American post office.

And within days, new attacks were reported. Eventually, weapons-grade anthrax would be found in congressional offices in Washington and in the New York news offices of ABC, CBS, NBC and the New York *Post*. Post offices in Washington, New Jersey and Palm Beach County also tested positive for the deadly bacteria.

The anthrax paranoia became a frenzy. Suspicious-package incidents soared in Florida and around the nation, as people reported anything resembling powder on mail, in trash bins and on other surfaces. Every spilled sugar packet, or envelope an office prankster had filled with baby powder, or popcorn ceiling flake falling to the floor, or pile of kitty litter, or spilled Tide detergent, prompted a panicked call to 911.

After a while, emergency workers couldn't respond to all the calls. Then some people started bringing items into the lobbies of police stations. Departments had to post signs telling people to leave the suspicious items outside.

A Delray Beach man told police he spotted anthrax in his yard. The police filed a report: "Moss growing on wood outside." A Palm Beach Gardens woman called police after discovering a white powdery substance falling from her... toilet paper. And a man reported finding a suspicious powder not long after eating a powdered jelly doughnut.

The clerk's office at a county courthouse in Delray Beach shut down for more than three hours because a woman who runs a marriage service sprinkled confetti made of tiny silver bells and glitter with a marriage license mailed to the office.

The Stuart Police Department seemed to be the first one to run out of patience. It advised residents to "exercise some individual protocols" before calling police about suspicious objects. The advisory was issued after a woman brought her morning newspaper to the police department to report a "suspicious smudge" of ink.

The anthrax attacks were almost as deadly to Boca Raton itself, a city that depended heavily on snowbirds, visitors to restaurants and shops, and tourists. Mayor Steven Abrams called his father, Dr. George Ehrlich, in Philadelphia. "Tell me about anthrax," the mayor said urgently. "It's the middle of the night," the rheumatologist said to his son. "Why are you calling about Amtrak?"

For the next 10 months, the FBI, the CDC, the Environmental Protection Agency and private maintenance crews walked the halls of the AMI building in Boca Raton in protective "moon suits," like extras in the bio-disaster film, *The Andromeda Strain*.

Drawers and cabinets were opened, and some items were removed as evidence. But most of the contents just collected dust. Dust that covered desks as ash covered the motionless dead of Pompeii. Dust—and perhaps anthrax spores.

In August 2002, executives who were allowed to don suits and masks and walk the deserted halls in the stifling 90-degree heat said it was like a scene from the *Twilight Zone*.

The parched bodies of fish lay at the bottom of aquariums, their water evaporated down to the gravel. Half-drunk coffee was reduced to gunk and mold. Refrigerators still held half-eaten sandwiches. Desk calendars still showed October 7. The paste-ups from an October 4 edition still hung on the wall

There were personnel files, unopened letters, Rolodexes, family pictures, notepads, Christmas gift lists. Plants, drooped and brown. Boxes full of floppy disks and CDs. Desktop computers, some of them still powered on, but with no way to remotely enter their electronic brains and retrieve their valuable contents. A main computer server still humming away for no one.

The air conditioner ran until some parts broke; workers tried to repair it from the roof but couldn't, and it finally shut down.

About five million photographs, most of them one-of-a-kind originals, sat in the company's news library. Heat had damaged most of them. The company had been just starting to transfer all the photos to CD-ROM. With the twenty-fifth anniversary of Elvis Presley's death coming up in the summer of 2002, AMI had several months earlier put several invaluable photos of the King onto CDs. They were able to retrieve those, but the anti-anthrax solution destroyed them. The paper had to lay out about $200,000 for new photos.

AMI got a few breaks — the company had copies of all its business records at a secondary office in nearby Delray Beach and had two issues assembled and sitting in computers in Dallas.

The EPA tested around files marked "Who's Who," "Oprah," "Prince Harry" (youngest son of England's Prince Charles), and "Nancy Kerrigan" (the skater attacked by a group of men that included the former husband of her rival, Tonya Harding.) The search list also mentions a file mysteriously marked "LOV" and another simply "X."

On top of everything, the publisher of "woman gives birth to two-headed alien" headlines had to deal with jokes such as the one where a headline says "Anthrax attacks *Enquirer*" and no one believes it.

In April 2004, a developer bought the quarantined multi-million-dollar building for all of $40,000. One of the first tenants: an international business specializing in the cleanup of anthrax, mold and other biohazards. A principal in the company: former New York Mayor Rudolph Giuliani, who knew a little about terrorism.

With a "let's go" from Rudy, a crew pumped sterilizing chemicals into the structure. Eventually the five million dollar spraying was completed and the building was declared clean and ready to reopen. Giuliani said he'd be one of the first people in the door.

Later, a glitch developed over the 4.5 million photos still in the place. They included the infamous shot of Elvis Presley in his open coffin. The photos were to be destroyed. But lawyers representing photographers called to warn that the photos belonged to their clients and couldn't be incinerated.

While no one ever made a direct link between anthrax and the September 11 hijackers, the fact that they and the substance had moved in the same circles was intriguing.

Some time in the summer of 2001, a man came into a downtown Delray Beach drug store. His hands were red and irritated. He wouldn't give pharmacist Gregg Chatterton a straight answer about how they got that way. After the attacks, Chatterton recognized the man from newspapers as Mohamed Atta.

Chatterton quizzed Atta about his line of work, hoping to get clues about the source of the irritation. He asked if the men were in construction; the rough concrete and its chemical makeup, heavy in lime, can be irritants. The man said no. Chatterton asked if he worked with toluene or other cleaning solvents. He asked, "Do you work with some sort of chemical?" No. "Do you work in a garden?" Atta laughed, "No."

Finally, Atta said, "computers." He changed the subject. He was evasive. The pharmacist figured the man had been around some chemicals that were basic rather than acidic, so he sold him a one-ounce tube of a medicine called "acid mantle" for $5.49. He also sold Atta's friend, Marwan Al-Shehhi, a bottle of Robitussin for a nasty chest cold and directed him to a nearby walk-in clinic.

Chatterton later identified hijacking suspects Waleed Alshehri and Wail Alshehri as having come in several times to buy snacks and toiletries. He said they never came in at the same time as the men identified as Atta and Al-Shehhi.

The pharmacist said the anthrax case in Boca Raton later had him wondering if Atta's hand irritation was the result of exposure to chemicals such as chlorine or ammonia or from repeated hand washing with regular soap.

Later, it was learned that agents never checked the apartments and hotel rooms in South Florida where at least 12 of the 19 presumed September 11 hijackers lived. The FBI did test for anthrax in some cars believed used by the hijackers, but not their residences

Chatterton said the men who had come into his store definitely had not asked for any of the antibiotics suggested for exposure to anthrax.

As of this writing, the anthrax mystery remains unsolved.

"YOU WILL PAY"

On January 5, 2002, a 15-year-old straight-A student, who had often volunteered to carry the American flag and lead the student body at his private academy in patriotic assemblies, stole a Cessna plane and crashed into the 28th floor of a downtown Tampa high-rise.

Near Charles Bishop's body in the plane, obscenely jutting from a corner office of the Bank of America tower, authorities found on plain white paper a few scribbled paragraphs expressing admiration for the September 11 attacks four months earlier.

Teenager Charles Bishop flew a small plane into a Tampa high-rise.

"Osama bin Laden is absolutely justified in the terror he has caused on 9-11," the note said. "You will pay—God help you—and I will make you pay!"

The ease with which Bishop stole the plane prompted calls from Florida Governor Jeb Bush and others for tighter regulations on civilian aircraft and flight schools.

The boy said in his note that he acted alone.

Bishop had transferred to another school by the time of the September 11 attacks and one teacher said the boy was so outraged he wore an Air Force T-shirt to school and vowed to become a military pilot. He started taking flying lessons in March at a Clearwater-based school.

On the day of his fateful flight, his flight instructor at St. Petersburg-Clearwater International Airport had told him to check out a four-seat Cessna 172 and wait for him by the plane. Instead, Bishop, who had fewer than 20 hours of flying time, started the engine, taxied to a runway and took off without contacting controllers in the airport's tower.

The controllers alerted the tower at Tampa International Airport and a Coast Guard helicopter in the area of the unauthorized flight. As they tried unsuccessfully to contact Bishop, the young pilot flew southeast across Tampa Bay. The Coast Guard helicopter was asked to intercept the Cessna as it flew toward MacDill Air Force Base.

Before the helicopter caught up with Bishop, he buzzed the MacDill tower, at one point flying below the windows, then flew within a few feet of two fully loaded tanker aircraft on a MacDill runway and three aircraft hangars.

Coast Guard pilots got close enough to give him hand signals to land. The pilots said they thought Bishop saw their signals and signaled back, but they couldn't tell what gestures he was making. At 5:30 p.m., Bishop hit the tower.

Bishop's family later filed a $70-million lawsuit against the manufacturer of the acne medication Accutane, claiming it caused the teenager to become severely psychotic. The manufacturer denied a link.

HOW COULD THEY?

Perhaps because of the larger picture, the government couldn't or wouldn't be specific of what the September 11 terrorists had been doing in South Florida.

Amazingly, a 900-page congressional report, issued in July 2003, has only a single mention of the terrorists' movements in Palm Beach County.

One of those concerned about the dearth of Florida details was U.S. Representative Porter Goss, a Republican congressman from southwest Florida and co-chair of the committee. In August 2004, Goss went to the other side when President Bush named him head of the CIA.

And when the long-awaited "9/11 Commission" report came out in July 2004, it also gave scant attention to the place where so many had planned the greatest criminal act in U.S. history.

For residents of the area, it will always be more than just the creepy feeling of knowing the terrorists were in their midst.

Try as they might, they can't figure out how these people could live among them, see them shop and eat and play and take their children to lunch or the park or school, and still be so convinced that killing them and their children would be such a privilege, they would give their lives in the process.

That probably will never be explained.

Miami *Herald*, September 14, 2001
South Florida Sun-Sentinel, September 16, 2001
Chicago *Tribune*, January 8, 2002
St. Petersburg *Times*, January 18, 2003
Palm Beach *Post*, September 12-18, September 24, October 11, October 14,
October 17, October 19, November, 2, December 9, 2001; March 13, October 4,
2002; August 27, 2002; September 11, 2003; July 12, October 22,
December 17, 2004

SEPTEMBER 11 FALLOUT

A Miami company withdrew from shelves 14,000 bags of candy containing a small toy showing an airplane flying into one of two towers. The wholesaler said workers did not look closely at the figurines until people complained they appeared to represent the September 11 terrorist attacks. The product number at the bottom of each figure: 9011. The candy had been distributed to small, mostly Hispanic groceries around Florida.

Associated Press, August 27, 2004

A 79-year-old grandmother was arrested after a security checkpoint at the Fort Lauderdale-Hollywood International Airport uncovered a tote bag shaped like a book that contained an unloaded single-shot Colt derringer and seven .22 caliber bullets. The Bonita Springs woman, who was heading to the Bahamas, said her husband was a gun collector. She said she had recently moved and had placed the case in the tote bag to keep it with her.

Miami *Herald*, November 24, 2004

An agent at the Orlando International Airport noticed the shape of a pistol inside a teddy bear on an X-ray monitor. The gun turned out to be a .22-caliber derringer. The teddy bear belonged to a member of an Ohio family going through security before boarding the flight home. Instead, they were detained. An Orlando police officer who ripped a hole in the stuffed animal retrieved the concealed weapon, a live round in its chamber. The family said a young girl at their hotel had given the teddy bear to their 10-year-old son two days before they were to go home. FBI agents said they were satisfied the family had not known about the gun.

Orlando *Sentinel*, July 19, 2003

A man who drove a shuttle bus at Palm Beach International Airport was heading to a secure area for a sandwich when he remembered he was carrying a folding knife. Rather than return it to his car or throw it away, he hid it in his shoe. But the airport's X-ray machine caught the knife. The man picked a bad day to try to sneak it through; it was the first anniversary of the terrorist attacks.

Palm Beach *Post*, September 12, 2002

A teacher was charged with carrying a concealed weapon—a bookmark—as she tried to get on a flight in Tampa. The bookmark was an 8 1/2-inch leather strap with small weights at each end. Screeners thought it could be used to knock people unconscious.

Associated Press, January 1, 2005

Federal agents in Miami hauled a teachers' aide off a cruise ship in handcuffs. They mistakenly thought she didn't pay a $50 fine for leaving marshmallows out while camping in Yellowstone National Park.

Associated Press, January 1, 2005

On September 13, 2002, a terror scare closed Alligator Alley between Naples and Fort Lauderdale for most of a day when a woman said she heard three medical students discussing terrorist acts at a Shoney's restaurant in North Georgia. She said the men were talking about how they were headed to Miami to commit some act that would make September 13 a more infamous date than September 11.

Authorities throughout the southeast were put on alert and one of two cars carrying the men was stopped when, police say, it ran a toll on Alligator Alley early Friday morning. Reportedly, the driver of the other car then pulled over on his own.

The men were detained for seventeen long hours in the hot sun, amid asphalt, scrub and swamp.

With authorities not talking, local television stations had to fill time with absolutely nothing substantive to say. While one opted to return to normal programming with a promise to break back in when they knew more, news managers at two others, in a game of TV news "chicken," dared not cut away before their competitor.

So they embarked on a brutal eight-hour marathon of speculation and moronic comments that led one TV critic to bemoan, "TV wouldn't let go" and another to describe coverage as "a wretched performance."

Among the inaccurate reports:

The woman in Georgia had told police the men were coming to Miami to blow something up.

Police spotted the men after they roared past a tollbooth (One car rolled by at a normal rate of speed; the other stopped and paid the tolls for both.).

Police used explosives to detonate a suspicious knapsack found in one car.

Explosive "triggers" were found in one of the cars.

Police were searching for a third car.

One anchor noted that Naples is very close to Venice, where one of the September 11 hijackers got flying lessons (at that point, the cars, which weren't moving anyway, were a full 100 miles from Venice, and only a little further, about 120 miles, from Miami).

One reporter said, breathlessly, that the two cars, which had been parked one behind the other, were now side by side. Another confirmed an anchor's inquiry about whether the trunks contained luggage, as trunks are known to do.

One anchor wondered if "these guys, apparently on their way to Miami to do some harm to the city of Miami" were tied to al Qaeda. "This looks like some loosely pulled together plot," he added. Later, he called them, "three men apparently on their way to Miami with some ill intentions."

Local stations weren't the only offenders. On CNN, also refusing to let go of a story that hadn't moved for hours, anchor Paula Zahn speculated the three were on their way to blow up the Turkey Point nuclear power plant south of Miami.

The men later denied the charges and were cleared, but their clinical rotation at a South Miami hospital was postponed.

South Florida Sun-Sentinel, September 14, 2002;
Miami *Herald*, September 14, September 22, 2002

A man flying from Philadelphia to West Palm Beach made the wrong decision in the post-September 11 era. Forty-five minutes before landing, he grew loud and boisterous and shouted profanity. He then shouted he was going to "bring the plane down" and appeared to charge the cockpit, allegedly telling a flight attendant, "This will put me on the map." Passengers leaped up and helped tackle the man and lock plastic handcuffs on his hands and feet. The man, who was removed from the plane after it landed and taken to jail, later admitted he'd smoked two or three marijuana joints and drank beer, whiskey and vodka at a bar in the Philadelphia airport. He said he didn't remember anything about the flight.

Fort Pierce *Tribune*, January 27, 2005

RUSH TO JUDGMENT

It was the juiciest of Palm Beach scandals.

A wealthy denizen of the exclusive island has a dirty little secret. It's not booze, or a secret crush on the nanny, or an alternative lifestyle, or the fact that the family is actually broke.

In this case, the patron can't get off the pain-killers.

The housekeeper knows.

In fact, the master of the house has let her in on his indiscretion. Not only that, he's sent her out to get his fix. She makes clandestine trips to a small pharmacy on the mainland and slips the goodies to the boss in the parking lot of a diner near the airport.

It's the stuff that makes the tabloids drool.

But that wasn't the tenth of it.

The boss was Rush Limbaugh. Yeah. That guy.

The conservative commentator who changed the face of talk radio found himself in a bit of a pickle when his former $370-a-week

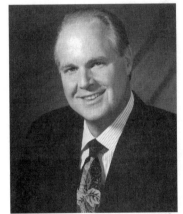

Conservative radio talk icon Rush Limbaugh admitted to being addicted to painkillers. (EIB Broadcasting)

housekeeper took her story to prosecutors, who gave her immunity, then sold it to the *National Enquirer*, which, of course, is headquartered in the same county.

The story broke the day after Limbaugh had quit the ESPN cable TV sports network over remarks he had made about a black NFL quarterback that offended some.

A week later, Rush "Rusty" Hudson Limbaugh, III made a remarkable confession. With as many as 15 million fans listening on more than 500 stations, Limbaugh admitted he had become hooked on painkillers while recovering from back injuries. He said he was leaving his $24 million mansion, for now, to check himself into a 30-day drug treatment program and would be off the air for a while.

But the story wouldn't. The local state attorney — a Democrat — let it slip that his office was investigating whether Limbaugh "doctor shopped," going from doctor to doctor to hoard as many separate prescriptions as possible in order to load up on the pills.

Prosecutors looked like the cat that swallowed the canary, but kept their mouths shut, yellow feathers at the edges, when asked what they had on the man and whether or when they would press charges. But week after week, Limbaugh reminded his listeners, and everyone else, that so far he'd not been charged with anything.

Then, investigators went to doctors' offices and grabbed Limbaugh's medical records.

"Limbaugh the commentator" put on his "Limbaugh the citizen" hat. The seizure, he argued, violated his right to privacy. He took the prosecutor to court.

And who stood beside him in the halls of justice?

The American Civil Liberties Union.

The same ACLU conservatives love so to bash as left leaning.

Remember back in the 1988 presidential debates, when then-Vice President Bush had delivered the most vicious of attacks on challenger Michael Dukakis just by calling him a "card carrying member" of the organization? That ACLU.

And why would anyone be surprised? This is Florida.

"GET ME SOME MORE!"

"Rush Limbaugh caught in drug ring," the *Enquirer's* October 2, 2003, headline blared.

Its source was Wilma Cline, Limbaugh's former housekeeper, and her husband David. The tabloid would not say what, if anything, it paid the Clines, but it's notorious for buying stories.

The couple told the tabloid that, from 1998 to 2002, Rush had paid them tens of thousands of dollars for the pills. They said they sold him 11,900 tablets in a six-month stretch of 2001 alone. They said they made the exchange in the parking lot of a Denny's restaurant near Palm Beach International Airport, with Wilma passing the pills in a cigar box through the open window of Rush's Mercedes. She said she secretly audiotaped two such transactions.

The *Enquirer* said the Clines provided e-mails Limbaugh allegedly sent them with such messages as, "You know how this stuff works…the more you get used to it, the more it takes."

Cline said she had mentioned to Limbaugh that her husband was taking the powerful narcotic *Hydrocodone*, after he was hurt falling off a ladder. Court records showed he had fallen in March 1998 at another island mansion and unsuccessfully sued the owner.

"To my astonishment," Cline told the tabloid, "he [Rush] said, 'Can you spare a couple of them?'" She said she gave him 10 from her husband's prescription. The next day, he asked for more. Soon the couple was supplying him 80 pills a month. She claimed that when her husband's doctor cut off the prescription, Limbaugh shouted, "I don't care how or what you do but you'd better — better — get me some more!"

She said she got more through another mansion employee, hiding them under Limbaugh's mattress so his wife wouldn't find them. She said Rush finally told her was going to rehab. But a month later, she said, he asked her to get him the even more powerful *Oxycontin*. She said she started a log of her purchases and, in forty-seven days, delivered 4,350 pills. She said Rush became increasingly paranoid, at one point groping her to see if she was wired. She said he tried to kick his habit at a New York hospital, to no avail.

Eventually, Cline said, a lawyer twice gave her $100,000 checks and eventually told her to stop supplying pills. He told her to hand over the computer containing Rush's e-mails. But she said she took the hard drive from another computer and smashed it in front of him.

That's when, she said, she and her husband got nervous and contacted a lawyer, who took them to prosecutors. They gave the couple immunity and used information the couple gave them to bust another couple who ran a pharmacy in nearby suburban Lake Worth.

Investigators said they tracked 450,000 doses of *Hydrocodone* to the small drug store. They seized 73,000 pills and unearthed $806,000 in cash. Authorities said they believed that little pharmacy was the source for the Clines.

Legal experts and leaks in the prosecutor's office told reporters that if what the Clines said about Limbaugh was true, he wouldn't be charged with possession because he hadn't been caught red-handed. The lead prosecutor in the bust of the Lake Worth pharmacy said he was more interested in finding the heads of big distribution cells than busting low-level drug users, celebrity or not.

One week after the *Enquirer* story broke, Limbaugh read a statement on the air: "You know I have always tried to be honest with you and open about my life," he said. "So I need to tell you that part of what you have heard and read is correct."

He went on to say he had taken prescription painkillers for five or six years after undergoing spinal surgery and had twice before checked into facilities to try to overcome his addiction. He said he was trying a 30-day program to "once and for all break the hold this highly addictive medication has on me."

He said he would be checking in immediately after the end of his show, which would be helmed by guest hosts until his return.

But he also said, "The stories you have read and heard contain inaccuracies and distortions, which I will clear up when I am free to speak about them."

And, he said, "I am no victim and do not portray myself as such. I take full responsibility for my problem."

Limbaugh would spend five weeks in the center, returning November 17, 2003.

And he wasted no time going after Barry Krischer.

A FISHING EXPEDITION

Palm Beach County State Attorney Barry Krischer's office obtained Limbaugh's records from a Palm Beach pharmacy, then used those to get a search warrant to seize medical records in November 2003 from his doctors in offices in Jupiter, West Palm Beach and Los Angeles. Prosecutors said those records contained enough information to charge Limbaugh with at least ten felony counts of doctor shopping, something that is rarely pursued.

Palm Beach County State Attorney Barry Krischer's office investigated "doctor shopping" allegations against Rush Limbaugh.

A lawyer and pharmacist, who was a former assistant public defender, reviewed the records and said most were written by one doctor.

"It's the actions of an addict, not a doctor-shopper," Randy Berman said. "Either he was stockpiling or really taking too much."

Limbaugh hired as his attorney Roy Black of Miami, who has been a side player in many other modern tales of weird Florida. He represented William Kennedy Smith, acquitted of raping a woman at the Palm Beach Kennedy mansion. He represented sportscaster Marv Albert, accused of biting a woman on the back during a sexual encounter. He represented actor Kelsey Grammer, who grew up in South Florida, during an investigation of statutory rape; the charges were dismissed by a grand jury. He won acquittal for Willie Falcon, the Miami powerboat racer accused of smuggling seventy-five tons of cocaine.

High-profile attorney Roy Black defended radio talk host Rush Limbaugh.

Limbaugh insisted investigators needed to get not just a search warrant, which they could hand someone on the way in, but also a subpoena, which provides advance notice. Prosecutors said they last thing they want to do, or should be required to do, is tell someone they're coming when they're about to seize evidence.

And, Limbaugh said, local lawmen were going on a fishing expedition, looking to land a big one.

"Rush Limbaugh's celebrity status is secondary to the fundamental privacy issues that arise in this case," said Randall Marshall, legal director of the ACLU of Florida. "What is at stake here is the medical privacy of millions of people in Florida and the need to protect people against unnecessary government intrusion into their medical records."

Limbaugh later slammed Krischer when the state attorney's office let leak that it had held talks with Limbaugh in which he had requested a pretrial diversion program while not having to plead guilty.

Black sought to keep these medical records under seal and tried to formalize a plea deal to bring the investigation of Limbaugh to a halt.

"The public is better served by treating addicts as patients rather than criminals," Black had written.

Prosecutors had offered a much tougher deal. Limbaugh would have to plead guilty to a felony, then be placed on three years probation, subjected to random drug testing, continuing treatment and community service to "raise public awareness of the dangers of prescription drug addiction."

Black called the counteroffer "ludicrous."

Prosecutors defended their release of the plea negotiations and said that Limbaugh's camp had already discussed them. They pointed to a December 22, 2003, interview on CNN in which a spokesman for the company that carries Limbaugh's radio show said discussions had taken place between Black and prosecutors.

An appeals court later ruled prosecutors were permitted to obtain medical records without a subpoena.

Krischer said that "Mr. Limbaugh's rights have been and will continue to be scrupulously protected, as are the rights of all individuals investigated by my office."

Roy Black, at a news conference later in the afternoon at a private club overlooking Miami's Biscayne Bay, scoffed at Krischer's use of the word "scrupulously," saying, "It's hardly scrupulous when armed officers enter a doctor's office and seize records in plain view of patients."

Meanwhile, the whole thing had Rush bashers salivating. Imagine the delicious irony:

The man who had said that "drug use destroys societies," that "too many whites are getting away with drug use," and that drug users should be prosecuted to the full extent of the law had admitted he was an addict and had reportedly sought a plea deal.

The man who had said "activist judges" endanger America was balking at a court that strictly interpreted the law.

The law-and-order champion, who wouldn't want courts to hinder prosecutors, was fighting their most coveted weapon — the search warrant.

The man who said in one of his books that "there is no basis in the Constitution for the privacy right" cited in allowing abortion rights was fighting to protect the privacy of his medical records. In fact, his lawyer was the man who, in defending William Kennedy Smith on rape charges, had tried to portray the alleged victim as psychologically unstable. To do that, Roy Black had repeatedly sought access to the woman's...medical records.

The man who compared the torture of Iraqi prisoners at the Abu Ghraib prison to fraternity hijinks was pontificating on the rights of the accused and the presumption of innocence. (By the way, Limbaugh, who fearlessly supported the Iraq war, had himself avoided the draft because of anal cysts.)

The champion of family values, who opposes gay weddings to protect the sanctity of marriage, announced he was divorcing his third wife. Attendees at that wedding had included former Education Secretary William Bennett, another family values advocate who later admitted to a multi-million-dollar gambling habit. The marriage had lasted ten years; the others lasted five years and eighteen months respectively. Rush also reportedly had a new girlfriend, a CNN anchor.

And, of course, the ACLU, which Rush regularly trashed, was coming to his defense.

Limbaugh had his own charges of hypocrisy. He wanted to know why Palm Beach County prosecutors continued to torment him — still without filing charges — while their counterparts in Tallahassee's Leon County had dropped felony prescription fraud charges against State Senator Mandy Dawson, a Democrat, who allegedly changed the "60" on a *Lorcet* prescription to "160."

Dawson said the charges were dropped after she entered a pre-trial intervention program and rehab. She said Limbaugh had not yet been arrested, but she had.

"Now who's getting preferential treatment here?" Dawson asked. "I was on everything but the milk carton."

State Representative Mandy Dawson was charged with tampering with a prescription.

Rush even went after the local newspaper, buying a full-page ad in the Palm Beach *Post* to reprint a supportive editorial from the Washington *Times*.

"I, El Rushbo, have to buy my way into this paper in order to get some modicum of fairness," Limbaugh said on his radio show.

Post Executive Editor Edward Sears said he found it "amusing that opinions disturb Rush Limbaugh." He said Limbaugh had never returned calls from the staff, adding, "I hope he will comment as fully to our news reporters as he has to our advertising staff."

Here's the final twist. Krischer, whom Limbaugh accused of conducting a "political" investigation, believes that the Legislature should rewrite the doctor-shopping law. He thinks lawmakers should specify search warrants before prosecutors can obtain medical records. Why? Because, he said, that would best protect patients' privacy.

Palm Beach *Post*, Oct, 3, October 4, October 8, October 11, 2003; February 4, May 4, May 14, June 12, June 25, October 7, 2004

OUT OF SIGHT: THE GCI PRISON BREAK

The escape of six killers from the Glades Correctional Institution in Belle Glade on January 2, 1995 was such an all-star performance of weirdness that it inspired the Elmore Leonard novel, and later movie, *Out of Sight.*

One of the six escapees never got off the grounds and was captured within an hour. One was killed and another captured a week later. A fourth was arrested the next day walking through Miami's Little Havana. A fifth was caught in the same neighborhood the day after that. The last one hid out for 2-1/2 years before being nabbed in Mexico, where he made the mistake of posing as a Mexican despite a Cuban accent that any self-respecting Hispanic would spot in a second.

The escape prompted a probe that uncovered inadequate security, failing facilities and corruption. Three employees were fired. One, a former administrator, was dismissed for beating the first recaptured escapee. A former inspector was later indicted on charges that he failed to investigate a tip that could have foiled the breakout. His job was taken by a man who had been fired from his previous job for doing the same thing.

Meanwhile, the warden, for having such a dramatic escape and an ensuing scandal occur on his watch, received…a promotion.

DIG TO FREEDOM

The inmates had started digging three to four months before the escape but were delayed by heavy rains that flooded the hole. They had dug into the same tunnel that had been filled in after a 1980s escape try, using shovels that were left there and flashlights bought from a guard and found in a trash can.

The tunnel was four to eight feet deep and two feet wide and stretched about 35 feet. It extended underneath a razor-wire fence and concrete slab.

The men dug four to five feet on each of twenty digging days, suffered two cave-ins and dragged dirt out of the tunnel on a blanket, then spread it under the chapel.

The chapel sits on blocks about 3 feet above ground. The men pried loose a grate to climb into the crawl space and then worked in shifts.

The six had taken the blessing of extra holiday church activities in recent weeks to make repeated trips to the prison chapel. While others prayed or sang hymns, they slipped underneath the red brick chapel, secretly changed into dirty clothes and inch, by muck-filled inch, burrowed their way to freedom.

The conspirators, who bunked together in one of the 120-person dorms, used the old piece of shovel, a couple of two-by-fours and a broken broom handle to dig and support the structure in the soft black earth. Checking beneath the chapel is routine for guards, but inmates scattered the dirt out very thin.

They stashed extra uniforms under the church that they would change into for digging. They changed back into their clean, blue prison uniforms when they finished so they would not raise any suspicion by having muddy clothes.

They were digging in the perfect soil—a compact type of muck found almost exclusively within a mile of Lake Okeechobee.

Noise from the fence's construction and other projects might have given the escapees extra protection. And anyone who asked about the long hours they spent in the chapel was told they were in choir practice or rehearsing a Christmas play.

The men timed their exodus during the time when prisoners are moved from the athletic fields on the compound's south end into the dorms for lockdown. They also knew the middle watch tower adjacent to their tunnel would be unoccupied then. Hurrying to beat construction of another fence going up around the prison, they made their final push and slipped into the darkness.

A relative of one of the six was in a waiting car outside. One was caught. But the rest kept going. In minutes, they were gone.

KEYSTONE COPS

The immediate reaction to the escape was like an episode of Keystone Cops.

A tower radioed the prison control room three times that inmates were escaping. The operator said she didn't hear the call. Radios were too cluttered with guards and supervisors talking simultaneously. Dogs didn't show for more than a half hour. A sergeant heading out of the prison was delayed six to eight minutes by a guard new to the front gate assignment.

One guard was so distrustful of prison vehicles' reliability that he took part in the search with his personal car. Another car failed to start right away. The radio in a third had to be repaired. Guards were given pictures of escapees that were photocopies and in poor condition.

One off-duty guard offered a ride to a man walking along the road. The guard felt something was strange about the man and stopped at the Belle Glade police station. He learned later the man was one of the escapees.

While it was later discovered a relative had driven the five to the Miami area, for several days after the escape, jailers believed that one or more of the escapees was still hiding out in the miles of tall, thick brush surrounding GCI. Two days after the men fled, 100 corrections officers were concentrating their search within a 25-mile radius of the prison.

Six months after the escape, authorities found the start of another escape tunnel beneath a trailer. Also found: two homemade knives, twelve feet of rope, three pairs of inmate pants, two pairs of gloves, two five-gallon buckets, two homemade masks, a shovel with no handle, a bag, a cup and a two-week-old newspaper. Six inmates suspected of involvement were transferred.

Governor Lawton Chiles ordered an investigation. He wanted to know how inmates could dig a tunnel without anyone noticing. Authorities soon learned that wasn't the half of it.

Investigations showed one in five guards had arrest records. Inmates had been caught using the chapel phone to make "900" phone sex calls and sexual liaisons occasionally occurred beneath the chapel. A typist was fired for having sex with an inmate in her office.

A December 1995 investigation named eight GCI corrections officers, including two sergeants and a lieutenant, as suspects in crimes ranging from gambling with inmates to smuggling drugs inside basketballs to calling inmates' families to arrange drug deals.

Former inspector Paul Welborn was fired on charges he got wind of the escape and failed to stop it. He was replaced by a Broward County jail superintendent who had been fired in Broward on charges he got wind of an escape and failed to stop it.

And prison superintendent Gerald Abdul-Wasi later took a regional job overseeing eight South Florida institutions. Officials said the move was, in part, because of what he was able to learn from the break-out.

Felix Carbonell, one of six prisoners who tunneled out of the Glades Correctional Institute, was quickly captured.

THE FATE OF THE SIX

And what about the six escapees?

Felix Carbonell never made it to the car. He fell while running and was kicked in the chest by one of his cohorts. He was caught outside the prison. An assistant superintendent grabbed him by the throat and threatened him; that officer was later fired. Carbonell's life sentence for murder later was extended by three years.

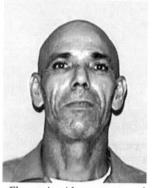

Florencio Alvarez, one of six prisoners who tunneled out of the Glades Correctional Institute.

Eight days after the escape, on January 10, sixty-five to seventy law enforcement officers raided a squatters' camp northwest of Miami. Helicopter searchlights turned night into day. Florencio Alvarez ducked for cover. Armando Junco darted out the back and through some bushes. An officer shot him in the chest. Junco, sentenced to life for machine-gunning two rival drug dealers, died at a nearby hospital. Florencio Alvarez was captured. Alvarez, already serving a life term for shooting his roommate in the head in an argument over drugs, was later sentenced to an extra fifteen years.

Two homeless men who tipped off authorities each received $10,000 in reward money.

The day after the raid on the squatters' camp, a Miami police officer recognized and arrested escapee Hector Rivas, who was walking through Little Havana. Rivas was serving a life term for murdering a Key West charter boat captain.

And the following day, Jesus Martinez was captured a few blocks from where Rivas had been caught and not far from the restaurant where he had robbed a patron and killed another fourteen years earlier. He later had three years added to his 25-year minimum life sentence and a 30-year sentence for first degree and attempted murder.

Juan Jesus Fleitas, serving a life term for murdering a college student during a home invasion, was the last to be captured. He was on the lam for 2-1/2 years, working for the last seventeen months at a seafood restaurant in a mall food court in the Mexican resort city of Cancun. But he made the mistake of shooting a woman during a botched home invasion.

As Fleitas sat in jail, a tipster told authorities he looked like a man being featured on TV's *America's Most Wanted*. The victim's Cuban-born father flew from South Florida to be with her. After sitting in on a police interrogation of Fleitas, he went to his daughter's computer, called up the Florida Department of Law Enforcement web site, and made the match from a poster showing the state's eight most wanted fugitives.

Also, Fleitas had told everyone he was a Mexican from Veracruz, but he couldn't hide his Cuban accent. He was later sentenced to nine years in a Mexican prison for the Cancun attack.

Hector Rivas was the only one of the six to fight his escape charges, despite the fact that he had been inside the prison and was later found outside.

Remarkably, he was found not guilty — but by reason of insanity, even though the judge had said, outside the jury's ears, that he was convinced Rivas was "putting on one heck of a show."

Also, this was his third try at a trial.

He'd been convicted in the first one after only 15 minutes of deliberation, despite his argument that he had fled because he had simply decided he had served enough of his sentence. But an appeals court had ordered a new trial, saying the judge had not properly questioned Rivas about his ability to represent himself.

Hector Rivas was the only one of the six inmates who escaped Glades Correctional Institution to fight his escape charges.

The second trial had been stopped when the Cuban-born Rivas, who claimed not to speak English, let loose a string of English expletives at his own lawyer, then lunged at the attorney but was tackled.

An escape conviction would have added just 20 months to his life sentence for murder, which had no parole possibility before 2017.

Jurors heard testimony from Rivas and examined medical records saying he had suffered from schizophrenia for years. But they also heard a psychologist testify for prosecutors that Rivas was competent to stand trial and probably was faking mental symptoms. The judge had refused to let prosecutors call deputies to testify Rivas behaved normally outside the courtroom.

Rivas had come to court with a bizarre patchwork haircut, pretended to sleep through part of his trial, snored in response to questions, and at times seemed overcome with anger. And that doesn't count what jurors didn't see: Rivas had smeared feces on himself, but was hosed down before court.

South Florida Sun-Sentinel, November 19, 1997
Palm Beach *Post*, January 4, January 12, January 13, February 11, March 1, March 10, March 11, April 7, April 11, October 6, December 7, 1995; January 1, August 7, September 12, November 8, 1996; August 23, August 27, September 1, September 10, 1997; February 20, April 23, 1998

MORE PRISON BLUES

An alleged burglar broke all the rules by breaking into Glades Correctional Institution. Authorities said the man had no idea what he was doing there and might have been drunk.

Palm Beach *Post*, August 25, 1995

A child molester and the helicopter pilot who aided him in a Hollywood-style escape from a treatment center in western Martin County were captured the next day in a ditch a few miles away. The helicopter crashed minutes after plucking the man from the recreation yard.

Palm Beach *Post*, June 4, 2000; April 1, 2004

An escapee from Cross City Correctional Institution borrowed a page from *Cool Hand Luke*, scattering pepper to throw off bloodhounds. The film, in which Luke (Paul Newman) used the same trick, had been shown on cable television exactly a week before the man escaped. He was serving a life sentence for murder and burglary.

Associated Press, September 30, 1987

Jail staffers in Titusville overdosed a murder suspect with anxiety and depression medications, forcing a mistrial.

Associated Press/Miami *Herald*, December 19, 1999

A man who spent nearly two years in Fort Lauderdale's Broward County jail before anyone noticed he shouldn't have been there sued the county for one million dollars. The 55-year-old formerly homeless man was in no hurry to leave for 607 days. He enjoyed three meals a day, jail food, and free health care before officials noticed he'd never come before a judge on a petit theft charge and a nine-year-old drunk driving warrant. Both are misdemeanors. The man finally appeared before a judge and said no one would listen to him. He was sentenced to time served and released.

Miami *Herald*, September 24, 1995

After totaling more than 500 days of delays, the contractor building a Broward County jail facility in Pompano Beach lost the master key, forcing the county to change about 800 locks.

Miami *Herald*, March 12, 1999

The contractor building the new $34 million county jail in Jacksonville forgot something—doors. Redoing plans to put doors in the jail's 195 cells added $1.5 million to the price tag, but the county had a two million dollar cost-over-run fund.

Associated Press, December 3, 1988

THE GOATSUCKER

Who needs Bigfoot? Florida has the goatsucker.

The legend of the *chupacabras*, prevalent in the Caribbean and Hispanic cultures, describes it as some type of nocturnal creature with a vampire's taste for blood. In this case, just animal blood. And internal organs.

In 1996, terror swept a mostly-Hispanic neighborhood in Sweetwater, near Miami. Dozens of animals, including chickens and goats, had died mysteriously in a matter of weeks.

Each of the animals had a large, round puncture wound that looked like a canine tooth. Chickens had broken necks with chunks of flesh ripped from them. The fence that confined the animals was pushed up from the bottom and dug out underneath. Patches of gray fur clung to the fence. Huge paw prints led away from the bodies.

One woman lost two goats and 28 chickens in one night. She said she awoke in the morning to find carcasses in her yard, each with deep puncture wounds but no blood. Her property and a neighbor's together accounted for 69 dead animals.

A rancher in northwest Miami-Dade County found two of his heifers had been reduced to just their heads and some assorted innards. Later, a woman in north-

The goatsucker allegedly attacked animals in South Florida.

ern Broward County said something had left fang marks on the plastic bumper of her Lexus. Nearby, something tore through chicken wire and devoured a pet rabbit.

47

The police proffered the usual suspects: rustlers, dogs, and raccoons. But who else could it be but the goatsucker?

THE GOATSUCKER GONNA GET ME

For six months, the hideous bloodsucking beast had reportedly been terrorizing the central mountains of Puerto Rico, but it had a large following in Latino communities from New Jersey to California.

It was described as part reptile, part insect, part extraterrestrial, with scaly skin, an oval-head and bulging red-eyes that stood on two legs.

One college student described it as three or four feet tall, with skin like that of a dinosaur. It had bright red eyes the size of eggs, long fangs and multi-colored spikes down its head and back. The creature reportedly disemboweled the family goat, draining the blood from its neck.

In South Florida, one Sweetwater resident came out of her home and, as television cameras rolled, demonstrated how she had confronted the goatsucker.

It stood up on two legs and was hunched over like this with big arms, she said, hunching, and looked at me with these red eyes.

In South Florida, a county commissioner called for a police inquest into the local goatsucker attacks. The police considered setting traps with a goat inside.

One of Latin America's most watched Spanish-language TV chat shows, *Cristina*, which is recorded in Miami, where it has a large audience, gave credence to the chupacabras phenomenon with an hour-long program.

On the show was Jose Chemo Soto, the mayor of Canovanas, a town in Puerto Rico where the chupacabras supposedly has claimed more than 100 victims—none human, at least so far. Fifteen people claimed to have seen the thing.

Soto offered viewers this grim warning: "Whatever it is, it's highly intelligent. Today it is attacking animals, but tomorrow it may attack people."

The former police detective, using caged goats as bait, was leading a weekly monster hunt of local volunteers who patrolled the Puerto Rican town's surrounding hills.

Also on the show: a Puerto Rican veterinarian who called the bites "abnormal," a writer on UFOs who believed the beast was an alien, and a publisher of a UFO magazine who said the things were drawn from space to Puerto Rico's Arecibo Observatory, the world's largest radio-radar telescope.

Across South Florida, there were T-shirts, a chupacabras sandwich, live morning radio and a Spanish pop song with a chorus that roughly translated goes like this, "Gotta have fun and party. In case the Goatsucker gonna get me."

Even English-language radio got in on the act when the popular station Y-100 ran a weeklong Search for the Elusive *Chupacabras!* It offered a $1,000 prize for a real photo of the creature. The station made its own mock effort, sending a reporter into the Sweetwater woods dressed in a goat costume.

At an FM rock station, disc jockeys created two songs in the creature's honor. One, called "Goatsuckers," is sung to the tune of *Ghostbusters*. The other is Chupacabrafraglisticexpialidotious, a spin on the song from *Mary Poppins*.

IT ENDS HERE

Ron Magill, communications director of the Miami Metrozoo, knew what it was. A dog. Just a dog.

Magill, who is part Cuban, was sensitive to Hispanic folklore. And as someone who believes in life on other planets, he understood the need to have an open mind. But as a scientist, he knew that there was a very pedestrian explanation for what was happening.

Magill said the bite marks on the animals looked like those of a garden variety dog and threw cold water on the vampire theory by saying he had cut into the animals and they were full of blood.

In fact, two years earlier, dogs had killed fifteen antelopes at the zoo in the same fashion.

One resident hypothesized it was a creature called a marsupial wolf that escaped from a circus. But zoo officials said such an animal had not been seen alive since the 1930s.

Finally, to try to put the panic to rest, a University of Miami veterinarian and professor of pathology performed a necropsy on a goat as reporters scrambled to get a better look. His conclusion—a dog.

"There is nothing to be afraid of out there," Magill announced. "It ends here."

Or does it?

St. Petersburg *Times*, March 21, 1996
Miami *Herald*, April 9, 1996; October 31, 2001, November 14, 2001
Wall Street Journal/Palm Beach *Post*, September 6, 1998

THE AMAZING RANDI

The Amazing Randi bends a fork with his mind. Right in front of you. He shakes it back and forth in his palms, and sure enough, a tine bends.

Except that James Randi bent it, with his hand, when you weren't looking, even though you thought you were staring right at it.

"They're tricks, pure and simple," he smiles. "Well, not so pure and simple."

He used good old distraction, the forte of any professional illusionist. Randi was once one himself. But he's spent most of his life shattering others' illusions.

For Randi, every day is April Fools' Day. He's one of the world's top debunkers (he prefers the terms "skeptic" and "investigator").

He crashes the party. He spoils the fun. He's the guy who says there's no Santa Claus — or ghosts, or alien abductions, or the ability to bend forks just by staring at them really, really, hard.

Simply put, he says that just about everything that's unexplained can be explained.

"The Amazing Randi" offers $1 million to anyone who can prove paranormal activity. (Randi Foundation)

His Fort Lauderdale-based foundation offers a million dollars "to anyone who can show, under proper observing conditions, evidence of any paranormal, supernatural or occult power or event." Since 1968, starting with $1,000 of his own money and building up to one million dollars, he has fielded attempts by hundreds. But none has claimed the prize.

He scoffs at claims that he makes the conditions too onerous, saying he and the challengers always agree on the terms in advance.

"Ninety-nine percent of them are people that believe they've got the powers," Randi says. "The charlatans don't come anywhere near us."

He never says he doesn't believe. He just says, "I don't have any evidence to support it. I wasn't there. When I get evidence, I'll believe it.

"There's lots of evidence for Santa, but it's all bad," Randi said. "A quantity of evidence doesn't make up for the quality of it."

Religion and belief in the paranormal, he says, are "exactly the same thing. It's based on the same evidence, which is no evidence."

Randi says he has no problem with people whose faith is based on faith— "except that they vote."

And, that their beliefs leave them vulnerable to people out to make a buck. "They're victims," he says. "They make themselves victims."

"THE AMAZING RANDI"

Now in his late 70s, the short, bald man with the thick beard doesn't look much like a dashing magician or an inspired slayer of myths.

Randall James Hamilton Zwinge, born in Toronto, dropped out of high school and joined a carnival road show. He later worked Canadian nightclubs as the illusionist "The Amazing Randi."

He fled twenty-eight jail cells, escaped while hanging upside-down in a straitjacket over the Niagara Falls and survived being frozen in blocks of ice. He appeared as a magician on the *Tonight Show* thirty-two times.

His debunking act started as early as age 15, when he was tossed out of a Toronto church and into jail for confronting a preacher who claimed to be "channeling" messages from the dead.

Professed psychic Uri Geller has sued Randi several times. (Uri Geller)

It was Randi's challenge of famous spoon-bender Uri Geller in the late 1970s that helped earn him fame. The first of his eleven books was *The Truth about Uri Geller.*

One night on the *Tonight Show*, Geller, also a regular on the program, was to determine which of several small metal film canisters was filled with water. Geller bumped the table several times, apparently by accident; Randi argues it was to see which can wouldn't slide because it was heavy with water. Randi had directed the show's crew by telephone to secretly coat the bottom of each can with rubber cement. Geller finally gave up.

In 1986, Randi went on Johnny Carson's show to expose a television preacher named Peter Popoff. The evangelist claimed he could tell strangers their names and maladies and then use the power of the Lord to heal them. Randi revealed that Popoff's wife was feeding him information through a secret earphone.

He will not expose the secrets of magicians—or more accurately, Randi argues, illusionists. He describes as "mean-spirited" a 1998 television show that did just that.

"The magician is the most honest performer in the world," Randi says. "He says up front, 'I'm going to deceive you,' and then he does it."

Randi's debunking crusade took off in 1986, when he got a $272,000 stipend from the MacArthur Foundation, founded by Palm Beach Gardens developer and multimillionaire John D. MacArthur. Randi had moved a few years earlier to Florida from New Jersey.

In 1996, he set up the not-for-profit James Randi Educational Foundation with two million dollars in stock from a computer magnate Randi won't name. The foundation operates out of a home just south of downtown Fort Lauderdale with an annual budget of $600,000 and a staff of five. It boasts more than three hundred members. Randi is actively seeking an heir to carry on his mission.

His library is filled with about 1,600 books on religion, UFOs, ghosts and other odd topics. A few debunk, but probably ninety-five percent support various theories and claims.

"You've got to find out what they're saying," Randi explains. One conclusion he's reached: the "experts" on these topics tend to refute each other.

Also on a shelf are various medicines, many of which can be found in your neighborhood drugstore. He describes them as "homeopathic crapola."

The foundation maintains a legal defense fund for people who are sued by believers in the paranormal. Randi has spent hundreds of thousands of his own dollars on such lawsuits.

A few thousand years ago, Randi might have been burned at the stake. These days, his foes use lawyers.

He has been sued more than a dozen times, six of those by Geller. He's lost only one case—and that was to Geller. He lost when he refused to challenge the suit in Japan because of the expense. Geller had asked for thousands, but

Japanese courts eventually awarded a few hundred dollars, which Geller was never able to collect.

"I DON'T GET SCARED"

Randi is also a founder of the Committee for the Scientific Investigation of Claims of the Paranormal, or CSICOP. Started in 1976 and based in Amherst, New York, it counts among its founders the late scientist Carl Sagan and science fiction writer Isaac Asimov.

The committee posted a lengthy website that trashes the urban legends which grew out of the September 11, 2001, terrorist attacks: supposed predictions by Nostradamus, the face of Satan—or God—in the collapsing World Trade Center towers, a man posing for a picture on an observation deck as a plane bears down on him, and various coincidences (the towers form the number 11, etc.). The site especially attacks a French leftist's book that, at one point, was a bestseller; it claims the United States orchestrated the attacks to justify its campaigns in the Middle East.

CSICOP publishes *The Skeptical Inquirer,* a crusading publication that regularly discredits claims of paranormal events.

It also runs the Council for Media Integrity, founded in 1996. The council has urged newspapers to place disclaimers next to horoscopes; more than seventy have.

The council's "Candle in the Dark Award" honors accurate science reporting; the 1997 winner was TV's Bill "the Science Guy" Nye. Its "Snuffed Candle Award" is less glowing. The 1998 "winner" was Art Bell, then host of the late-night paranormal radio program *Coast to Coast AM.*

Randi still supports CSICOP, but in 1991, he says, after Geller sued him for $15 million, CSICOP "got chicken" and asked him to leave Geller alone. Instead, he quit the group.

"They got scared," he says, "and I don't get scared."

James Randi Educational Foundation: www.randi.org
Palm Beach *Post*, March 31, 2004

SECTION II

THE QUEST FOR WEIRD FLORIDA

SECTION TWO CHAPTER 1

INGLIS: A SATAN-FREE TOWN

The tiny coastal town of Inglis, north of Tampa, placed itself on the national map when the mayor issued a proclamation outlawing Satan.

"Be it known from this day forward," the proclamation said, "that Satan, ruler of darkness, giver of evil, destroyer of what is good and just, is not now, nor ever again will be, a part of this town."

The proclamation concluded, "We exercise our authority over the devil in Jesus' name. By that authority, and through His Blessed Name, we command all satanic and demonic forces to cease their activities and depart the town of Inglis."

Mayor Carolyn Risher wrote the proclamation on her kitchen table on Halloween night in 2002. She said she was convinced Satan had a grip on the small town, where a man had molested a child, teens were dressing in goth black, and use of the deadly drug crystal methamphetamine was on the rise. The mayor printed the proclamation on town stationery, stamped it with a gold seal, stuffed copies into four hollowed wooden posts, and, with the help of other town officials, planted one at each of four entrances to the town.

Inglis mayor Carolyn Risher wrote the proclamation banning Satan.

"My main goal was to wake Inglis up," the mayor said in March 2004. "If the proclamation could get people to wake up and realize that they needed God, then it would be a success. Then Inglis would be saved."

Inglis hadn't made the news like this since Elvis Presley came in the early 1960s to film *Follow that Dream*. More than 200 news organizations from around the world came to the town, as well as the American Civil Liberties Union, whose Florida chief described the proclamation as "the most extreme intrusion into religion by a public official that I have ever seen in my twenty-seven years as a director of the ACLU."

Comedy Central's *The Daily Show* sent a correspondent who dressed in a red devil's costume, stood in front of a convenience store, and slipped passersby twenty dollars to "chase him out of town" for the camera. More than one prankster called the mayor, including one who said, "This is Satan. I want you, baby."

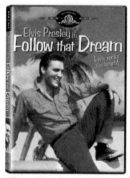

But letters from supportive Christians filled five binders. One Canadian couple said they were so inspired, they planned to move to Inglis.

The ACLU dropped a lawsuit after Risher agreed to reimburse the town for the thirteen dollars spent on the proclamation, which was never voted on by commissioners and so was not an official town act. In fact, the commission had voted once before to bar her from using town stationery for personal use.

Elvis Presley came to Inglis to film Follow that Dream. (MGM)

The commotion settled down and the bad habits never went away, residents said.

"Only thing it did was make us a laughing stock," the owner of one bar said.

But a captain on the five-man police force said drug use and burglary were down and arrests were up. He didn't have exact numbers, saying only that the numbers were up "significantly. And the Big Man upstairs is the reason."

Another businessman, however, noted that the number of officers jumped from two to five, adding, "If that proclamation had worked, why did we need more?"

And Floyd Craig, a produce market owner who unsuccessfully challenged Risher for reelection, said, "Our drunks still drink, our hookers still hook and truckers still ride like the devil up and down the highway. People are going to sin, plain and simple. No proclamation is going to stop that."

Associated Press/Miami *Herald,* March 14, 2004
Newscaster Publishing, Inglis, Fla.

135 Highway 40 West
Post Office Drawer 429
Inglis, Florida 34449

(352) 447-2203
(352) 447-2204
Fax (352) 447-1879

PROCLAMATION

Be it known from this day forward that Satan, ruler of darkness, giver of evil, destroyer of what is good and just, is not now, nor ever again will be, a part of this town of Inglis. Satan is hereby declared powerless, no longer ruling over, nor influencing, our citizens.

In the past, Satan has caused division, animosity, hate, confusion, ungodly acts on our youth, and discord amoung our friends and loved ones. NO LONGER!

The body of Jesus Christ, those citizens cleansed by the Blood of the Lamb, hereby join together to bind the forces of evil in the Holy Name of Jesus. We have taken our town back for the Kingdom of God. We are taking everything back that the devil ever stole from us. We will never again be deceived by satanic and demonic forces.

As blood-bought children of God, we exercise our authority over the devil in Jesus' name. By that authority, and through His Blessed Name, we command all satanic and demonic forces to cease their activities and depart the town of Inglis.

As the Mayor of Inglis, duly elected by the citizens of this town, and appointed by God to this position of leadership, I proclaim victory over Satan, freedom for our citizens, and liberty to worship our Creator and Heavenly Father, the God of Israel. I take this action in accordance with the words of our Lord and Savior, Jesus Christ, as recorded in Matthew 28:18-20 and Mark 16:15-18.

Signed and seal this 5th day of November, 2001.

Carolyn Risher
CAROLYN RISHER, MAYOR

Sally G. McCranie
SALLY McCRANIE, TOWN CLERK

"Gateway to the Gulf"

STILTSVILLE

Stiltsville, a symbol of South Florida individuality for six decades, was supposed to go the way of progress. The collection of homes built on stilts six miles out in Biscayne Bay, about a mile south of the Cape Florida lighthouse, was scheduled for oblivion by July 1, 1999. But by the mid-2000s, it was still standing strong.

There was no phone, electricity or water line; you brought it with you. Rain was collected in cisterns; waste in holding tanks for disposal ashore. Boats ferried construction materials, furnishings and provisions.

The sea and sun pounded relentlessly on the wood structures and their frail legs. What the homes did provide was a weekend getaway; a quiet but spectacular lifestyle among the fish, the waves, and the sky. Step off your porch and snorkel among the sea life. Drop a fishing line out the front door. Listen to the waves lap. And see the sun drop behind the downtown Miami skyline.

Stiltsville had its origins around 1939, when Commodore Edward Turner created the Quarterdeck Club on stilts in the shoals below Cape Florida. The club had electricity, heating, refrigeration, a bar, a dining room, a bridge deck, a dining deck — and a remarkable view.

Life Magazine, in February 1941, said the club "hovers between sea and sky, a $100,000 play-place equipped with a bar, lounge, bridge deck, dining room and dock slips for yachts. Ranged about it in the bay's wide watery acreage are the green-and-white shacks of members and vice-commodores."

One maverick enterprise led to another, and soon, houses were built on the submerged land without benefit of any legal transaction. By 1945, twelve houses and two clubs existed.

The stilt houses were a haven for — what else — booze, gambling and women. At the Bikini Club, a pink card gained entry day or night. The Quarterdeck Club had a bar, gaming tables and slot machines.

In July 1965, state beverage agents raided the Bikini Club, which was nothing more than a 150-foot yacht hard aground on the flats. The raiders charged the proprietor with selling alcoholic beverages without a license.

Two months later, Stiltsville took a hit from Hurricane Betsy. Where twenty houses had perched atop stilts, less than a half dozen remained, and the Bikini Club was listing twenty degrees to port.

Some of the houses were replaced, at which time the state began to take notice of Stiltsville.

In 1968, the Florida Cabinet issued leases on the properties. By 1975, however, the state was looking at Stiltsville as not being worth the small lease stipends, particularly because the Biscayne Aquatic Act of 1974, creating a park of much of south Biscayne Bay, had included Stiltsville. The Department of Natural Resources tried to evict everyone.

Calmer heads prevailed, maybe because the leaseholders included a local judge, attorneys, a realtor, corporate executives, and corporations. In 1976, a deal was struck: The Cabinet renewed leases for fifteen stilt houses for twenty-three years, on the condition that the houses be vacated by 1999. The area officially became part of the 173,000-acre Biscayne National Park in 1980.

In 1992, Hurricane Andrew blew away seven of the houses. The seven that survived were atop pilings anchored into bedrock on the floor of the bay. They stood in water from one to three feet deep at low tide.

As the 1999 deadline for the future of Stiltsville approached, leaseholders fought attempts to raze the homes, and that led to, of course, lawsuits.

In 1998, the Florida National Register Review Board recommended Stiltsville be added to the National Register of Historic Places. Seven months later, on March 18, 1999, the Register rejected the site, saying the remaining seven houses were less than 50 years old.

The National Park Service then said it wouldn't extend the leases when they ran out in June 1999. But 10 days before the deadline, the Park Service granted a 5-month stay. In November 1999, it extended that another year.

In 2003, the federal government announced plans to transfer the remaining seven cottages from private leases to public use. The Stiltsville Trust, a 15-member non-profit group would raise money to rehabilitate cabins for uses such as artist-in-residence programs, community meeting spaces, even a bed and breakfast inn.

Meanwhile a group called "Save Old Stiltsville" gathered more than 55,000 signatures in an effort to get the historic designation that would preserve Stiltsville permanently.

"Save Old Stiltsville" Web page: www.stiltsville.org

"Fishermen Get Away from it all at a Club Knee-deep in Biscayne Bay," *Life Magazine,* February 10, 1941 Walewski, Sandra, Associated Press, "Biscayne Bay's stilt structures on last legs," *Palm Beach Post,* December 25, 1989

McLeod, Beth, "Stilt City," Palm Beach *Post,* August 13, 1992

Rubin, Aaron, "Seven Homes in Stiltsville Fall in Storm," Miami *Herald,* August 30, 1992

Kleinberg, Howard, "Trying to Keep Stiltsville, Its Stories and Legends," Miami *Herald,* September 9, 1995

Morgan, Curtis, "Stiltsville Adrift," Miami *Herald,* May 2, 1999

Rabin, Charles, "Elevated Future: Stiltsville Could Open to Public," Miami *Herald,* August 2, 2003

Stiltsville stands in Biscayne Bay near downtown Miami (Save Old Stiltsville)

THE WAKULLA VOLCANO

What caused the great Wakulla volcano, which mystified North Floridians for decades, brought death to those who sought it, and abruptly vanished?

It was a column of smoke, hidden in the Wacissa Swamp about 30 miles southeast of Tallahassee. No records show when it started, but as far back as 1830, residents reportedly climbed onto rooftops, and later the top of the old capitol building, to see the smoke pouring into the sky.

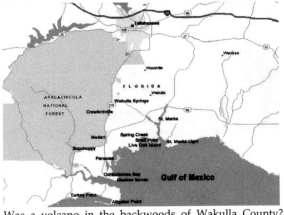

Was a volcano in the backwoods of Wakulla County? (Wakulla County)

Speculation over the years had it coming from the campfires of local natives or runaway slaves or pirates, or spewing from one heck of a moonshiner's still. Sailors approaching the nearby port of St. Marks used the smoke for bearings and were said to have remarked that the old man of the swamp was smoking his pipe again. It was first dubbed "The Wakulla Volcano" in 1882, in a piece by a writer named Barton Jones in *Lippincott's Magazine*. Accounts say it suddenly disappeared after a famed August 31, 1886, earthquake that was centered in South Carolina and, in a rarity, was felt as far south as St. Augustine, where it rang church bells.

Geologists say a volcano is a physical impossibility in Florida. They say volcanoes are usually found in places such as Hawaii where a stream of molten rock shoots up from hundreds of miles under the surface, or places where the planet's tectonic plates interact. Igneous rocks, those generally created from the cooling of molten rock either deep inside the Earth or by volcanic action, should be found at and just under the ground near volcanoes, but none have been seen in the Wakulla area, and any igneous rocks are 7,000 feet underground and likely formed millions of years ago.

In a November 1, 1934, letter to state geologist Herman Gunter, state librarian W.T. Cash said his own mother had seen the smoke as a child.

"It was claimed by some that their compasses wouldn't work in parts of the Wacissa Swamp, which I believe is all bosh," Cash wrote. "Others said that quagmires, floating tussocks, etc., were so thick they couldn't go any farther in the swamp."

In the mid-1990s, the volcano became an obsession for Sonny "The Round Man" Branch, a used car salesman and former talk-radio host. He collected news articles, maps, photos and letters about the thing for years and led volunteers on many expeditions into the swamp in search of what he called, "the Big Belch."

Sonny Branch

In 1997, he took with him two state geologists, a wildlife officer and reporters. Branch was not the first.

A New York *Herald Tribune* reporter had made the trek in the 1870s with a large entourage, but they had turned back and the correspondent "inexplicably sickened and died...before high land could be reached," scientist and writer Wilfred T. Neill wrote in a June 1963 edition of *Florida Wildlife*. He wrote that two other explorers tried in 1891 but also turned back, with one nearly losing his life in the process.

In the 1920s, A.L. Porter, a Wakulla County judge, and James Kirkland, a forester, reported they had been deer hunting in nearby Jefferson County's Gum Swamp when the judge climbed some rocks and spied a crater.

William Wyatt, a Tallahassee office-supply businessman, and Fred Wimpee, a Jacksonville businessman, set out for it in 1932, following directions left by a Chicago reporter who had reportedly gotten close to the smoke but grew exhausted and had to retreat. The two drove as far as they could, then hacked their way through the swamp. Soon, they reported, they came across a four-mile-square spread of great sinkholes and boulders that appeared to have been blown out of the ground.

In 1996, another Tallahassee-area radio personality, Julian Roberts, planned his own expedition. Roberts said he'd met a retired Pentecostal minister who said he saw a crater in the swamps northeast of the St. Marks lighthouse while working with a government surveying team in the early 1960s. The minister said the crater was about one hundred feet across and surrounded by oak trees but contained melted rocks as black as charcoal. He said the group threw rocks in the hole but could not hear them hit bottom.

In his 1997 expedition, Sonny Branch passed through a swampland known as Hell's Half Acre, to a football-field-sized area of swamp, and declared it to be his Holy Grail. He then announced to his entourage, "The Wakulla Volcano is in Jefferson County, not Wakulla, and it's not a volcano. My theory is that it was a peat-bog fire that started in one place and burnt different types of vegetation."

Branch said the large boulders seen by the earlier expedition were probably blasted out to make way for U.S. Highway 98.

He had no evidence to back his peat fire theory, but it is one others have proffered. In fact, state librarian W.T. Cash had suggested it in his 1934 letter. And Wilfred Neill's articles suggested the 1886 earthquake opened a sinkhole that devoured the peat and smothered the fire.

A peat fire would explain why people reported seeing the smoke change colors. Tom Scott, one of the two geologists in Branch's group, said a drought could drop the water table and spark the peat fire. His colleague, Harvey Means, said, "If I'd found a volcano, I wouldn't have called the (newspaper). I would have called David Letterman."

Wakulla Volcano web page: www.wakullavolcano.vashti.net

Laufenberg, Kathleen, "Searching for the Wakulla Volcano," Tallahassee *Democrat*, April 20, 1997

Christensen, Sig, "Adventurers to seek Wakulla volcano," *Florida Times-Union*, February 8, 1996

Tallahassee Bar Association Bulletin, April 2002

"Geology of Jefferson County, Florida." *Geological Bulletin 48*, Florida Geological Survey, 1966

Letter from State Librarian W.T. Cash to State Geologist Herman Gunter, November 1, 1934 (Wakulla Volcano Archive)

THE MERRITT ISLAND DRAGON

For more than three decades, the Melbourne Dragon guarded "Dragon Point," at the confluence of the Indian and Banana Rivers at the southernmost tip of Merritt Island. Now it might rise again.

The 70-foot-long, 35-foot-high, sea green sculpture, nicknamed "Annie," was built in 1970.

The Merritt Island Dragon

An Illinois couple, Aynn and Jeff Christal, hired Miami sculptor and card-carrying warlock Lewis Van Dercar to create it from twenty tons of concrete and steel. Van Dercar said a woman in white told him how to build the thing in a dream. He named it after Aynn.

When residents caught wind that a huge beast was being built on the river, they launched an unsuccessful "Ban the Dragon" campaign.

In 1974, another couple bought the property and installed red lights in the dragon's eyes and a gas apparatus in its mouth, giving it the ability to breathe fire.

Warren McFadden, a prominent businessman and political organizer from Fort Lauderdale, bought the 7,800-square-foot home at Dragon Point in 1981. He hired Van Dercar to add a curling tail and two back legs, elongate the neck, and add a cave man, a woman and four hatchlings named Joy, Sunshine, Charity and Freedom.

Van Dercar also added some Flintstone-style furniture, sculptures of Fred and Wilma and a sunroof. An icebox and three telephones were installed inside and Annie was wired with electricity to light tables, chairs and stairs that led up to the nostrils. Looking out the nostrils, visitors could watch the sun rise and set.

McFadden, who filled his home with dragon figurines, said he often invited groups to tour Annie, walk inside her hollow body, and climb to the sun deck on her back. He sometimes used tours to raise money for charity.

Annie was a fanciful navigational guide for mariners. At Christmas, the massive serpent was strung with lights. And every July 4, she drew thousands to the Eau Gallie Causeway and brigades of boats to the river when she belched a fifteen-foot-long flame over the Indian River Lagoon—just like the legendary dragon that natives claimed to have seen on the spot hundreds of years ago.

The Merritt Island Dragon was a landmark. (City-data.com)

Some locals stirred up stories that glows and ghostly figures, including the woman in white, enveloped the beast. But McFadden said it was sadly untrue.

It wasn't just children who were drawn to the dragon. Lee Scherer, director of the nearby Kennedy Space Center from 1975 to 1979, climbed on it. So did Colonel Oscar Payne, a former commander at nearby Patrick Air Force Base.

Through the years, while most admired the dragon, some did not. Vandals knocked holes in its belly with a sledgehammer, stole one of its legs and made off with Fred's arm. A boater took one of its concrete teeth for a souvenir.

Finally, the vandals, along with storms and erosion, took their toll on Annie. In August 2002, she crumbled into the water, leaving only her tail and the four hatchlings intact and parts lying on the coquina rock that had protected her from the currents.

Local authorities and engineers had inspected the dragon seven months earlier, had declared it was deteriorating and had ordered it closed to visitors.

Rebuilding it appeared out of the question. McFadden said Van Dercar died in 1989 at the age of seventy-five.

Businessman Bob Hereford, who bought the property in 2003, he'd received numerous e-mails and phone calls and offers from groups who wanted to donate toward rebuilding Annie. As far back as 1996, residents had formed the Hope Dragon Foundation to raise money for Annie's maintenance

Hereford eventually announced he would build a new Annie. His business partner, Tom Palumbo, said the dragon would resemble the old one but might be more modern. He said he was looking at some of the dragon designs from nearby Walt Disney World. The dragon's demise and possible rebirth sparked a children's book, a play script, a coloring book and sheet music.

Hereford said he hoped to build a new dragon by 2006. This one would be not concrete, but a sturdier fiberglass. But, it would still be green.

Interview with Warren McFadden, September 7, 1995

Florida Today, August 6, 2002; December 13, 2003; July 4, July 21, 2004

Associated Press, August 7, 2002

Orlando *Sentinel,* August 7, 2002

.

SECTION TWO
CHAPTER
5

SOLOMON'S CASTLE

For three decades, Solomon's Castle, a full-sized replica of a 16th-century castle, has stood in the middle of nowhere, near the settlement of Ona, in Florida's interior near Arcadia.

The sixteen-room, thirty-foot-tall, 12,000-square foot building, surrounded by horse and cow pastures, has spires and minarets. At first glance, it looks like a collection of large cutout boxes wrapped in aluminum foil. The foil is actually old aluminum printing plates. Most of the castle and the art within is made from recycled material.

Sculptor Howard Solomon built Solomon's Castle in southwest Florida. (Solomon's Castle)

The castle, believed to be the only tourist attraction in Hardee County, has drawn tens of thousands of tourists. But its creator, junk artist Howard Solomon, eventually put it on the market.

A CHAIR MADE OF BEER CANS

The sculptor, a native of Rochester, New York, closed galleries of his work in the Bahamas and Miami and bought 70 acres of land in Ona, about seventy miles southeast of Tampa. The idea was to retire and sculpt. He began building the castle in 1972 as his retirement home. But, he says on his web page, he decided the castle needed something to make it look "big and shiny, as castles are meant to be."

Then Solomon read in the *Herald Advocate*, a weekly in nearby Wauchula, that the newspaper was selling used 22-by-34-inch offset aluminum printing plates, suggesting chicken farmers use them to repair their coops. He said he developed a hobby that got out of hand. Every few months over the next fourteen years, he bought stacks of plates for a dime each. He coated the castle in

12,000 square feet of plates, their shiny blank sides on the outside and old news stories hidden on the inside.

Solomon still sculpts, working in a 2,000-square-foot studio in the woods a short walk from the castle. He has turned beer cans and clothes hangers into giraffes, chairs and other creations. He used old oil drums, worn-out food processors, gas tanks, metal scraps and other debris. The hair on many sculptures is made from roller chains. Solomon took 50 pounds of clothes hangers to make sculptures of a giraffe, elephant, shark and penguin. He has interpretations of *Star Wars* villain Darth Vader, former Ugandan dictator Idi Amin and other characters.

Other sculptures:

A knight fashioned from Volkswagen parts.

1948 Triple Crown winners Eddie Arcaro and Citation assembled with universal joints.

A large engine made from Xerox parts, kerosene lamps and other debris and powered by an old Hoover vacuum engine.

A chair made from 86 beer cans.

A giant 190-pound lion made from five oil drums.

An elephant made from seven oil drums with old clam shells for toenails.

Solomon originally opened his home up to the curious once a month for 12 years, giving a free tour. Then his daughter told him he ought to charge admission and hold regular hours. Since then, tour groups have made regular trips to the castle, and it's now featured in a wide variety of books and enjoys regular exposure in the press and on television.

A tour leads through the lower level of the castle where visitors explore the unique art that fills several rooms.

When guests arrive, they're greeted by an iguana that lives in a circular cage built around a tree in front of the castle. The tour runs about thirty-five minutes, but visitors can also walk a nature trail lined with Spanish moss-covered live oaks and cypress trees along the creek.

Visitors get a glimpse of the living room and kitchen of the Solomon family. When the trap door is open, guests get a peek at a small, dark underground room complete with the sculpture of a large green-faced monster.

A guide elicits groans from visitors with one-liners associated with each piece of art. A tortoise shell with a wig dangling beneath it is "the tortoise and the hair." A piece described as suicide doctor Jack Kevorkian's dueling pistols has the barrels of both bent back toward the holder. A half-gondola hanging lengthwise on a wall is "Cleopatra's Gondola;" she lost the other half in the divorce and is now "in de-Nile."

Outside are more than 80 stained glass windows, each with a story or message in them. Some represent the nine planets, nursery rhymes such as the cow jumps over the moon and Humpty Dumpty, the eight arts, various coats of arms and other scenes.

Solomon built a moat around the castle and a drawbridge that led to a large boat that serves as a restaurant. The sixty-foot replica of a 16th century Spanish galleon is called "Boat in the Moat." Solomon also built a three-story lighthouse to stand over the boat. Beyond that is a gift shop and outdoor cafe.

One of the towers holds the Blue Moon Room, which Solomon rents out for overnight or weekend stays. A balcony overlooks the boat/restaurant. The suite contains a kitchen and satellite TV. The charge includes a bottle of wine, a tour of the castle and a full breakfast for two.

Solomon lives in the castle with his wife Peggy and son Ben. His daughter Alane and her husband run the restaurant.

MISSING: ONE ALLIGATOR

Wanting to slow down, Solomon finally put the place up for sale either as a tourist attraction "or to some crackpot that wants it as an unusual home." He started at five million dollars, but more recently was down to $2.5 million.

When Hurricane Charley came through in the summer of 2004, Solomon, then sixty-nine, rode it out in his truck. He watched the roof of his daughter's home blow off. The rest of his family stayed in the castle. An alligator that patrolled the moat surrounding his Spanish galleon-like Boat in the Moat Restaurant went missing. But the 'gator later showed up.

Web site: www.solomonscastle.com
Orlando *Sentinel*, October 16, 1988
Associated Press, July 13, 2003
St. Petersburg *Times*, January 30, 2004
Fort Myers *News-Press*, April 4, 2004
Presstime, June 2004
Tampa *Tribune*, August 23, 2004
E-mail correspondence with Solomon's Castle, December 2004

SECTION TWO
CHAPTER
6

AFRICA U.S.A.

In 1960, *Life Magazine* did a cover story on amusement parks. Inside was a mention of a little place in California called Disneyland. On the cover was Africa U.S.A. in Boca Raton.

Never heard of it?

Fifteen years before neighbor Lion Country Safari opened, Africa U.S.A. was the wildest attraction this side of the Serengeti. When its creator, John P. "Pete" Pedersen, died in 1996 at ninety-eight, part of Florida's colorful, kitschy past went with him.

The Wisconsin native had worked for the Southern Pacific Railroad in California and came to Florida in 1934. He bought up property in Broward County at Depression-era prices.

Boca Raton, which had been a bustling military town during World War II, reverted to a population of less than 1,000 after the flyboys left. By the late 1950s, Pedersen considered Boca "the deadest town" he'd ever seen.

The "Masai Warriors" were actual locals. (Africa-USA.com)

But he had an idea to liven up the place—buy 350 acres, bring in some big game animals, build a 30-foot waterfall and thrill tourists with the sight of "Masai warriors."

"THE POISON ARROW GOT HIM"

Pedersen, fascinated with Africa, had never been there.

But in a plan that would be copied in the 1960s nearby Lion Country Safari, he planted thousands of tropical trees—3,000 Royal Poincianas alone—and let animals roam in an environment similar to their native lands, surrounded by double 8-foot fences.

His son went to Africa and returned with ostriches, giraffes, colorful birds, and Abyssinian asses. He got 60 nearly-extinct Grevey zebras under a special permit for $1,000 each.

Africa U.S.A opened in February 1953. The 177-acre spread, one of Florida's original wild animal attractions, hosted hundreds of exotic animals and drew as many as 2,000 tourists a day to sparse Boca Raton.

Billboards up and down the state told how many miles left to get to the attraction. On a large sign on Federal Highway in Deerfield Beach — this was before Interstate 95 — a big arrow guided motorists.

Admission was free, but visitors paid to ride trams for a six-mile, one-hour tour of Tanziniki, the country Pedersen invented.

Pete Stumberger, who would stay on in Boca Raton, got a job driving the tram in the summer of 1955.

At Jungle Town, Stumberger recalled in 1996, visitors were greeted by "Masai Warriors" — most of whom had grown up in nearby Pompano Beach.

"We had a big fellow dressed up as a warrior," Stumberger said. "It was so hot. He just passed out. I didn't know what to tell people. I said, 'Well, the poison arrow got him.'"

The 30-foot "Zambezi Falls" waterfall sent 275,000 gallons of water a minute cascading down a built-up hill into flower-covered rapids and on to a seven-acre lake.

In their tour boats, visitors watched the Watusi Geyser send up a 165-foot plume of water from the lake. The tourists didn't know it was Pedersen peeking from his home and turning the switch.

"At 3:30, we had to stop that tram at a certain spot," Stumberger recalled. "We'd say, 'That's Old Faithful. It could go at any time. Get your cameras ready.' Meanwhile, Pete was watching out the window."

Sometimes, the wild animals stampeded, Stumberger recalled.

"We were going through the area where the herd of cud-chewing animals were when something set them off," he said. "They were coming right for the tram. I was trying to figure how to get out of there and wondering if they were going to stop. At the last second, they did stop, and everybody thought it was a part of the show."

Another time, he said, a herd of giraffes stampeded as he was driving an empty tram through their area. One struck the last car and shattered its leg.

Pedersen's son would ride around town in his convertible with cheetahs Mojah and Mbili riding shotgun. A Hollywood producer spotted the pair and they were featured in the film *Quo Vadis* as Emperor Nero's wife's personal pets. And Princess Margaret, a chimp who was featured on *The Tonight Show* with Jack Paar, was dressed in lacy outfits and taught to kiss people.

By the early 1960s, housing was going up on both sides of the park and neighbors were complaining about the sounds of the Serengeti disturbing their sleep. Pedersen had an extended battle with the city, which condemned some of his land for a right-of-way.

In early 1960, federal agriculture agents found the first-ever North American outbreak of African red ticks among Pedersen's herd. He had to destroy thousands of dollars worth of animals. Others died from the anti-tick spraying or after being tranquilized.

Finally, fed up, Pedersen sent his animals to zoos as far away as Canada and Mexico and closed down.

"We are not closing because Africa was not a success," Pedersen said at the time. "We made in three years close to $420,000. We closed the place because we are tried of fighting the continual harassment by Boca Raton City officials."

In October 1961, he sold the land he had purchased for about $10,000 to the developers of Camino Gardens for $1.1 million. He promptly retired, declaring he was "going to Australia!"

In 1968, the successor to Africa U.S.A., Lion Country Safari, opened on 320 acres in Loxahatchee, west of West Palm Beach.

Pedersen spent his last years living in suburban Lake Worth and died in a West Palm Beach nursing home.

For years, peacocks, monkeys and parrots that had eluded captors remained in the Africa U.S.A. property. Boca Raton's omnipresent and annoying Muscovy ducks are said to be courtesy of Mr. Pedersen.

The Camino Gardens homeowners' association, which owns the island, dismantled the bridge in 1987. Boca Raton posted "peacock crossing" signs that soon disappeared as souvenirs. And neighbors continue to spot parrots at their bird feeders.

In 2003, descendants of Pete Pedersen came to honor what his daughter called "a little boy's wish that came true." On the edge of the lagoon that had once been a centerpiece of Pedersen's "Africa U.S.A.," his relatives and residents of the neighborhood that replaced the wild animal park gathered to honor its fiftieth anniversary.

Pedersen's daughter, Shirley Pedersen Schneider, helped dedicate a brass marker that tells the story of the park. Most of the 50 or so attending were Camino Gardens residents. Eight raised their hands when Shirley Schneider's niece, Ginger Pedersen, asked if anyone had attended the park.

Schneider told about fifty people her father had set three goals as a child — become wealthy, live past 100 "and find land that looked like Africa and let animals run free, not caged." She said her father died two months shy of ninety-nine but met the other two objectives. And Ginger Pedersen said her grandfather, who had only a sixth-grade education, "was an extremely determined and motivated person who did not take no for an answer."

The Palm Beach Community College dean, born after the park closed, has kept her grandfather's vision alive through a Web page. She said one woman who'd visited as a child wrote in an e-mail, "Thanks for helping me feel like I was six years old again."

Web page: www.africa-usa.com

Palm Beach *Post*, May 1, 1996; July 10, 2002; March 20, 2003

South Florida Sun Sentinel, December 29, 1995

Glimpses of South Florida History, by Stuart McIver

"Boca Raton's 'Africa, U.S.A.'" by Donald W. Curl.

EVERGLADES CITY

On the morning of July 7, 1983, dawn sent its rays onto the tiny village of Everglades City, a dot of some five hundred people on the southwest corner of the Florida peninsula, hard between the cypress swamps and the Gulf of Mexico.

On State Road 29, the only highway that connected the town, at least by land, lawmen had put up a roadblock.

Then, more than two hundred federal and state officers charged into the hamlet. They kicked down doors and carted off two airplanes, five vehicles, and fourteen fishing boats. They cuffed fifteen people in town and another nineteen in the vicinity and were hot in the pursuit of seven more.

The big bust, one of the largest pot smuggling crackdowns in U.S. history, wrapped up a two year operation called "Operation Everglades" that netted authorities more than 450,000 pounds — 225 tons — of pot, then worth about $179 million. They'd arrested 153 people, a third of them local residents.

The law had come down like a hammer on a town that had sold its collective soul.

"THE LAST FRONTIER"

Everglades City called itself "The Last Frontier." The gateway to the Ten Thousand Islands is separated from most of the rest of the world by sea, swamp and scrub. For decades, residents made a living from fishing, or guiding hunters, or serving tourists. Rum-running was big business during Prohibition and ship-wrecking was before that.

The place had become the county seat in 1923, when developer Barron Collier grew impatient at delays in the building of the Tamiami Trail. He got the state legislature to carve Collier County from Lee County, and, since he owned 90 percent of the new county, he arranged for its commissioners to approve bonds to build the road.

In 1960, Hurricane Donna sent a seven-foot wall of water through the town. The seat was moved twenty-two miles west to Naples. By the mid 1970s, the town had no movie theater, no car dealership, not even a gas station.

At that time, the South Florida drug trade, then approaching its zenith, had bought many of the people in town and turned it into a distribution center that would make Wal-Mart proud. Only this was for marijuana. It came and went in boats and in semi-trailers hauling fifty tons.

What made Everglades City so attractive was the miles of waterways, too many even to count or chart. Some were so covered over by mangroves that tourists would get lost for days nearly within shouting distance of help.

It had started slowly, with strangers rolling into town, dripping with conspicuous consumption. They'd flash their nice clothes and jewelry and fancy cars and homes and top-of-the-line pleasure boats. And they'd disappear periodically on "fishing trips" that didn't fool anyone.

They'd meet their mother ships, unload bales of pot—"square grouper"— and load them in fishing boats or airboats or vehicles or aircraft, then send them down various conduits to the outside world.

The top cop in town, deputy sheriff Charlie Sanders, had made his share of arrests, sometimes busting a friend. He'd watched people fudge their morals amid the tantalizing scent of big money. The temptation was hard to resist for someone who worked a fourteen-hour day in the blistering sun for a decent wage but could earn $10,000 cash in one night.

Add to that the distrust and resentment of a big government that infringed on fishing rights, zoned everything to death and chased little guys while the big smugglers walked.

And even those who didn't participate in the illicit activities benefited from the money that poured into the local economy as smugglers bought homes and cars and food and drink.

Sanders said he'd been offered bribes that would have made him a rich man, and turned them all down. It didn't matter; he had just six officers for a huge area, and the smugglers knew it. Usually they just had to wait for a wreck on the highway, which would send the lawmen out of town and free them to do their smuggling with impunity.

Eventually, the sheriff of the 2,000 square mile county, the state's largest in area, had called the feds for help.

Infiltrating had not been easy in the small clannish town, where it seemed everyone was related by blood or marriage.

Agents had posed as buyers, sellers and handlers. Some had worked as crew and off-loaders in smuggling runs. When they made busts, they towed the vessels hundreds of miles to other ports and reported they'd been nabbed during routine patrols.

But in the months leading up to the raid, residents had been called to a federal grand jury in Miami, so pretty much everyone in town knew something big was brewing. But the feds had not told Sanders or the mayor or even the local newspaper publisher about their big bust.

They had, however, tipped big city reporters two days ahead of the raid. One had called the deputy sheriff four hours before. Another had called the mayor asking for an advance comment.

"THESE ARE GOOD PEOPLE HERE"

One resident, Ada Collins, recalled being awakened about 6:00 a.m. by loud talking, then a crash, and opening her eyes to see a man holding a revolver in her husband's face. Four men were in the home, and they'd come to take four of Ada's seven children.

"Those agents went around afterwards saying we were nothing but bums," Ada Collins said later. "But all seven of my children finished high school and one of them went on to junior college, and if they'd have said they had a warrant for their arrest, they would have surrendered themselves. There was no need to shut down the town with roadblocks. These are good people here."

Residents later said many of those arrested had previous arrests and that most of the boats were eventually returned for lack of evidence that they took part in smuggling. Eventually, most of the forty-one people arrested in connection with the raid would be convicted or plead guilty. And a second raid took place in July 1984 after a grand jury indicted forty people.

For years, locals would bitterly criticize the authorities for the 1983 raid. They called it a well-planned publicity stunt, with the press brought in for maximum exposure—and humiliation—of a little town that had gone from nothing to boom to a very big bust.

Williams, Christian, "Smugglers' Paradise Lost,"
Washington *Post*, July 15, 1983
Hiaasen, Carl, "Marijuana Bust nets 28 in Collier,"
Miami *Herald*, July 8, 1983
Cosco, Joseph, "Everglades City Bitter over Busted Reputation,"
South Florida Sun-Sentinel, October 30, 1983
Associated Press, "Drug Notoriety on Overdose," December 8, 1984
Kleinberg, Eliot, *Florida Fun Facts*, 2004

ANDYTOWN

If you want to find Andytown, you'll need to work your way along the shadow of Interstate 595, west of Fort Lauderdale, to a bar behind a chain link fence and next to a convenience store.

Andy's Lounge and Package is nondescript except for one feature, above the front door—an old highway sign, its green background not yet faded. It says simply, "Andytown."

It's been a quarter century since the Halloween night when the state shut down the metropolis, population never more than fifteen citizens.

For three decades, the dusty fifteen-acre clearing at the corner of U.S. 27 and Alligator Alley was a haven for truckers crossing the endless expanse of saw grass and water and darkness between coasts, or fishermen hauling their johnboats, or hunters chasing white-tail deer.

They would crunch to a stop in the gravel parking lot and slog through the stifling humidity and swarming mosquitoes toward that haven in the heat or

Andytown, on the edge of the Everglades

the bright light in the darkness. They knew it meant a fill-er-up, a bucket of bait, and some chow and a cold one to wash away the dirt and sweat and the glare of the headlights.

But it was also a beloved South Florida oddity that inspired forecasters, editors and mapmakers.

Weather forecasters mentioned it, and more than one editor had a little fun directing a rookie reporter to run out to Andytown City Hall and pick up the agenda for the next council meeting. And dozens of boilerplate web pages refer to it, even though it's been gone for years.

"GOD BLESS ANDY"

Andytown was a restaurant, bar, gas station and bait shop. Behind it was a six-unit motel. At first Andy rented out the rooms. Later, employees lived there.

The saloon that was the town's centerpiece was never fancy. It had the usual Formica tables, about a dozen of them, along with a long, thirty-stool bar, pinball machines and illuminated beer signs.

One would expect an oasis in the Everglades to smell like frying catfish and sound like Johnny Cash. Andytown was all that, but it was also *gyros* and *ouzo* and plinking mandolins.

A sign over the bar said, "This is the town that Andy built. God Bless Andy."

Greek immigrant Andy Poulos had come to the spot in 1947, when Fort Lauderdale had only about 90,000 people and there were only about 2.7 million souls in all of Florida, about as many as there are in Miami-Dade County today.

Andy, then a linen service operator in Philadelphia, got lost looking for Hollywood one day and stopped for a cup of coffee at a small cafe at U.S. 27 and State Road 84. He returned the next day and bought the café and a gas station and the surrounding 10 acres for $50,000. He brought down nephew Konstantinos "Gus" Tsanos in 1964 and John Theodore, brother of Gus' wife, in 1967. Both were fellow Greek immigrants who had been living in Indiana.

It was the early 1970s before the phone company finally ran a line out there for a bank of pay phones. Visitors included Telly Savalas, Bob Hope, and adult film star Linda Lovelace. The priest at the Greek Orthodox church in Fort Lauderdale, where the denizens of Andytown worshipped, came out every year to bless Andy's empire.

Andy died in 1972 during a visit to his birthplace of Kostana, in Greece, the country he had left at the age of ten. He was buried there.

But Andytown's clock was already ticking. Five years earlier, the Florida Department of Transportation had bought up the whole place for $180,000. Its

Andytown on the final night in 1979 (Palm Beach *Post*)

buildings would be knocked down to make way for the Interstate 75 interchange.

"Last call" came on Halloween night in 1979. Tsanos and Theodore, their wives, their barmaid, and a crush of friends packed the place. The liquor flowed for free. Tsanos wept.

"I spent an hour and a half with radio stations over the phone," Theodore recalled in October 2004 from his home in Coral Springs. Tsanos did not respond to several telephone calls or a note left for him at the bar.

The morning after the party, November 1, 1979, Tsanos handed the state the keys to Andytown.

"THE LEGACY GOES ON."

The owners vowed Andytown would rise from the ashes somewhere else on State Road 84. But they parted ways. Gus opened Andy's Lounge. Theodore bought a service station in Coral Springs.

Tragedy struck the two in recent years. In January 2000, Evangelin "Litsa" Tsanos, 60, Gus Tsanos' wife and John Theodore's sister, was found by Gus, shot to death, in their Plantation home. The family posted billboards and offered an $11,000 reward, but Plantation police had no suspects or witnesses.

A quarter century after it vanished, Andytown still holds a place in John Theodore's heart.

"It was one of the nicest places I ever lived," he said in his thick Greek accent. "I get people who call me many times and say, 'I'm so and so. Do you remember me from Andytown?' The legacy goes on and on."

Actually, there is one other homage to the old place besides the sign at Andy's Lounge.

On the concrete median that separates the north and south lanes of I-75, where it crosses U.S. 27, state transportation officials used that bureaucratic black stencil usually reserved for more mundane information. They had painted: "Andytown. 1947-1979."

Palm Beach *Post*, October 30, 2004

SECTION III:

THE DAILY WEIRD REDUX

SECTION THREE
CHAPTER 1

BLASTS FROM THE PAST

John Henry Eaton, governor of the Florida territory from 1834 to 1835, ended up in what was then a sparsely-populated backwater after suffering through a class scandal. Eaton had been Secretary of War for Andrew Jackson, not one to stand on society, but even Old Hickory took heat over the fact that Eaton's wife, Peggy O'Neale, was a former barmaid in a Washington tavern. Wives of prominent politicians boycotted functions Peggy attended; even Vice President John C. Calhoun refused to force his aristocratic wife to attend. Eaton eventually resigned and went to his exile in Florida.

Florida Handbook

John Henry Eaton became a territorial governor of Florida after a society scandal ran him out of Washington, (Florida Photographic Collection)

On June 9, 1903, fire broke out in the famed Breakers hotel in Palm Beach, then only seven years old. As the fire, perhaps started by a plumber's torch, raced through the wooden structure, the alarm went out. Palm Beach had no fire department. The city of West Palm Beach had only a volunteer department. As "Flagler's Alerts" raced over the wooden railroad bridge, they were stopped by the toll keeper, who demanded a nickel from each man. The hotel eventually burned to the ground, but historians said the tollbooth delay probably made no difference. The Breakers was later rebuilt.

Palm Beach *Post,* March 22, 2000

Women working as telephone company change counters in the 1950s in Miami hired "a particularly ample-bosomed woman" by the name of Ruth

When The Breakers burned in 1903, arriving firefighters had to pay toll (Historical Society of Palm Beach County)

MacNabb and paid her $5 a week to stuff as many rolls of quarters as she could into her brassiere. The scam was exposed when police, dispatched to a brawl involving the women, found piles of quarters scattered throughout her house.

Associated Press, November 25, 1998

A wild shot from a .22 caliber revolver into the Reno Bar in Pahokee knocked a wig off the head of Rose Mary Cutter. A local man seen driving away from the area was arrested.

Palm Beach *Post*, January 17, 1967

When President Richard Nixon made his famous "I am not a crook" comment on November 17, 1973, he said it at Walt Disney World. Nixon was addressing the annual convention of the Associated Press Managing Editors Association.

The quote:

"I made my mistakes, but in all of my years of public life, I have never profited, never profited from public service. I have earned every cent. And in all of my years of public life, I

President Richard Nixon delivered his famous "I am not a crook" speech in Florida. (Florida Photographic Collection)

have never obstructed justice. And I think, too, that I could say that in my years of public life, that I welcome this kind of examination, because people have got to know whether or not their President is a crook. Well, I am not a crook. I have earned everything I have got."

University of California, Santa Barbara

At the December 28, 1978, Gator Bowl game in Jacksonville, famed Ohio State University coach Woody Hayes slugged a Clemson player who'd run out of bounds near Hayes after intercepting a pass. The Buckeyes lost 17-15 and fired Hayes two days later.

Florida Historical Society

In May 1983, eclectic artist Christo wrapped pink plastic around eleven islands in Biscayne Bay, The "surrounded islands" project used six million square feet of the stuff to give each island a 200-foot-wide ring. The project cost $3 million, $900,000 of that for the material. Officials said it spurred tourism.

Palm Beach *Post*, February 26, 1994

A barge carrying 1-1/2 tons of New York City garbage trekked from port to port in three nations and six states, including Panama City and Key West, but could find no takers. It finally gave up and returned home. Later, a freelance writer did a cover story in the *New York Times* weekly magazine titled "Can Miami Save Itself?" which included a picture of a drug bust that turned out to be staged. The Miami *Herald* wrote a satiric response showing the infamous garbage barge and the Manhattan skyline and titled, "Can New York Save Itself?"

Palm Beach *Post*, December 31, 1987

ROCK 'N ROLL FLORIDA

In 1956, a Jacksonville judge told Elvis Presley not to shake his pelvis because it might drive women to distraction. The King wiggled his pinky instead.

When Presley arrived in Jacksonville, *Hound Dog* and the record's flip-side, *Don't Be Cruel*, were near the top of the charts. A week after the Jacksonville show, he would head to Hollywood to make his first movie, *Love Me Tender*. Elvis was set to perform six shows August 10-11, a Friday and Saturday, at the Florida Theatre. Tickets were $1.25.

When Presley and his Blue Moon Boys arrived in Jacksonville, Juvenile Court Judge Marion Gooding ordered "Elvis the Pelvis" not to wiggle and actually monitored the first matinee performance with a local contingent of "morally upright citizens." Later, Presley was summoned to meet with Gooding, who witnesses say rambled on about maintaining order. Gooding concluded by ordering Presley, then the most powerful force in entertainment, to tone down his act.

Presley swore privately he'd never forget the incident. When asked later by reporters about Gooding's order, Presley shrugged and mumbled, "I can't figure out what I'm doing wrong. I know my mother approves of what I'm doing."

Florida Times-Union, August 10, 1996

On November 16, 1969, Janis Joplin was arrested after a show in Tampa for screaming obscenities at police during a concert.

Joplin was fresh off her electrifying performance three months earlier at Woodstock. She showed up with a full bottle of Southern Comfort, which she promptly upended and drained.

Halfway through the show, and in the middle of *Summertime*, an officer with a bullhorn had climbed onstage, warning fans who were dancing to the music to clear the aisles. With 3,500 fans watching, at five dollars a head, Joplin screamed into the microphone, "Leave my (expletive) people alone."

She was allowed to finish her 90-minute performance but police later went to her dressing room and took her out in handcuffs, charged with two counts of public use of profanity. The mayor later had to defend the actions of police.

Joplin was fined $200 in March 1970 for what she said was her first arrest. But for months since the incident, many promoters had shunned her, fearful of riots. Four months after her court appearance, in October 1970, Joplin was dead of a heroin overdose.

Rocker Janis Joplin was arrested for cursing during a concert.

Tampa *Tribune*, November 16, 1994

In 1969, Jim Morrison of *The Doors* was charged with exposing himself at a concert at the Dinner Key Auditorium in Miami's Coconut Grove. He was convicted but the case was on appeal when he drowned in Paris

Palm Beach *Post*, July 22, 2001; November 22, 2002

Jim Morrison was charged with exposing himself at a Miami concert.

From November 24 to November 27, 1975, Tallahassee minister Charles Boykin conducted a public burning of $2,000 worth of rock 'n roll records to protest their evil effects on America's youth. Boykin, saying lyrics promoted promiscuity, claimed that 984 out of 1,000 unwed mothers were impregnated with rock music in the background. How he conducted his survey was not recorded. State pollution control officials later ordered Boykin to quit burning the vinyl records because they gave off hazardous fumes. The reverend, who had been in a rock band in high school, took his show on the road, burning records around the country.

WPLG-TV; United Press International, January 25, 1977

In 1983, Sly Stone, of *Sly and the Family Stone*, was arrested when police found him and a woman unconscious in a Fort Myers hotel room. Police said they found a "free basing" kit. He had just finished a performance so dismal the club owner refused to pay him. Four years later, Stone spent a week in jail on probation charges relating to the original arrest.

Miami *Herald*, December 14, 1985; June 13, 1987

In 1985, rock hero David Crosby docked his boat and surrendered to the FBI in West Palm Beach for two 1983 drugs and weapons convictions from Texas. He later served nine months of a 5-year sentence.

Palm Beach *Post*, July 22, 2001; November 22, 2002

In 1986, Richard Manuel, 42, pianist for the group *The Band*, was found dead in his hotel room in Winter Park, near Orlando. He had hanged himself.

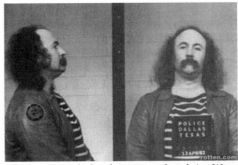

Rocker David Crosby surrendered in West Palm Beach on drug and weapons charges. (Dallas County, Texas, Sheriff's Office)

St. Petersburg *Times*, January 6, 1987

Rocker Gregg Allman was convicted of drunk driving.

In 1987, Gregg Allman served three days in jail in Ocala for drunk driving. He was supposed to serve five days, but was released early after agreeing to perform at a graduation party for area high schools.

Palm Beach *Post*, July 22, 2001, November 22, 2002

In 1990, raunchy Miami rappers 2 *Live Crew* ran afoul of the

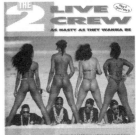

The state of Florida charged rappers 2 Live Crew with obscenity.

law in Broward County, where a federal judge in 1990 ruled their record, *As Nasty as They Wanna Be*, was obscene. The ruling was, of course, manna for the crew. Governor Bob Martinez' public pursuit of the rappers had helped shoot album sales to two million. One columnist wrote, "People will crawl naked over broken glass to get what someone tells them they're not supposed to." The verdict was eventually rejected by an appeals court. The group and its leader, Luther Campbell, were also arrested on obscenity charges for performing the music at a Broward club, but were later acquitted. Soon they had been replaced by raunchier groups and had faded into obscurity.

Denver *Post/South Florida Sun-Sentinel*, January 2, 1987

In 1995, rocker Courtney Love, widow of *Nirvana's* Curt Cobain, was charged with slugging two teens at an Orlando concert of her band *Hole*. Charges were later dropped, the judge saying the teens weren't exposed to any greater amount of violence than could reasonably be expected at an alternative rock concert. But Love said the place is violent. "Even the state of Florida is shaped like a gun."

Orlando *Sentinel,* December 6, 1997

Courtney Love was charged with slugging fans at a concert.

SECTION THREE
CHAPTER
3

CELEBRITY CORNER

Former football star and actor O.J. Simpson, acquitted of killing his ex-wife Nicole and her friend Ron Goldman in 1994 and later successfully sued for $33.5 million for wrongful death, left southern California and moved to South Florida. Florida law protects Simpson's home against such civil judgments, and federal law protects his pension from his years in the NFL. Simpson had not worked since, because any money he made could be used to satisfy the judgment, which is mostly unpaid.

Simpson said at the time he moved in part to escape the glare of publicity and to protect his fourteen-year-old daughter, Sydney, and son, Justin, twelve.

In South Florida, Simpson was the 911 caller, or the subject of a call, in numerous domestic incidents. Officers had to break up a fight between him and a girlfriend at a Miami hotel and ended up asking the girlfriend to leave for assaulting Simpson.

In October 2000, a jury cleared him of charges after he allegedly snatched off the glasses and scratched the face of another motorist after a traffic altercation in a Miami neighborhood.

In December 2001, federal agents searched Simpson's suburban Miami home as part of an investigation into *ecstasy* drug sales and money laundering. A TV news helicopter showed Simp-

O.J. Simpson moved to Florida. (Los Angeles County, Calif., Sheriff's Office)

son, not in the back of a white Ford Bronco, as he was during his famed 1994 "low speed chase," but rather standing in his white bathrobe.

Simpson also ran afoul of DirecTV. The satellite company sued him, alleging he pirated the firm's television signal. The firm sought at least $20,000, plus attorney's fees. Federal agents removed satellite equipment from Simpson's home during the December 2001 search. DirecTV said agents removed two "bootleg" signal-pirating devices.

That prompted comedian David Letterman to comment on CBS' *The Late Show*, "The lesson here is, it's OK to kill your wife, but DON'T MESS WITH DIRECTV!"

Los Angeles *Times*, February 10, 2001; Miami *Herald*, December 5, 2001; newsmax.com

Police in Davenport, about twenty miles south of Walt Disney World, said they confiscated a camera from singer R. Kelly's vacation home, where he lived with his wife and three children, and found pictures of him involved in sex acts, but not intercourse, with a girl under eighteen. But a judge ruled they couldn't be used to prosecute Kelly because police had obtained them while searching the home for drugs. Kelly still faced charges in Chicago of child pornography in connection with videotapes found there that allegedly showed him having sex with underage girls.

Police arrested hip-hop artist R. Kelly after finding pornographic tapes.

Orlando *Sentinel*/Chicago *Tribune*, June 6, August 31, 2002, January 23, 2003; March 18, 2004

Singer Bobby Brown spent five days in jail in 1998 after he crashed the black Porsche 911 belonged to his wife, pop star Whitney Houston, into a signpost in Hollywood. He was sentenced to seventy-five days in jail in 1999 after repeatedly violating the drunk driving conviction.

Associated Press
Quincy (Massachusetts) *Patriot Ledger*, July 7, 2000

Police admitted they kept dossiers on hip-hop artist P. Diddy and others.

Police in Miami and Miami Beach confirmed they secretly watched, and kept dossiers on, hip-hop celebrities and rappers such as P. Diddy and DMX and their entourages when they come to South Florida. Authorities insisted they were acting to protect the celebrities from the public. Officers said they photographed the stars at the airport, staked out hotels and night clubs and kept thick binders on each one. Industry observers called the work unfair stereotyping and profiling.

Chicago *Tribune*, March 11, 2004

Actor Jeffrey Jones, who played the high school principal in the film *Ferris Bueller's Day Off*, was charged in Sarasota with violating the terms of his probation for employing a fourteen-year-old to pose for sexually explicit photos. Jones had failed to officially register as a sex offender.

Associated Press/*South Florida Sun Sentinel*, July 4, 2004

Actor Jeffrey Jones failed to register as a sex offender.

Actress Yancy Butler, who appeared in films and television and starred in the TV series *Witchblade*, was arrested in Delray Beach after she was found staggering into traffic. She later admitted she had a long battle with alcoholism. A family attorney said she had come to the area to take part in a rehabilitation program after getting into similar trouble during altercations with relatives in Long Island.

Palm Beach *Post*, November 25, 2003

After police arrested Hollywood radio disc jockey Bill Tanner on charges he got a 16-year-old high and molested him, they learned information that led to the arrest, a week later, of Tanner's colleague sportscaster Gary Hopfmann—known as G. Michael McKay—for allegedly getting a fourteen-year-old boy high on drugs and performing a sex act on him.

Associated Press/Palm Beach *Post*, November 28, 1991

Actress Yancy Butler was arrested in Florida.

Miami weatherman Bill Kamal was busted for soliciting a teenaged boy. (*WSVN*)

Longtime Miami weatherman Bill Kamal, after several talks with a fourteen-year-old boy over the Internet and by phone, arranged to drive up to St. Lucie County for a meeting. But the boy turned out to be a St. Lucie County detective. Kamal was arrested on federal charges of child enticement. He was immediately fired by his employer, *WSVN-TV*, Channel 7. The station, which specializes in sensational stories, especially crime stories, did not spare Kamal, giving his fall the same breathless, wall-to-wall coverage the station reserved for other celebrities. Kamal eventually pleaded guilty and was sentenced to five years in prison.

Associated Press, December 9, 2004

101

WSVN-TV, Channel 7 anchor Rick Sanchez struck a man who ran out into traffic leaving Joe Robbie Stadium during a Miami Dolphins football game. The man was paralyzed and died about five years later. Sanchez was charged with DUI after a test showed his blood alcohol level at 0.15, over the legal minimum. The victim's blood level was 0.23.

Miami *Herald*, November 2, 1995

Gregory Hemingway, 69-year-old son of famed writer Ernest Hemingway, died of natural causes in a South Florida jail after being arrested for indecent exposure. The man, who often dressed as a woman and went by the name of Gloria, was found dead in a private cell at the Miami-Dade women's detention center.

Miami *Herald*/Philadelphia *Inquirer*, October 4, 2001

Silver screen actress Hedy Lamarr was arrested for shoplifting. (United Artists)

Hedy Lamarr, who was a film beauty and glamour queen in the 1930s and 1940s and wrote a scandalous tell-all in the mid-1960s, later slipped into obscurity and financial straits.

In 1991, while living at a condominium in Altamonte Springs, near Orlando, she was charged with shoplifting $21.48 worth of personal care items from an Eckerd Drugs store in Casselberry. Her lawyer blamed absentmindedness and the charges were later dropped.

Lamarr had also been charged with taking eighty-six dollars worth of merchandise from a Los Angeles department store in 1966 but had been acquitted.

On January 19, 2000, Lamarr was found dead in her bed. She was eighty-six.

United Press International, August 2, 1991;
Palm Beach *Post*, January 20, 2000

Aileen Wuornous, one of America's few female serial killers, smiled at witnesses, made a bizarre final statement and then succumbed to a lethal injection at the Florida State Prison in October 2002.

Her last words, "Yes, I'd just like to say I'm sailing with the Rock, and I'll be back. Like Independence Day with Jesus, June 6, like the movie, big mother ship and all. I'll be back."

Wuornous had been given six death sentences and admitted to killing a seventh person. She had lived in motels and rented rooms and on the streets among Florida's drifters and earned her living as a prostitute along an interstate highway. In late 1989, she killed one of the men who picked her up, and, over the next year killed at least five more.

Actress Charlize Theron later won an Academy Award for her uncanny portrayal of Wuornous in the film, *Monster*.

St. Petersburg *Times*, October 10, 2002; AMPAS, 2003

THE PERFORMING ARTS

When Miami-based *WTMI*, the only commercial classical music station in South Florida, switched to an all-dance format, it followed its last classical piece, *Beethoven's Ninth Symphony*, with *Shut the F — Up and Dance*.

Associated Press, December 31, 2001

A nude dancing establishment in Casselberry, north of Orlando, found a novel way to get around a new Seminole County anti-nudity ordinance. The Club Juana had the exotic dancers perform Shakespeare.

"They're very good-looking young witches," said Morris Sullivan, entertainment critic for the Daytona Beach *News-Journal* and author of *Femmes Fatales*, the 45-minute playlet presented twice each Friday at Club Juana. It was a series of five sketches based on the works of Shakespeare and the Marquis de Sade, as well as several performance art pieces.

After business dropped by more than half following passage of the ordinance, a lawyer hired by the owner found an exemption for "*bona fide* performances and demonstrations, which have a genuine message."

"Not only were we acting, we were acting in the nude, and the sheriff's office was there, videotaping with the little red 'Record' light lit," a dancer known as "Scarlet" said. "I figured we'd all be arrested. I made no social plans for Saturday. I figured I'd be in the tank."

And Sullivan said, "I've done eight plays, but now that I've done a forty-minute play for a strip club, I'm getting calls from the New York *Times*. That's the world we live in, I guess."

Palm Beach *Post*, June 7, 1999

Retiree Bernie Barker, 62, of Hollywood, made the Guinness Book of World Records as the world's oldest male stripper. "At least I'm not sitting around growing old, watching television," the grandfather of two said. The retired real estate broker said he tried out for the gig on a dare and was collecting as much in his G-string as he did in his Social Security check, dancing in a western thong and white loafers. "I feel like I'm watching my grandfather dance naked. Talk about dirty," one twenty-year-old patron said.

Bernie Barker was listed as the old world's oldest male stripper.

Miami *Herald*, January 19, 2003

A couple appeared on an episode of *The Jerry Springer Show* called "Secret Mistresses Confronted" to accuse the man's former wife of stalking them. The show aired three months later. Within hours, authorities said, the man murdered his ex-wife in Sarasota. The man was later convicted and received a life sentence. The judge in the case told Springer and his producers, "Are ratings more important than the dignity of human life? Shame on you."

Miami *Herald*, May 25, 2002

"The Human Blockhead" died in 2001 of a stroke at age ninety-four in Gibsonton, the circus and carnival workers' retirement town near Tampa. Melvin Burkhardt could hammer a spike into his head through a cavity behind his nostril. "He was 60 years in the sideshows, and he's the last of them," friend and fellow magician Bill Dahlquist said. Others who died in Gibsonton in recent years were the 2-1/2 foot tall "Half Girl," the pincer-handed "Lobster Boy" and the rigid "Ossified Lady."

Associated Press/Miami *Herald*, November 11, 2001

A man who made a living dressing as the bright orange "Tigger" at Walt Disney World was acquitted of charges he fondled a thirteen-year-old girl and her mother as they posed for a photo at the theme park. His defense attorney dressed up as Tigger to show how the character's oversized hands couldn't possibly fondle a young girl and that it was impossible at the time to know exactly who was in the costume.

Miami *Herald*, August 5, 2004

A fifty-year-old Miami-Dade Community College professor filed state and federal complaints, saying the producers of *American Idol* violated anti-discrimination laws when they turned him away from a tryout in Miami Beach. The Fox-TV show said auditioners had to be twenty-four or younger.

South Florida Sun-Sentinel, January 21, 2003

An adult film actress who used the screen name Bianca Trump became an activist in her West Palm Beach neighborhood, not far from Donald Trump's Mar-a-Lago mansion in Palm Beach. Trump helped plant trees, wrote a neighborhood newsletter and battled city code enforcement officers.

Palm Beach *Post*, January 6, 2001

Passersby in Miami Beach were startled to see a sculpture of a battered woman crawling from two rapists who hung from the ceiling by their genitals. The artist said he did the sculpture to show the horrors of rape and the idea that women could defend themselves. Identical copies went on display in four other cities.

Miami *Herald*, May 5, 1994

SECTION THREE
CHAPTER

5

FLORIDA FAMILY VALUES

Investigators found a man living in a rural home near Moore Haven with his sister and their thirteen children and grandchildren. Also, a tiny casket containing the body of an infant son. The man and his sister had apparently exhumed the body of the eight-month-old, who'd died of natural causes, and kept it in their home for twelve years. The couple was charged with incest and the children were placed in the care of state officials. According to authorities, no charges were filed in the exhumation because the statute of limitations had expired.

Associated Press, February 28, 2002

Kimberly Mays Twigg, who was taken from the parents who'd raised her after tests showed they weren't her real parents, had her own family issues as an adult.

In 1988, it was discovered that Kim, then ten, and another baby had been mistakenly switched at the hospital and sent home with the wrong parents. Regina and Ernest Twigg, who then lived in Pennsylvania, learned this after Arlena, the child they had thought was their daughter died of heart disease and genetic testing revealed that she had not been their biological child.

The Twiggs launched a five-year custody battle against Robert Mays, who had raised Kimberly alone after his wife died in 1981.

A court ordered visitation rights for the Twiggs, and Kimberly spent an increasing amount of time with them, until 1993, when, at her request, a judge denied the Twiggs further involvement with her. She then went to live with Mays, but not happily. At one point she ran away to a homeless shelter.

Through her teen years, Kimberly alternated between living with the Twiggs and Mays.

At age nineteen, she married and said then she had at last found happiness, but her marriage was marred by so much discord that the Florida State

Department of Children and Families took away the couple's two-year old son. He was returned a year later after the couple received counseling.

Philadelphia *Daily News*, March 3, 2004

Because of a series of bureaucratic blunders, five-year-old Rilya Wilson was missing for more than a year before anyone noticed. The case mortified Floridians and led to wholesale firings, demotions and resignations at the Florida Department of Children and Families.

Five-year-old Rilya Wilson was missing for more than a year before anyone noticed.

The girl's grandmother said in May 2002 that someone who claimed to be from the agency took the girl in late 2000 or early 2001, saying she needed a neurological evaluation. She said she thought the agency still had the girl. State officials said they never learned about the disappearance because the caseworker faked paperwork, saying she had visited the home when she hadn't. The director of the state's Children's Advocacy Foundation said a supervisor should have reviewed the case every month, another supervisor every three months and a judge every six months.

The grandmother and her companion were later charged with various counts ranging from neglect to abuse. The girl remained missing. In March 2005, the companion was charged with murder after she confessed to a cellmate that she smothered Rilya and buried her.

Associated Press, May 1, 2002
Miami *Herald*, April 7, 2005

In North Port, near Sarasota, an eight-year-old girl was banned from singing *Kumbayah* at a talent show at the Boys and Girls Club of Sarasota County. Organizers said the classic African folk song violated their ban on religious songs because it repeated the word "Lord." An official said, "We don't want to take the chance of a child offending another child's religion." The girl's mother said, "It's a crock! I learned that song in Girl Scouts, not in church. It's a campfire song, for goodness sakes."

Associated Press, August 13, 2000

A couple in Deltona, near Daytona Beach, got fed up with their messy kids, set up a tent in their front yard and moved into it. For several days, Cat and Harlan Barnard were media darlings, appearing in newspapers everywhere and on national television. But along with the TV trucks came the crazies. One pickup drove by with someone yelling, "Somebody should come by and shoot you in the head." Then temperatures dropped into the lower 40s. But the parents toughed it out. By mid-January 2005, however, the tent showed no signs of habitation and the parents, who were not responding to media inquiries, appeared to have moved back in.

South Florida Sun-Sentinel, December 13, 2004;
Daytona Beach *News-Journal,* January 15, 2005

A Fort Pierce woman pointed a gun at her pregnant sixteen-year-old daughter's belly, drove her sixty-seven miles to a clinic near West Palm Beach, and told a nurse, "If my daughter doesn't have this abortion, I'm going to blow her brains out." The mother was arrested. A detective said the mother had also threatened to beat the girl until she miscarried. The teen returned home with a family friend who supported her desire to have the baby.

Palm Beach *Post,* August 2, 2000

A nineteen-year-old St. Petersburg woman who shot herself in the abdomen while she was pregnant because she couldn't afford an abortion was charged with manslaughter. Under Florida law, a fetus able to live outside the womb would be considered a person.

Palm Beach *Post,* January 24, 1995

Christian Scientists from Sarasota were charged with letting their seven-year-old daughter die of diabetes. The charges challenged a 1975 Florida law that maintained, parents who withhold medical care may not be considered abusive or neglectful if they acted out of a deep religious belief. After the couple's only daughter, a straight-A student, went from chubby and gregarious to thin and listless, dozing in doorways and buckling under the weight of her schoolbooks, the couple consulted spiritual healers but not doctors. The parents said it was their daughter's choice to die.

Miami *Herald,* April 10, 1989

A Melbourne couple, part of a sect that doesn't believe in medical treatment, were cleared of neglect charges in the death of their two-year-old son, stung 432 times by yellow jackets in September 1988 while the family visited friends near Tampa. They treated the boy with only a bath and some juice and waited seven hours, until he was unconscious, to call 911. Prosecution witnesses said the boy could have survived with proper medical attention. But jurors said the parents' actions didn't amount to willful neglect.

Tampa *Tribune,* August 4, 2000

An Orange County six-year-old, who brought more than $1,000 worth of crack cocaine to school, said she found the bag of more than a dozen rocks at home. But her mother said she must have gotten them trick-or-treating.

Associated Press/*South-Florida Sun-Sentinel,* November 5, 2004

The mother of a nine-year-old boy accused of bringing fifteen bags of marijuana to a Port St. Lucie school said her son is sorry. She and the boy said he found the pot, worth about $75, on the ground next to his father's Fort Pierce home and "kind of knew" what it was.

Palm Beach *Post*/Miami *Herald*, December 15, 2002

A 16-year-old boy was arrested near Fort Myers after police said he fought with his mother because she wouldn't share her marijuana.

Associated Press, December 19, 1999

Police cited a seven-year-old boy in New Port Richey after he ran a stop sign and crashed into another car. His father said he gave him permission to drive, saying, "I'm not irresponsible. I just had a few beers."

Associated Press, December 27, 2002

When three U.S. Marines showed up at the Hollywood home of Carlos Arredondo to notify him his 20-year-old son Alexander had died in Iraq, the man became overcome with grief and torched the $15,000 government van. The vehicle was destroyed and Arredondo, a former bullfighter in Costa Rica, was hospitalized with second-degree burns on a fourth of his body. Military authorities decided not to press charges.

South Florida Sun-Sentinel, August 27, 2004

A fifty-year-old Boca Raton man was charged with trying to electrocute his 77-year-old mother in a bubble bath to get his inheritance. The woman said she was about to take a shower in the oceanfront apartment she shares with her son when the man suggested a bubble bath would ease her stress. She said she was looking into the tub when her son placed something against her back and tried to push her in. She said she heard a buzzing sound and felt a burning sensation. After she struggled free, her son handed her a handgun and told her to shoot him. When she wouldn't, he fled. He was later arrested near Tampa.

Palm Beach *Post*, December 29, 2000

Two Ocala boys admitted to dressing in white robes, like members of the Ku Klux Klan, to scare a black school bus driver. The two said they pulled the prank because the older sister of one disliked the driver.

Associated Press/*South Florida Sun Sentinel*, June 26, 2004

While schoolteacher Mary Kay Letourneau's romance with a student led to a prison sentence, two children, two movies and three books, four Florida women had their own moments in the sordid spotlight:

Debra Beasley LaFave, a 23-year-old Tampa area middle school teacher, was charged with having sex numerous times with a 14-year-old student, including in a classroom, in her apartment, and in a vehicle while the boy's 15-year-old cousin drove around Ocala.

Schoolteacher Debra LaFave was charged with having sex with a 14-year-old student.

Amy Duane, 37, of Greenacres, near West Palm Beach, a mother of three, was sentenced to four years in prison for having sex with a 13 year old during parties at her home.

Girl Scout registrar Debra Favre, 39, Duane's friend, got two years in prison and two years of probation after pleading guilty to having sex with a 16-year-old boy and serving alcohol to minors at Duane's home.

Carol Flannigan, a Boynton Beach music teacher at Rolling Green Elementary, was charged with having a 19-month-long sexual relationship with a former student that started when the boy was 11. The case got even more bizarre when the boy's father later revealed he had been having an affair with Flannigan at the same time she, unknown to him, was having sex with his son.

Palm Beach *Post*, January 10, 2004; March 10, 2005; Miami *Herald*, June 30, 2004

Palm Beach County Commissioner Addie Greene campaigned to pass an ordinance to ticket men and women who wore pants low enough to expose their underthings. A county attorney advised Greene that while extremely specific — and graphic — anti-nudity language has been upheld, fashion laws, including one that targeted a topless male Palm Beach jogger, have been ruled unconstitutional.

Palm Beach *Post*, July 26, 2004

A man caught streaking near a Broward County playground turned out to be a supervisor for counselors of foster children. He was also charged with carrying a concealed weapon.

Associated Press, December 27, 2002

A sect that believes life on earth was created by extraterrestrials held a news conference in Hollywood to say it had produced the world's first human clone, a baby girl.

Leaders promised to allow DNA tests but later reneged. When a Coral Gables lawyer filed suit to determine the well being of the child, a judge eventually closed his inquiry after leaders said in court she was longer in Broward County, but in Israel. The group had recently announced a second cloned child had been born.

South Florida Sun-Sentinel, December 28, 2002;
Miami *Herald*, January 5, January 30, 2003

A man on his way to a business meeting near West Palm Beach called a co-worker from his cell phone to say his car had stalled along Interstate 95 in Boca Raton. That's the last anyone heard of James Cuddy for a while. That sparked one of South Florida's most extensive searches, with Cuddy's name splashed across newspapers and television, on T-shirts, and on banners behind airplanes. His family hired a private investigator and got him on the program *America's Most Wanted*, which sparked 50 tips. When his credit card showed no activity, relatives feared the worst. Two weeks later, he called his mother-in-law from a California gas station. Police in California said Cuddy, who'd recently moved to Florida from Virginia for a new job, told them that he'd felt pressure and home at work. As he embraced his wife at the Ontario, California, airport, he told reporters, "I've been through a lot of (expletive) and now my name's got to be in the paper?" Apparently he had not yet learned how much it already had been.

Abducted & In Danger
Father of 2
$10,000 Reward
(For Information Leading To Location)

James Cuddy

Abducted From Northbound I-95 Near Boca Raton / Delray Beach, Between 9:00 A.M. & 10:00 A.M., **Tuesday, April 3, 2001** By Two Unknown Men.

Missing -1998 Jeep Cherokee (Forest Green 4-door) Virginia License Plates ZCX - 3102

Please Contact the Boca Raton Police Department At **561-338-1258** Or Steve Kiraly **305-586-8622 (cell) P.I.**

Businessman James Cuddy disappeared, sparking a nationwide search.

Palm Beach *Post*, April 17, 2001

When 800 parents paid ten dollars so their children could see Barney the Dinosaur at a Sunny Isles theater, they expected a six-foot purple people pleaser. When a skinny, faded fake sauntered in, children cried. The show shut down. Police were called.

South Florida Sun-Sentinel, December 29, 1993

An employee of a pharmacy near West Palm Beach made hundreds of harassing phone calls to women who were pregnant or seeking medical treatment to try to get pregnant. She swore at them in an attempt to get them to adopt. "You infertile bitch," she would say. "You would have more luck fertilizing your lawn."

Palm Beach *Post*, October 1, 1998;
Associated Press, November 28, 1998

Six years after his two-year-old son died in an explosion when a car slammed into their vehicle at a gas station, a man in Town 'N Country, near Tampa, tried to kill his wife with a flare gun and ended up burning down their house, police said. The wife, who survived, told policed she was watching TV when her husband began arguing with her, then pulled out a flare gun and pulled the trigger. The woman's clothes caught fire and spread to a nearby bed.

Associated Press, July 10, 1998

Steven and Marlene Aisenberg, who said their 5-month-old daughter, Sabrina, was kidnapped from their suburban Tampa home in 1997, were later charged with conspiracy and lying to investigators after prosecutors in Maryland, where they'd moved, produced surveillance audio tapes that suggested Aisenberg killed the baby and blamed it on cocaine. The charges were later dropped. The child has never been found, and no one has been charged in her disappearance.

Associated Press, November 6, 2003

A 49-year-old man who married an 82-year-old woman fought the woman's grown children in the courts, even after his wife died.

Stephen Sheaffer married widow Dorothy Robinson Millman. Dorothy's daughter, Diane Trask, said the two should be separated. Trask was fifty-five; her husband was ninety-two.

Trask said the age difference was not a factor. She said she believed Sheaffer was sponging off his wife's life savings and wasn't able to properly care for the woman, who suffered from dementia. A judge had ruled her incompetent a month after the September 1996 marriage.

Eventually, Trask was granted custody of her mother and hid her away from Sheaffer in an undisclosed Boca Raton home.

Months later, he learned his wife had been dead for five days, and an emergency court hearing was slated for the next day to approve her cremation. That night, Sheaffer left eight voice mails for Palm Beach County Circuit Judge John Wessel, trying to stop the hearing. They grew increasingly desperate, and the last one, made at 2:00 a.m., said, "You'd better have an armed guard."

Sheaffer later apologized, saying he was distraught and had had too much to drink.

Palm Beach *Post*, March 12, October 13, October 14, 2000

When a woman picking up her child at a Fort Lauderdale daycare center accused one of the staffers of twisting the four-year-old boy's ear to make him sit, the mother punched the staffer in the face as she held her own fourteen-month-old. She then chased the staffer into a kitchen, breaking another worker's foot in the process, but retreated when she saw the staffer had grabbed a 13-inch butcher's knife. The staffer then chased her out and fatally stabbed the woman in the back and chest as dozens of children watched. The worker was later sentenced to twenty years in prison. Witnesses had testified the 24-year-old mother of four was a good mother and a caring worker, and that fatally stabbing the mother of one of her charges during pickup was an isolated incident.

South Florida Sun-Sentinel, April 1, 1999

A woman in Port St. Lucie, worried about Hurricane Isabel, wanted her husband to help brace their home, but he said he wanted to keep watching a football game on television. At halftime, he finally confronted her about the issue, and she threw an 8-inch kitchen knife which struck him in the leg. The woman was charged with domestic aggravated battery. The storm eventually missed Florida and struck the mid-Atlantic seaboard.

Palm Beach *Post*, September 16, 2003

Bruce Richenthal, 51, who pumped four bullets into his seventy-year-old mother and another two into his seventy-four-year-old dad, later told jurors he had a troubled life marred by parents who didn't love him or acknowledge their grandchildren. But prosecutors said he just couldn't wait to get his hands on their North Miami home. Richenthal was sentenced to life in prison. Richenthal was one of three children. A second had not spoken to his parents for the last ten years of their lives and a third had leaped off a New York sky-scraper. Richenthal's marriage had ended when he went to prison in the late 1980s for faking his own death to scam an insurance company.

Miami *Herald*, November 20, 1999

In 1992, in Orlando, Gregory Kingsley, 12, successfully sued his mother for divorce so a foster family could adopt him. He claimed that his mother turned him over at age four to an alcoholic father who abused him and that he was later abandoned to a succession of foster homes. The foster family eventually adopted him and Gregory changed his name to Shawn Russ.

Palm Beach *Post*, September 24, 1992;
South Florida Sun-Sentinel, November 22, 1998

A Jupiter Farms four-year-old collected more than fifty toothpaste tubes, earning him visits on several television talk shows, including David Letterman's.

Palm Beach *Post*, November 24, 1994

The homeowner's association board in a condominium near Jupiter fought the mother of a fourteen-year-old boy with muscular dystrophy.

The association complained that the boy zoomed around the complex in his motorized wheelchair, running over sprinklers and making marks on the inside walls of the elevators. They said the boy also broke association rules by using the whirlpool spa, which was off limits to kids under fourteen. His mother argued the pool was therapeutic for her son.

The owner of the condo unit the family was renting decided to sell, and the family tried to buy another, but the board blocked them. The boy and his mother settled and moved. The boy later graduated high school with a 3.45 grade point average.

Palm Beach *Post*, July 19, 1998; May 25, 2004

A couple in Citrus County, north of Tampa, was arrested in Utah, ending a nationwide search that began when authorities found evidence they'd mistreated and underfed their seven adopted children, ages twelve to seventeen, leaving them weighing no more than elementary school students. The children said their parents subjected them to electric shocks and beatings and tore out their toenails with pliers.

USA Today, February 7, 2005

SEX

The case of the bosom-bonked bachelor was finally settled on national television by a former New York mayor, but only after a pair of breasts became Exhibit B.

Paul Shimkonis, a 38-year-old physical therapist, had said he went to the Diamond Dolls club in Clearwater in September 1996, days before his wedding,

According to Shimkonis' 1998 suit, "The guest of honor was requested by the star dancer to sit low in a chair, resting his neck to the back of the chair with his eyes closed to be specially entertained by the star dancer."

Then, Tawny Peaks, who boasts a 60-HH bust, jumped up and slammed her ample bosom into Shimkonis' head, rocking it backwards.

Stripper Tawny Peaks was sued for injuring a man with her breasts.

"I saw stars," he said. "It was like two cement blocks hit me."

Former Mayor Ed Koch presided over a dispute involving a stripper's attributes.

Shimkonis said he was too embarrassed to see a doctor for three months and, two years later, he was still in pain. He sued when the club wouldn't pay his medical bills.

Days later, the two took their dispute to New York, to the television program *The Peoples Court*, before celebrity judge and former mayor Ed Koch.

Koch instructed a court officer to take Peaks into his chambers and examine her breasts. They were later estimated to weigh about two pounds each and were twenty percent silicone and the rest natural.

Koch later ruled against Shimkonis.

Associated Press, July 1, July 10, 1998

A former nude dancer received two years of house arrest for knocking out a colleague's tooth with her high-heel shoes.

Associated Press, December 27, 2002

A Palm Beach County Circuit Judge struck down as unconstitutional a law requiring strippers to register with the county, saying it violated their privacy. The county had hoped to keep underage women from working in clubs. Nearly 1,000 registered. An appeals court later reinstated the requirements.

Palm Beach *Post,* May 17, 2001

Fearing the job would go to a foreigner, Florida's Department of Labor, Bureau of Workforce Program Support, placed an ad in a local newspaper for a nude dancer. A Stuart club had wanted to hire a foreign dancer, but under federal law, the state was required to first see if a Floridian wanted the job. The ad said the job required four years of experience and paid $11 an hour.

Associated Press, April 16, 1999

Manatee County passed a law barring women from exposing more than three-fourths of their breasts or anyone from showing more than two-thirds of their buttocks. "I don't think we'll be tape-measuring," spokesman Dave Bristow said.

Chicago *Tribune,* April 4, 1999

At a construction site in Pembroke Pines, near Fort Lauderdale, a worker found a naked man who had been chained to a bulldozer and spray-painted with anti-gay graffiti by a recent acquaintance. The victim, who was unhurt, declined to press charges, saying the acts were consensual.

South Florida Sun-Sentinel, December 18, 1999

A man was arrested in Bradenton on charges he attached nude photographs of himself to his van's sun visor and flashed children in other vehicles.

Associated Press/Miami *Herald,* December 19, 1999

Al Goldstein, once a sex industry giant, fell into financial ruin and lost his Pompano Beach mansion to bankruptcy.

Goldstein, arrested 21 times on obscenity charges in his career, published *Screw Magazine* and hosted the New York cable television show *Midnight Blue,* which was calm by today's standards but created an uproar when it debuted. A renowned gourmand, he had his stomach stapled and lost half his body weight.

His 10,000 square foot manse included five satellite dishes, 900 pairs of shoes, thousands of cigars and one dominatrix mannequin. An eleven-foot hand on the pool deck gave the finger to boaters passing by on the Intracoastal Waterway. In 1992, he ran for sheriff of Broward County, with bumper stickers that read, "Sheriff Al says, 'Fight Crime; Shoot Back.'"

In 2002, SWAT teams swarmed *Casa de Al* after a heavily armed and deeply depressed hooker barricaded herself in his guesthouse. Days later, police at Fort Lauderdale-Hollywood International Airport yanked him off a flight for making sexually suggestive comments to a security worker.

Screw shut down in 2003 after thirty-four years, a victim of competition from Internet porn sites. Goldstein later surfaced as a ten dollar an hour sales manager at New York's famed Second Avenue Deli. Goldstein, 68, said he alternated between living in a Manhattan homeless shelter

Porno publisher Al Goldstein fell on hard times (Palm Beach *Post*)

and sleeping on the floor of his in-laws' Queens apartment. He later became a national marketing director for an international company that offered X-rated films on demand.

Miami *Herald,* August 9, 1998; June 22, September 11, 2004;
Business Wire, April 11, 2005

When a man took his computer to a suburban Boca Raton Best Buy store, a technician found pornographic photographs of children on its hard drive and called authorities. The pictures showed naked children, some as young as four years old, engaged in explicit sex acts. The 47-year-old was charged with thirty felony counts.

The man's wife said he had asked permission to subscribe to an adult website, but that he later downloaded "the nastiest pictures he could find" because he couldn't believe such things existed on the Internet. That alleged noble motive rang hollow when investigators found more than 75,000 pictures, many of them kiddie porn.

The wife said she had canceled the account and didn't know her husband continued to download images.

Palm Beach *Post*, December 14, 2004;
Palm Beach County Sheriff's Office

A pilot for an air service for people who want to have sex in flight said he was hijacked by an older couple who wanted to fly the plane to Cuba. The pilot ditched the Piper Cherokee. The bodies of the couple were never recovered. The motto of "Fly Key West" was "Love is in the Air." The service offered passengers a chance to take part in the "Mile High Club," an unofficial association of people who've had sex on airplanes. Its web page said, "We fly at 5,280 feet, give or take six inches." It advertised a customized cabin with the pilot screened off and a price list of flights ranging from "The Quickie," twenty minutes at altitude, to the "Big Bone Islander," forty minutes long.

Palm Beach *Post*, August 12, 2001; Miami *Herald*, April 28, 2002

A male civilian Eglin Air Force Base employee fought orders to stop coming to work in a bra, makeup and earrings.

Associated Press, December 19, 1999

An 89-year-old Orlando-area widower was arrested after his thirty-four-year-old girlfriend told police he popped a *Viagra*, then clubbed her in the face with a crowbar because she wouldn't perform sex for money.

Associated Press/Palm Beach *Post*, June 13, 1998

An Orlando-area car dealer was charged with offering female customers price breaks in exchange for sexual favors. After a woman told police the man had offered her a $1,000 discount, Longwood police sent in a female undercover officer. This time, police said, the man offered only a $100 markdown. When he rubbed against her, he was arrested.

Associated Press, November 17, 2004

After the parents of a two-year-old boy in Palm Bay, near Melbourne, bought a *Tickles for Elmo* book with a strip of audio push-buttons, they were surprised when the strip fell off and they saw a photograph of an embracing nude couple. The Illinois publisher said the book was accidentally made from recycled paper from a porno-book cover.

Orlando *Sentinel*, July 13, 2000

When a seven-year-old in St. Petersburg showed his mother a toll-free phone number on the back of his Scooby-Doo book, she dialed it, and was connected to a phone sex line where she could "talk to hot, sexy girls."

Associated Press, December 27, 2002

A marketing flyer for Busch Gardens in Tampa urged Fun Card holders to call for a special offer. But because of a typographical error, the number rang to a phone sex line.

Palm Beach *Post*, March 21, 2004

A 22-year-old high school dropout was charged with having sex with the corpse of his friend's mother after helping the friend kill the woman. But police said they couldn't charge him with criminal sexual battery because necrophilia was not a crime in Florida. The man was charged with helping his seventeen-year-old friend strangle and bludgeon the 41-year-old Tallahassee woman because she had grounded the boy and forbidden him from hanging around with the older friend. He admitted to sexually assaulting the body before throwing it down an abandoned thirty-foot well shaft. The two were later sentenced to life in prison and the Legislature passed a bill making the sexual abuse or mutilation of a corpse a second-degree felony.

Associated Press/Miami *Herald*, July 12, 1995; June 4, June 25, 1996

A Palm Beach County Public Defender's Office investigator, on probation for stealing $2,000 from a police union, was charged with lewd conduct after deputies said they caught him having sex with his wife at a Broward County swingers' club.

Palm Beach *Post*, February 23, 1999

A man who attacked his ex-wife at a suburban Boca Raton stationery store threw a box of condoms, striking her in the head and tried to stretch a condom over her head before fleeing.

Palm Beach County Sheriff's Office

A 43-year-old man was arrested for installing a tiny camera embedded in his sneakers that looked up women's skirts at a Wal-Mart store in Plant City, near Tampa, and taped them on a video recorder he carried in a bag via a wire. While on probation for that, he was caught using the same setup to peep on women at his church. At his hearing for that offense, a prosecutor said he was even doing it to a cashier at the probation office. He was also caught doing it at a flea market in nearby Brandon. Investigators said they were reviewing about forty-five videotapes, some four hours long, that they seized from the man.

Tampa *Tribune*, December 12, 2001

Doctors amputated the left foot of a Boy Scout leader who was found hanging upside down from a tree in a Central Florida forest as part of what investigators called a solo sex act. Authorities said they found the 42-year-old man dangling from a rope about twelve feet off the ground. Blood flow to his feet had been cut off for more than twenty-four hours. The incident was captured on a camera the man had set up. "He was doing something sexually to himself," Lake County Sheriff's Sgt. Nick Pallitto said. "I guess that's his thing."

Associated Press/Fort Lauderdale *Sun-Sentinel*, August 8, 1999

After they seized more than 1,300 adult videos in a raid, deputies in Columbia County anticipated having to watch all 1,300 to determine if they were obscene. At issue was whether the videotapes violated community standards regarding obscenity, but there are no written guidelines that determine what community standards exist. Authorities later reached a deal with the store-owner in which the tapes were destroyed in exchange for his not being charged.

Associated Press, March 22, 2000

LOVE IS IN THE AIR

A Loxahatchee company called "Poop Poop We Do" delivered bouquets of horse manure. Arranged in floral boxes with tissue paper and ferns, the bouquets arrived with messages such as "Have a Crappy Day" and "Stinking Of You." Also available: "Meadow Muffins" delivered in a cupcake box.

Palm Beach *Post*, July 11, 1992

In Cooper City, in western Broward County, a couple exchanged wedding vows in the jewelry aisle of a Wal-Mart. The manager of the jewelry department said the couple had come to look at wedding rings and she told them she could hold the ceremony right there. She suggested decorating the ear-piercing hut with flowers. The manager of the pet supplies department, who was a notary public, did the honors.

Miami *Herald*, January 23, 1999

A Tampa man sued his former fiancée for $25,000 for breaking off their engagement. Jeffrey Kinner said the breakup cost him thousands of dollars in wedding preparations, including an expensive engagement ring. Former fiancée Marie Glinka said, "I think he has mental problems. I can't believe he's doing this." Kinner said he waited three months after their breakup to file suit because he hoped for a reconciliation.

United Press International, December 29, 1990

Fort Pierce disc-jockey Dennis Hart broadcast his marriage proposal to his girlfriend, Joann Mileni, during his morning show on *WKGR-FM*, and she and about 30,000 other people heard it. While Hart waited fifty-three minutes for Mileni to drive to the station to accept, several women named Joann — and several offering to change their names to Joann — called in case she said no.

Orlando *Sentinel*, December 31, 1989

Romanian gymnast and Olympic gold medalist Nadia Comaneci defected from Romania with the help of Hallandale roofer and émigré, Constantin Panait, 36. When the pair arrived in South Florida, they held a press conference to announce that Panait would be leaving his 25-year-old wife, Maria, and their four children and moving in with Nadia. Asked if she knew Panait was married and a father when their romance began, Nadia replied, "So what?"

Orlando *Sentinel*, December 31, 1989

Former Olympic gymnast Nadia Comaneci defected to Florida.

An Orlando man, whose wife of seventeen years had left him and gone to stay with her parents in Jacksonville, spent $17,000 to place a full page ad in Jacksonville's *Florida Times-Union* begging her to take him back. The man said his wife's parents had barred him from their gated community and she had changed her cell phone number.

Associated Press, January 27, 2005

SECTION THREE
CHAPTER 8

FLORIDA. OH. MY. GOD.

A Broward County woman who said her 10-year-old, partially-eaten grilled cheese sandwich bore the image of the Virgin Mary, put it up for sale on the eBay online auction service. It got more than 100,000 hits, and bids reached $22,000, until eBay yanked it hours before it was to end, telling the woman in an e-mail that it violated a policy against listings "that are intended as jokes."

Diana Duyser, a work-at-home jewelry designer, insisted her sandwich was no joke. The woman said she made the sandwich on plain white bread with American cheese 10 years earlier and had taken a bite when she saw a face starting back at her. She said she placed it in a clear plastic box with cotton balls and kept it on her nightstand. At first, she said, she was scared. But, she said, "now that I realize how unique it is, I wanted to share it with the world." She said it miraculously never drew mold.

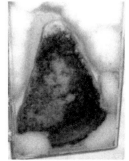

A South Florida woman said her cheese sandwich bore an image of the Virgin Mary. (GoldenPalace-Casino.com)

While the woman said the face was that of the Madonna, skeptics voted for another Madonna, the pop star, or 1930s actress Greta Garbo.

The folks at eBay finally relented and, after 1.7 million hits, the sandwich eventually sold, for $28,000, to an online casino known for promotional stunts. Not willing to trust the mail, two casino executives flew to South Florida for the sandwich, which they said they planned to take on a barnstorming tour around the world.

A Miami *Herald* columnist drove the sandwich across the country to deliver it to a Las Vegas casino where it would go on display.

Meanwhile, inspired by the success of the holy sandwich, a man in Canada posted a year-old burned fish stick on eBay he said bore the image of Jesus.

Miami *Herald*, November 17, 2004;
Miami *Herald, South-Florida Sun-Sentinel*, November 23, 2004;

Toronto *Globe and Mail,* November 24, 2004

For eight years, hundreds of thousands of the faithful gathered at a Clearwater office building where they believed they saw the image of the Virgin Mary. Experts said the image was created by mineral deposits from water on the building's side. Some said the likeness had healing powers.

Within three weeks of its initial discovery in 1996, police estimated almost a half-million people had come to see the image. In 1998, a Cincinnati-based ministry bought the building for more than $2 million. It later erected an 18-foot cedar crucifix out front.

But, in March 2004, someone smashed the three windows that comprised the image's face and veil. Police said someone shot three small ball bearings at them. A teen later admitted to using a slingshot to break the windows. A prosecutor likened his act to "slashing Mona Lisa." The boy was sentenced to ten days in jail and two years of probation and ordered to pay $1,200 for the damage. Authorities said the act was not a hate crime, just a lashing out by a youngster haunted by family problems and "mad at the world."

A Clearwater office building claimed to bear an image of the Virgin Mary. (Startime.com)

Later, people swore the surviving parts of the image also portrayed a fuzzy depiction of Jesus seeming to peer out from where Mary's womb would be.

St. Petersburg *Times,* March 2, July 13, July 18, 2004

A Lake City man asked a judge to legally change his name from Charles Haffey to "God." When that didn't work, he found a passage from the Bible where Moses asks God his name and hears, "I am who I am, or I will be who I will be." So he submitted that. Acknowledging it was pretty wordy, he said he was willing to settle for "I am who I am." His first name, he said, would be "I am." The judge finally granted his petition. The 55-year-old said he sought the name change as a way to gain release from feelings of "panic, anxiety, fear, rage, murder, and suicide" that had plagued him since he served in the Vietnam War.

Associated Press/Palm Beach *Post,* October 9, 2002

Police arrested a St. Petersburg-area podiatrist after finding guns and explosives in his home. They said he planned to destroy an Islamic education center and dozens of mosques. A friend said the man, who was Jewish, wanted to make a statement for "his people."

Associated Press/Chicago Tribune, August 24, 2002

A Muslim Daytona Beach woman took the state to court after she was denied an identification card because she refused to remove a head covering. The woman later agreed to adjust her scarf so her face could be photographed.

Associated Press/South Florida Sun-Sentinel, February 3, 2002

A Miami nursing home asked the National Labor Relations Board to toss out a union vote, saying a series of voodoo signs might have scared the mostly Haitian-American workers into voting to organize. Workers testified they saw lines of pennies, half-empty water cups and a pro-union employee twisting black beads in her hands before the vote. The board upheld the result.

Associated Press, December 27, 2002

A man who had robbed a Palm Beach Gardens bank three years earlier turned himself in, claiming he was inspired to confess after seeing the film *The Passion of the Christ*.

Palm Beach *Post*, March 21, 2004

Lady Ygraine, a witch who sold daggers and occult items, offered $250 to sponsor a youth baseball team in Port St. Lucie's Babe Ruth Bambino Baseball League. The league's president turned her down after visiting her shop. Lady, who belonged to the Church of Satan, said her religion doesn't promote hate but rather responsibility and self-empowerment. She said the league, which serves kids ages five to 12, had come to her. The local American Civil Liberties Union chapter said it was considering a lawsuit.

Palm Beach *Post*, February 4, 1999

A former nun became a police officer in Lake Helen, near Orlando. Anna Haskins, 60, had spent fourteen years as a nun before turning in her habit to spend a quarter-century as a Catholic school principal. As officer, she was assigned a pair of handcuffs and a .40 caliber Glock handgun.

Associated Press/Palm Beach *Post*, August 14, 2000

Palm Beach Atlantic University, a small Christian school in downtown West Palm Beach, held six performances of the musical, *Damn Yankees*, in which a man sells his soul to the devil to help his team with the pennant.

129

The school opted to replace the name in ads, calling it "*D@#$ Yankees*" in ads and spelling "Damn" in its program as a D, a baseball, a bat and a glove.

"We felt that using the name in the title would be offensive to some people," college spokeswoman Becky Peeling said.

Palm Beach *Post*, March 21, 2000

A youth minister in Jacksonville, who wanted to show congregants that sinning is like playing Russian Roulette, waved a .357 caliber handgun at his head, then shot himself with a blank. The cardboard was propelled by the blank, shattered the minister's skull and critically injured him.

Associated Press/Palm Beach *Post*, September 27, 1998

9

ANIMAL LIFE

An 800-pound cow and her three-week-old calf who had walked away from a northern Palm Beach County pasture led a frantic posse of police and paramedics on a three-mile-long slow-speed stampede before finally jumping off a sea wall into the Intracoastal Waterway in North Palm Beach. Police borrowed a fishing boat and finally managed to rope the animals, three quarters of a mile offshore, as they swam toward Singer Island. They weren't hurt, but one officer got kicked in the rear as the animals were pulled onto the boat.

Palm Beach *Post*, May 4, 1999

A cow meandered into a marshy field along Interstate 4 and held up traffic when drivers slowed to see if it was stuck. A road crew posted an electronic sign saying "The Cow is OK," but that only prompted more motorists to slow down.

Associated Press, December 19, 1999

A 600-pound pet tiger named Bobo, owned by a former B-movie Tarzan actor named Steve Sipek, escaped from a compound west of West Palm Beach, sparking a 26-hour hunt that ended when a state wildlife officer fatally shot the animal. Officials said the tiger, which shared the compound with other exotic animals, lunged at the officer.

"Bobo didn't have to die," a weeping Sipek said. While some argued Sipek's keeping of wild animals in an urban setting was a tragedy waiting to happen, neighbors later held a candlelight vigil for Bobo and the officer received death threats.

Also, a woman who'd brought a pet pig in her trunk as bait for Bobo was charged with animal cruelty.

Years earlier, another tiger had mauled a woman helping Sipek and fractured her skull. The woman's husband said she had thought the cage was empty when she entered it to do some touch-up painting. The couple was helping Sipek prepare for a photo shoot.

Palm Beach *Post*, February 4, 2002, July 14, 2004

Former Tarzan actor Steve Sipek's pet tiger Bobo escaped and was later killed by a state wildlife agent. (Steve Sipek)

In St. Augustine, the owner of a big cat wildlife sanctuary was injured when a 350-pound Siberian tiger he had brought to a county fair attacked him after being startled. Police used stun guns to get the animal to release the man, who was not seriously injured.

Associated Press, January 1, 2005

Firefighters searching for a cat in a burning garage in Sunrise, near Fort Lauderdale, found the animal—but it was a 90-pound puma. The animal, named Diamond, appeared ill from heat and smoke inhalation and was taken to a veterinarian.

South Florida Sun-Sentinel, April 16, 1994

When a 60-pound kangaroo and his companion, a goat, were found walking down a road in St. Lucie County, authorities were stumped as to how the exotic animals got there. Their owner finally showed up: Vanilla Ice, a rocker and former rapper. Real name: Robert Van Winkle.

"Ice," who lives in Broward County, later went to the county's animal control office and collected his pets. He said Bucky Buckaroo—actually a wallaroo, a kangaroo-wallaby hybrid—and Pancho the goat had apparently escaped a week earlier from the backyard of his wife's grandmother. He said he had left them there while he shot a commercial in California. They roamed the woods until a neighbor spotted them.

Former rapper Vanilla Ice had to reclaim his lost wallaroo and goat.

Van Winkle said he loved exotic animals. He said he once owned a Siberian lynx and planned to buy a pair of giraffes. He was cited twice in 1998 for not having a permit to keep his lynx in his Davie backyard. He had not renewed a permit to keep Bucky in Davie, but the animal was released to him on a neighbor's permit.

Palm Beach *Post*, November 20, 2004

GO GATORS

James Billie, chief of South Florida's Seminole Tribe, hadn't wrestled an alligator in ten years when he impulsively decided to try again at a show at the Billie Swamp Safari at the Big Cypress Indian Reservation. As about one hundred tourists looked on, he reached to grab the 7-foot gator's jaws and got only one. The animal clamped down on his right ring finger, tearing it off at the second joint. Billie said he planned to wear the finger on a necklace.

Miami *Herald*, February 2, 2000

In Everglades City, near Naples, an alligator wrestler continued to perform his act for two years after going blind. Odalph Stokes finally retired at seventy. A victim of macular degeneration, he could see only murky shapes. But, he said, "I can still see forms, and once I get ahold of that sucker, he's mine."

Associated Press, August 14, 1999

The Seminole Tribe of Florida advertised for non-Seminoles to perform the tribe's famed alligator wrestling — at $8 an hour — at its Okalee Village west of Hollywood. A tribal spokesman said that, while the tradition has been handed down for two centuries, members were now pursuing more mainstream careers.

Palm Beach *Post*, September 15, 2000

An alligator bit off a man's finger in Haines City, near Orlando, after he tried to pull it off Interstate 4. A state wildlife officer saw the incident but the injured man refused help, saying he would drive himself to a hospital. A licensed trapper later removed the animal.

Associated Press, April 26, 2002

A Gainesville man stabbed a six-foot alligator in the eye with a pocketknife to free his dog from the reptile's jaws. The man said he shoved the alligator away, the knife still lodged in its eye. The dog escaped with three teeth marks on its left shoulder, one on its head and one on its right ear.

Associated Press, August 26, 2004

A Palm Beach County woman was riding in the back of a pickup truck when a ten-foot alligator lunged up and bit her leg as the truck passed through a deep puddle.

Associated Press, January 1, 2005

A school bus driver in Lacoochee stopped to let four boys capture a four-foot gator. They brought it back on the bus and two brothers took it home.

Associated Press, January 1, 2005

A man in Port Orange, near Daytona Beach, was facing battery charges after authorities say he swung a three-foot alligator at his girlfriend during an argument. Volusia County officials said the man had been keeping the animal in his bathtub. It was turned over to wildlife officers. "This will be one more Volusia story that makes the national news," sheriff's spokesman Gary Davidson said.

Associated Press/Palm Beach *Post*, July 18, 2004

A Kentucky man who got lost in a swamp near Tampa during a trip to photograph alligators taped himself high in a tree with duct tape to make sure the animals didn't attack him while he slept. The 26-year-old man was later rescued.

Chicago *Tribune*/Reuters, April 20, 2000

In Palm Harbor, near Tampa, a 77-year-old retiree who, by his own admission, had been sleepwalking woke up armpit deep in a pond filled with alligators. As he tried to free himself from the muck he realized he was attracting the animals, all at least three feet long. He said he poked at them with his cane, to little avail. After an hour, he began shouting. His wife, who was asleep, didn't hear him, but a neighbor did and called authorities. Arriving firefighters and deputies could hear the man but not see him in the dark. They followed his voice with a flashlight and pulled him out, as eight to ten alligators hovered eight feet away.

Tampa *Tribune*, November 24, 1998

Trappers removed an American crocodile named "Snaggletooth" from a golf club south of Miami and removed it to a southwest Florida park. Somehow the animal found its away back. Wildlife experts believe it swam 140 miles around the peninsula.

Miami *Herald*, January 14, 2000

SPIDERS AND SNAKES

An 18-month-old boy underwent surgery to reattach his eyelids after a 13-foot-long pet python named Puppy bit him in the face. The boy's parents immediately killed the snake, which had been drinking water in the boy's bathtub earlier. Authorities later removed the boy from the home.

Orlando *Sentinel*, August 26, 1999

A 13-foot Burmese python named Sidney escaped a Lincoln Continental where its owner had been keeping it since it outgrew its cage. The snake was found two blocks away from its Boynton Beach home.

Palm Beach *Post*, December 29, 1993

Authorities said a Port St. Lucie snake handler was feeding his pet python live kittens. The man allegedly placed six of the cats in a cage with the 20-foot python after one of the kittens soiled his clothes. A former roommate said she found two kittens crushed to death in the python's cage and two others still alive inside a five-gallon bucket filled with water. The python had eaten two kittens, but the girlfriend saved two by pushing the snake away with a stick.

Palm Beach *Post*, June 3, 1998

A St. Petersburg man stole four Sinaloan milk snakes, a sword, two cell phones, $200 in cash and a purse from his roommates, then hailed a cab. The cabbie got suspicious when the man paid his fare from the purse and alerted police.

Palm Beach *Post*, July 5, 2002

A 15-year-old Palm Beach Gardens boy picked up what he thought was a harmless king snake and began mimicking it, only to have the two-foot-long deadly coral snake bite him on his tongue. He spent several days in critical condition and his mother said doctors told her the boy would have died had the family not acted quickly.

Palm Beach *Post*, April 6, 2000

FISH TALES

A nude man was found dead on the back of a killer whale at SeaWorld in Orlando. A medical examiner speculated that the 17-year-old man drowned after passing out in the 55-degree water, but his reasons for entering the pond were a mystery. The man, a drifter who had lived in a Hare Krishna temple in

Miami, either hid in the park until after closing or sneaked in during the night. His parents sued SeaWorld, but later withdrew the suit.

Orlando *Sentinel*, December 26, 1999

An eight-foot barracuda leaped from the water and latched onto the leg of a Tampa-area woman. While barracudas are not known for unprovoked attacks, the fish jumped twelve to fifteen feet into the boat, ripping the woman's left hand with its razor teeth, then clamped onto her hip. Her relatives were able to push it overboard. It took 200 stitches to close the wounds. The victim had to have tendons replaced in her hands and leg and got skin grafts. Her doctor told her the fish came within an inch of fatally severing her femoral artery.

Associated Press/Palm Beach *Post*, July 13, 1993

A man who was being hit by a beer bottle in Madeira Beach, near St. Petersburg, grabbed a swordfish and stabbed his attacker in the abdomen.

Associated Press, December 27, 2002

A woman called Port St. Lucie police to report that her 3-inch long Beta fish had vanished from her aquarium. "A BOLO (be on the lookout) for Rex could not be issued do to lack of description information," an officer with bad grammar but a sense of humor wrote in his report. He said the fish was valued at $3.95. The officer said the home had no pets that might be suspects and added, "It cannot be determined if Rex was taken against his will."

Port St. Lucie police, October 5, 2003

A 22-year-old surfer in New Smyrna Beach was knocked off his board by a 5 foot, 100-plus pound tarpon that left him out cold for four hours. He woke up with a broken nose and 15 stitches on his head.

Associated Press, July 8, 2001

A Brandon man who keeps sharks in a backyard swimming pool was cited for possessing a protected species.

Associated Press, December 19, 1999

A giant manta ray caught two fishermen, dragging their 16-foot boat miles out to sea near New Smyrna Beach.

Associated Press, December 19, 1999

SHAGGY DOGS

A Pensacola-area man who had already shot three of a litter of puppies was holding two of the dogs, trying to shoot them in the head; when one wiggled, sending a bullet into the man's wrist. The two surviving dogs and three others were rescued from the man's home. He was charged with animal cruelty.

Pensacola *News Journal,* October 23, 2004

A 73-year-old Tallahassee woman saved her 9-month-old Scottish terrier by biting the attacking pit bull. The dog had clamped its jaws around the terrier's head and she couldn't pry it loose, so she finally got on her knees and bit down on the back of the pit bull's neck. It let out a yip and let the terrier go, then bared its teeth at the woman, who bit it again. A neighbor with a baseball bat them scared the dog off. The woman got four stitches in her arm, and her dog also received stitches and had bruised eyes. The owner said neighborhood youngsters might have left his gate open. He said had he seen his dog attacking the terrier or the woman, he'd have shot it himself.

Associated Press/Palm Beach *Post,* June 17, 2001

A man in Oakland Park, near Fort Lauderdale, who was upset after a driver ran over and killed one of his two miniature schnauzers put up a 7-foot wooden hand, featuring "the finger," in an effort to slow motorists down.

South Florida Sun-Sentinel, December 15, 2002

A 90-pound German Shepherd mix and a 50-pound Labrador-pit bull mix attacked and killed an 18-day-old infant whose mother left him in a swing while she went to warm his bottle. The family had posted a "Beware of Dog" sign outside their Tampa home.

Associated Press/*South Florida Sun-Sentinel,* June 19, 2000

A Gainesville man was charged with biting his Jack Russell terrier on the paw as punishment.

Chicago *Tribune,* December 15, 2004

A man robbed a hotel, carjacked a taxi, and raced down Miami Beach's Collins Avenue, with police in pursuit. He then ditched the cab and took off on foot. When a police dog nipped his heel, the man grabbed the 90-pound German Shepherd and bit its neck, police said. For his trouble, the thief was pepper-sprayed, cuffed and hauled off to jail. Among his charges: biting the police dog, a third degree felony.

Miami *Herald,* October 31, 1996

A Palm Harbor company marketed "Fido Fun Hats." The foam hats could be soaked in water to keep a dog's head cool. Prices ranged from $8 for a Chihuahua size to $13 for a St. Bernard model.

Miami *Herald*, December 29, 1991

ON THE WING

Turkey vultures attacked several park cars at an industrial park in Sunrise, in western Broward County, tearing off wiper blades, the little tubes that squirt washer fluid, the gaskets on trunks and doors, and other rubber auto parts. Wildlife authorities were stymied.

The business owners tried scaring off the vultures with horns, squirting them with water, or stringing wires over the parking lot. Because the birds are protected and can't be harmed, strategies to move them were limited.

They usually arrive in South Florida in October and return north for the spring and summer. One of their favorite local perches is atop the Miami-Dade County Courthouse.

The birds, which are often seen at landfills, have disgusting habits such as defecating on their legs to keep cool and vomiting when they are harassed.

South Florida Sun-Sentinel, January 1, 1999

In Tampa, federal courthouse officials annoyed by vultures installed a device that screeches like a dying vulture every 45 seconds. It succeeded only in running off people.

Associated Press, December 19, 1999

A police officer in Greenacres, near West Palm Beach, shot a peahen to death. Wildlife authorities later captured two motherless chicks and the mate. The chief had declared the birds a nuisance after some neighbors complained they were aggressive and might carry disease. About 70 residents in the town of 1,700 protested the shooting. The chief said trappers had been unsuccessful.

Palm Beach *Post*, July 4, July 21, 2000

A Tamarac woman won a $250 prize for submitting a story to *Family Circle* about a pet parakeet that brought her together with a man she ended up marrying. She said the bird had bitten all her previous boyfriends, but it hopped onto the shoulder of this date and whispered "I love you" in his ear. Six months later, the story said, the two married. The story beat out 2,000 other entries. But it turned out to be fiction. The woman was a divorcée who owns six exotic birds and an iguana. The magazine said it preferred true stories but there was no rule that said they had to be true.

Miami *Herald*, October 11, 1993

A flock of crows sitting on a 1,500-foot-long ground wire spanning the Kissimmee River in western Okeechobee County suddenly flew away; the lifting of their combined weight sent the wire upward and into a live wire, causing a short that knocked out power to nearly 2,000 homes. Workers needed a crane to fix the wire, which topped 110-foot poles.

Palm Beach *Post*, November 30, 1999

A man was arrested at Miami International Airport as he tried to smuggle forty-four birds in his pants. The small finches were said to be worth hundreds of dollars. The man allegedly stuffed two birds each inside 22 empty cardboard toilet paper rolls, then taped the sealed tubes to his legs.

Palm Beach *Post*, November 18, 2001

Residents of a St. Petersburg condominium fought to have an African gray parrot named Bubba banned from the complex, saying the bird whistled, mimicked and shouted crude words down to them from a balcony as they lay around the pool. The city charged the owner with violating a city ordinance that forbid "loud and raucous" animal noises. The owner said the bird is his only companion.

St. Petersburg *Times*, September 28, 2000

A 31-year-old man drowned after a duck apparently struck him in the face and knocked him off a water scooter on a northern Broward County lake. The suburban Hollywood man, a technician and mechanic for a suburban Pompano Beach watercraft dealer who customized the vehicles, was testing the scooter when the accident occurred.

Palm Beach *Post*, November 20, 2001

A firefighter shooting pool with friends at a bar in New Smyrna Beach, near Daytona Beach, noticed a parrot sitting on one man's shoulder, grabbed it and bit its head off. The firefighter said later he'd been drinking and did not remember what happened but offered to replace the bird, worth about $200.

Daytona Beach *News-Journal*, February 8, 2005

Beekeepers reported someone stole 288 hives holding about fourteen million bees from their farm near Lakeland. The bees were valued at $21,000, their honey about $8,000. Owners of the family farm suspected the thief was a fellow beekeeper who knew how to work with the insects.

St. Petersburg *Times*, February 18, 1999

A Lake Worth man was living with hundreds of thousands of bees in his roof. He said he found the bees "mesmerizing." When they began stinging him, though, he called a beekeeper, who removed at least 700,000 bees.

Associated Press, January 1, 2005

Key West's first, and probably only, official chicken catcher, hired by the city to round up roaming fowl, quit after six months. Armando Parra Sr. had been hired to catch up to 900 chickens for twenty dollars each. In the end, he bagged only 542. He said he was frustrated by a bureaucracy that expected him to make sure he caught only certain chickens in certain yards.

Miami *Herald*, August 1, 2004

About 100 buffalo-like animals called beefalo roamed onto Florida's Turnpike in northern Dade County, causing five accidents that left seven of the animals dead.

Palm Beach *Post*, Sunday, December 25, 1988

When neighbors complained after a man in Pace, near Pensacola, tried to change his zoning from agriculture to business, Scott Teston retaliated by putting seventeen pigs in his yard. "God as my witness, that was his plan; to stink us out," neighbor Linda Brown said.

Associated Press/Miami *Herald*, July 28, 2004

Several employees of the Miami Seaquarium were disciplined after a rare sea turtle in captivity at the marine park died and the workers ate it. The leatherback turtle, part of an endangered species, had been hurt in a boat collision. "This is just the absolute height of stupidity," said Russ Rector, president of the Dolphin Freedom Foundation and a Seaquarium critic. "We're changing the name to the Miami Seaquarium and Barbecue." The workers admitted to putting some of the meat in a stew.

South Florida Sun-Sentinel, February 6, 2001

A pet store owner from Barbados said he had nothing to declare to Customs officers at Miami International Airport. But a search found he was wearing two pair of pants and stuffed between them were 55 four-inch-long endangered red-footed tortoises. The man confessed he'd hoped to sell the turtles, which are an endangered species and go for five dollars in Barbados but as much as $75 in the United States.

Chicago *Tribune*/Associated Press, December 5, 1999

Local governments spent more than one million dollars after thousands of mice swarmed some 10,000 homes in a fifty-mile zone in the Lake Apopka area, northwest of Orlando. Orange County Chairman Mel Martinez, who would later become a U.S. Senator, asked Governor Jeb Bush for $1.6 million for poison, traps and manpower. In all, some 7,000 mice were trapped, more than 3,775 traps and 38,816 poison packs were handed out, more than 1,870 acres of brush were mowed and more than 400 tons of debris were cleared.

Orlando *Sentinel*, December 26, 1999

A New Jersey man said he was driving to the Keys on vacation and saw hundreds of rabbits fleeing a burning sugar cane field off U.S. 27 near Lake Okeechobee. He said the animals were screaming and throwing themselves into a canal, with turkey buzzards in hot pursuit. He said he saved one and placed it in a milk crate. He later delivered it to a wildlife rescue group in the Keys, but it died.

Farm officials said animals often flee fields being burned to rid canes of leafy material so the crop can be harvested. But they said usually only a dozen or so rabbits will flee a particular fire, and usually they can outrun it.

"I don't know why anyone would pick up one of these marsh rabbits," U.S. Sugar Company spokeswoman Judy Sanchez said. "They're mangy and vermin-ridden. They're not pet rabbits."

Locals said they often lay in wait during cane fires and grab the rabbits on the way out for a meal.

Palm Beach *Post*, February 21, 2001

A man accidentally ran over and killed a wild monkey near the Intracoastal Waterway Bridge in Dania. As he stopped to push the dead animal to the side of the road, five monkeys lunged from the bushes. "They were so mad at me," the man said. "They were kind of grinning and sticking their teeth out and jumping up high." Authorities did not say what the monkeys were doing in Dania.

Miami *Herald*, October 11, 1993

A 79-year-old woman who fought off a rabid fox by holding onto it for twelve hours died two months later. Her son said it was unclear how much the injuries from the attack contributed to her death. The fifteen-pound animal had bitten and clawed her after she'd stepped outside her mobile home in Zephyrhills, about 45 miles north of Tampa. She fell to the ground, breaking a hip, but grabbed the fox and gripped its throat and tail during an all night struggle. It repeatedly bit and clawed the woman as she clutched it, until her landlord showed up and clubbed the animal to death.

Associated Press, April 6, June 20, 1999

A Broward County pest control company glued tiny bar codes to twenty-five live roaches, with one possibly worth a million dollars. The company released the bugs from southern Palm Beach County down to southern Broward County, as part of a release of 350 cockroaches in thirteen states. Besides the one insect with the bar code worth one million dollars, each of the fourteen companies participating also released a roach good for a new Volkswagen Bug. Gluing bar codes the size of a match head onto 25 cockroaches took nearly two hours.

Palm Beach *Post*, May 5, 2000

An eleven-year-old boy went door to door in his northern Broward County neighborhood for donations and recruited his classmates to spread the word to save Lucky, a 50-year-old lobster and longtime denizen of a supermarket tank. The boy raised enough money to save the lobster and arrange for it to be released into the waters off Maine.

Miami *Herald*, March 8, 1997

NASA officials had to deal with pigs roaming the Kennedy Space Center and the adjacent 140,000-acre Merritt Island National Wildlife Refuge. After pigs bolting from thickets struck twenty-two cars, NASA managers worried about one striking a space shuttle making a one-shot-only landing at 200 mph.

Miami *Herald*, March 19, 1997

A family renting a Hialeah home followed a strong chemical scent to a secret room filled with more than forty large jars of preserved animals, apparently collected by the home's former occupant, a world traveler and rare animal dealer who had died nearly two decades earlier. The animals, preserved in a transparent brown liquid, included a toucan, rats, birds, a small monkey, an iguana, and many snakes. After the family called police, officers found a trap door in a backyard tool shed that they say led to an underground laboratory.

Miami *Herald*, December 25, 1997

An emu that got loose tied up traffic on West Palm Beach's Forest Hill Boulevard for two hours as sheriff's deputies tried to corral it. They finally caught up with it and put a sock over its head.

South Florida Sun Sentinel, September 8, 1999

The dean of the University of Florida's veterinary school proposed a three million dollar retirement center for pets that outlive their owners. Dogs and cats would each have common living quarters with a television, upholstered furniture and carpeting.

Associated Press/Palm Beach *Post*, November 19, 2000

A 23-year-old University of Miami graduate working in the circulation department of the Miami *Herald* was diagnosed in 2002 with America's first known case of mad cow disease. British doctors said they believe the woman, born in England, contracted the disease from eating infected beef before she and her family moved to Florida. They said the disease could be dormant for five to 40 years and had no cure. The woman died about a year and a half later.

Miami *Herald*, October 20, 2002; June 25, 2004

SEE YOU IN COURT

A quadriplegic man from Orlando sued two West Palm Beach strip clubs because they didn't have wheelchair access to private areas where patrons could get lap dances. He also complained the counter around which women dance in the main part of the club was too high for him to place his drink.

South Florida Sun-Sentinel, January 20, 2002

An ex-Hooters waitress sued the Panama City Beach restaurant where she'd worked, saying she was promised a new Toyota for winning a beer sales contest but instead got a toy Yoda — the little green character from *Star Wars*. The manager said the whole thing had been an April Fool's joke, but the waitress later quit and sued. She eventually settled. Her attorney would not disclose terms, although he said the woman could now go to a local car dealership and "pick out whatever type of Toyota she wants."

Associated Press, July 27, 2001; May 9, 2002

A Hooters waitress turned police officer was unsuccessfully sued by a former customer who said she didn't repay the $3,940 he loaned her for breast enlargement surgery.

Associated Press, December 27, 2002

A lawsuit filed in Orlando claimed Dollar Rent-A-Car should have known a driver was prone to drinking because he was from Ireland. The man's lawyer later apologized and said he would omit reference to his client's Irish heritage.

The lawsuit said Dollar "either knew or should have known about the unique cultural and ethnic customs existing in Ireland which involve the regular consumption of alcohol at 'pubs' as a major component to Irish social life."

A local Irish American Club leader said, "That would be like saying all blacks steal." The lawyer said later he would emphasize the different driving conditions in Ireland, such as driving on the left side of the road.

Miami *Herald*, May 20, 1999

A teen driver seriously hurt after crashing his car sued the city of Bradenton for not arresting him earlier. The 16-year-old driver and his lawyer said police found him trying to climb into a relative's window, clearly intoxicated, but officers let him drive home. Minutes later he slammed into tree, rupturing his aorta. A test later showed his blood-alcohol level was double the legal minimum to be considered drunk and ten times the standard for minors.

Associated Press/Palm Beach *Post*, November 14, 2000

Timothy John Marshall of South Bay escaped a Florida Keys road prison in 1987 after serving two years of a fifteen-year sentence for cocaine trafficking. He was at large for nine years and four months before authorities finally tracked him down in Orlando—married, with a stepson and regular job.

He then asked to be released, saying his term would be over if they only gave him credit for the more than nine years he was on the lam. Marshall argued the state didn't try hard enough to find him. When a lower court refused, he went to the Fourth District Court of Appeal.

Escapee Timothy Marshall asked for credit for the time he was on the lam.

Two of the three judges on the panel were Jewish, but it was Gentile Gary Farmer who wrote, "This petition may take the prize for chutzpah." The Yiddish term refers to a special kind of gall and arrogance, such as that employed by a man who would kill his parents, then ask for mercy because he was an orphan.

Fourth District Court of Appeal, November 17, 1999;
Palm Beach *Post*, November 18, 1999

The clubhouse at a neighborhood in Weston, in Broward County, banned soap in its locker room showers to keep people from slipping, falling and suing. The association had recently paid $50,000 to settle such a lawsuit. Signs also advised those taking showers not to bring their own soap either.

South Florida Sun-Sentinel, March 13, 1999

Two men police suspect were shot in a fouled drug deal at a Hialeah hotel won a $1.7 million verdict against the inn for failing to provide them proper security. The judge excluded any evidence about the alleged drug deal on grounds it could have unfairly tainted the case. The hotel's lawyer said the jury heard only half the story.

Chicago *Tribune*, November 26, 1999

A man unhappy about the outcome of a domestic violence case took a Jacksonville lawyer hostage in his office and threatened to set off a bomb unless the judge in the case stepped down. Later, Duval County Judge Sharon Tanner walked up to a television reporter covering the standoff and said she was resigning immediately. The man later surrendered. Police said he probably wasn't taken in by the phony resignation, adding that he told police he didn't expect it to be accepted anyway and had just wanted to make a point.

Associated Press, August 5, 2004

Broward County Circuit Judge Joyce Julian was found half-clothed and drunk in the hallway of a hotel near Jacksonville. Police found the judge, attending a judicial conference at the Amelia Island Plantation resort, lying in a public area wearing only a shirt. At first, she said she had been drugged and assaulted. Hotel employees said she had been drinking heavily and fell down. One employee said he saw her remove her pants. Records showed police called to her home two years earlier had found her

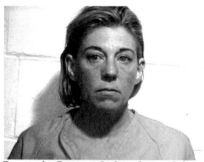

Broward County Judge Joyce Julian resigned after she was found half-naked at a North Florida hotel.

drunk. Julian underwent rehabilitation and the misdemeanor charge was dropped. She lost her bid for reelection.

Miami *Herald*, February 20, 2002; Associated Press, January 12, 2003

A Stuart nurse hired a Palm Beach Gardens lawyer to represent her in a bankruptcy dispute; she felt a female lawyer could best relate to her. She later learned her counsel used to be a man and had undergone a sex change operation. She argued the lawyer had misrepresented her credentials. The lawyer sued her for non-payment of legal fees.

Palm Beach *Post*, September 17, 2000

When a woman sued the Boynton Beach location of the Italian restaurant chain Romano's Macaroni Grill in November 1999 after claiming to have bitten into a quarter-sized key ring in her *pesto capellini*, her lawyers got a little carried away, arguing that "The said *pesto capellini* entree was not fit for use as food but was defective, unwholesome, and unfit for human consumption."

The suit, parroting a standard lawsuit passage, said that biting into the key ring caused the woman, among other things, disfigurement, humiliation, impairment of her working ability, and, the classic, "loss of enjoyment of life."

Palm Beach County Circuit Court

A woman was awarded $100,000 in a suit that claimed her boss bit her on the neck, fondled her and made unwanted sexual advances. Carol Moniz said she had tolerated the groping because she had two children to support but quit and contacted police after the biting incident.

Palm Beach *Post,* August 5, 2000

A Tampa judge ruled a local television reporter had to stay 300 feet from a man who claimed the reporter was stalking him in pursuit of a story. The 30-year-old cook, subject of a series of stories about his multiple DUI arrests, said the reporter had been harassing him. The reporter called the injunction an affront to the First Amendment.

Associated Press, December 11, 2002

A potential juror who wasn't picked in a first-degree murder case thought he was, then sat through the four-day trial, then got selected foreman, and even recited the guilty verdict. It was only after the nineteen-year-old defendant was sentenced to life, shackled and cuffed, and led away did anyone realize the mistake. The man, Fred Burtz, apparently misheard a bailiff as he called Robert Burns. Burns apparently didn't hear his name. Burtz then joined the jury. While he was called "Burns" several times, court officials figured he just thought his name was being mangled. He even signed his proper name. The mistake wasn't discovered until jurors were preparing to go home. A judge later refused to grant the defendant a new trial.

Miami *Herald*, September 4, 1999;
South Florida Sun-Sentinel, September 10, 1999

A man charged with drunk driving and his alleged victim struck up a friendship of sorts during jury selection and went to lunch together, where the victim knocked back two beers in front of one of the jurors. After the defendant told his lawyer, a judge ordered a mistrial.

Palm Beach *Post*, March 4, 1999

Four people were sent flying when the small elevator they were riding in at a suburban Boynton Beach condominium suddenly dropped eight feet. All four were hospitalized and one died six weeks later. The two couples then sued the condo's owner, the builder and the elevator maker. But defendants said the elevator clearly posted a 500-pound weight limit, and between them, the four people weighed about 800 pounds. The case was later settled; terms were not disclosed.

Palm Beach *Post*, September 18, 1995;
interview with attorney Paul Nemiroff, December 20, 2004

A Jacksonville man was sentenced to two days in jail for cutting a hole in an American flag and wearing it as a dress.

Associated Press/Miami *Herald*, December 19, 1999

Famed insurer Lloyd's of London sued a West Palm Beach Sheraton hotel in January 2000, claiming it botched the February 1998 delivery of a $40,000 manuscript by 19th century poet Percy Bysshe Shelley to a British book dealer in town for a book fair. According to the suit, the dealer's London office sent the package by Federal Express to the man, in care of the hotel, but he wasn't told of its arrival until after he'd checked out. Lloyd's claimed an employee of the dealer was told a bellhop had delivered the package to an "unaccompanied minor" who checked into the room the dealer had left. The child's mother denied knowing about the package.

Palm Beach *Post*, January 7, 2000

The family of a fisherman from the Florida Keys who was killed in a thunderstorm tried to sue the Weather Channel for ten million dollars, saying it failed to predict the storm. A judge threw out the suit, saying weather forecasts are, not guarantees.

Associated Press, March 24, 1999

A Miami administrative law judge who wrote a memo threatening to use a baseball bat against his two fellow judges and an office manager was removed from the bench. The judge said the memo had been an exaggeration.

Miami *Herald*, August 29, 1998

Shakespeare must have rolled in his grave during the October 6, 1999, exchange between a lawyer and judge who both revered the bard. Attorney Barry Silver, fighting a fine from the Florida Elections commission, told a three-judge Fourth District Court of Appeal panel, "If you steal my purse, you take nothing, but if you steal my reputation, you take everything." He'd heard the line from *Othello* on the radio that week. Judge Gary Farmer responded, "Men at some time are masters of their fates. The fault, dear Brutus, is not in our stars but in ourselves." That, of course, from *Julius Caesar*.

Attorney Barry Silver traded Shakespeare quotes with a judge.

Palm Beach *Post*, October 7, 1999

The operator of a Miami Beach restaurant agreed to pay $15,000 for sensitivity training a month after he added an automatic fifteen percent tip to two black patrons and, after they complained, explained, "You black people don't tip well." The agreement settled a suit against the Thai Toni restaurant by Florida Attorney General Bob Butterworth. The manager later appeared on the *Leeza* daytime television talk show to apologize to the two patrons.

Palm Beach *Post,* November 25, 1999;
Miami *Herald,* December 14, 1999

GO FIGURE

An Altamonte Springs man sold insurance against abduction by aliens.

"You don't want to leave earth without it," president Mike St. Lawrence said. The single lifetime premium of twenty dollars bought a $10 million policy.

Miami *Herald*, March 9, 1997

U.S. Food and Drug Administration officials were searching for the source of a hoax flier that warned Miami Beach residents their water had been poisoned as part of an ongoing mind control experiment being conducted by the Central Intelligence Agency. It warned them to wrap their heads in aluminum foil and drink plenty of alcoholic beverages. The circular, which was left at hotels, restaurants and bars, listed the telephone numbers of the FDA and then U.S. Senator Jesse Helms of North Carolina.

South Florida Sun-Sentinel, December 9, 1993

Volunteer firefighters in Chumuckla, north of Pensacola, answered an alarm, only to find the blaze was at their own firehouse. Two trucks were saved but the building burned down in thirty minutes.

Associated Press/Chicago *Tribune*, January 30, 2000.

At least a half dozen people reported they'd been duped by a man in Punta Gorda who staged realistic-looking choking incidents with the aim of being "rescued" and eliciting sympathy. Police said the man had committed no crime.

Associated Press/*South Florida Sun-Sentinel*, March 9, 2003

A Tampa television reporter house-hunting on the Internet learned a neighborhood commonly known as Interbay was actually called "Swastika." While the term is best known for the Nazi symbol, it also refers to a good luck symbol used by Native Americans and ancient Greek cultures.

Associated Press, November 7, 1999

A woman bought an ink-and-water color painting of a dancer in a Fort Myers thrift shop for $1.99. It turned out to be an original by French sculptor Auguste Rodin and was valued at more than $14,000. The painting, in a worn frame in a corner of the shop, bore the signature "A. Rodin." The woman was skeptical but was willing to gamble for two dollars. No local appraisers would inspect the painting and she had nearly abandoned it when she heard the Oprah Winfrey program was having a special called "Hidden Treasures." Appraisers on the show told her the painting was authentic.

Fort Myers *News-Press*, February 10, 2000

An antiques dealer from Oviedo, near Orlando, bought a mahogany card table at a Stuart estate sale for $1,650. It later sold at auction in New England for $1.32 million. It turned out to be an original Chippendale-period table from the early 1760s. The dealer called it "the Mona Lisa of card tables."

Associated Press, December 17, 2001

A veteran motorcycle safety instructor on his way to teach a class in Fort Lauderdale was fatally struck by a sports utility vehicle.

Miami *Herald*, September 11, 2000

Workmen tearing down walls for renovations at a Panama City school found a wallet that Sara Frank Renfroe had lost when she was twelve — in 1965. The billfold had no money but did contain invaluable photos of Sara, now forty-seven and living in Wyoming, and her sisters. Also inside — a Barbie fashion catalog and Beatles trading cards. Authorities tracked down the woman through her library card, which held the address where her parents still live.

Associated Press/Palm Beach *Post*, November 19, 2000

In December 2002, three friends were fishing off Fort Lauderdale. One, Eric Bartos, was in the middle of a break-up and the three decided that if they hooked a sailfish, they would hold an informal ceremony — Bartos would place his gold wedding band on the fish's bill and let it go. That's what they did. More than two years later, in January 2005, the three said, they and two other men were fishing further south, off Fowey Light, near Miami. Bartos reeled in another sailfish. It had the ring on its bill. The men said they took pictures, removed the ring, and released the fish. Bartos later passed a polygraph test.

Miami *Herald*, February 3, February 8, 2005

WHOOPS

Three drug dealers who'd hidden their cocaine deep in the vents of their car's air conditioner broke into a sweat when they were pulled over on a routine traffic stop in Callaway, near Panama City. So they turned on the air conditioning. The fan broke the plastic bag open and showered the crooks' faces with their contraband.

Associated Press, February 19, 1998

A federal Drug Enforcement Agent, giving a gun safety presentation to about fifty adults and students at the Orlando Minority Youth Golf Association, shot himself in the left thigh. The agent was treated and later returned to work.

Associated Press, April 30, 2004

A man posing as an undercover cop, complete with a *Miami Vice* badge and flashing lights but armed with a real gun, pulled over a woman on a dark road in Hobe Sound, near Jupiter. She turned out to be an off duty Palm Beach County Sheriff's Deputy and another deputy was following her. Martin County deputies charged the man with impersonating an officer.

Stuart *News/South Florida Sun-Sentinel*, May 14, 2004

A man called police in Greenacres, near Lake Worth, to say he thought he had found cocaine in a bag. It was an onion.

Palm Beach *Post*, July 4, 2001

A man who was attacked by an eleven-foot, 385-pound alligator as he pulled weeds along the shore of a lake in Tavares, but saved himself by punching the beast in the nose, was later arrested on unrelated grand theft charges.

Chicago *Tribune*, July 29, 2004

Actor James Earl Jones was misidentified as James Earl Ray. (Lorimar)

The city of Lauderhill created a plaque to honor James Earl Jones, the guest speaker at a local Martin Luther King celebration. But the plaque said, "Thank you James Earl Ray, for keeping the dream alive." While Jones might be keeping the dream alive, it was Ray who was convicted of murdering the civil rights icon. The plaque maker said it would fix the plaque for free.

Associated Press/Palm Beach *Post*, January 20, 2002

James Earl Ray, convicted assassin of Martin Luther King. (FBI)

A woman who pulled into a McDonald's drive-through in Weston, west of Fort Lauderdale, decided her bag was a bit too heavy for a bagel and drink. She looked inside and found hundreds of dollars in a sealed bag. It was the restaurant's bank deposit. McDonald's officials, who wouldn't reveal the total amount, said the money had been placed in the food bag to make it less conspicuous and the bag was accidentally left too close to the pickup window. The woman returned the money and got a "thank you" note and fifty dollars in gift certificates.

Chicago *Tribune*, December 21, 2003

A man fleeing deputies at the Seminole County courthouse, north of Orlando, lost his low-slung baggy jeans when he jumped over some shrubs. He was found a few blocks away in his boxer shorts.

Associated Press December 27, 2002

A man in Tallahassee who was urinating in public spotted some police, slipped his lit cigarette in his pants and took off. By the time officers caught up with him, his pants were in flames. They let him drop the pants to his ankles before they arrested him.

Associated Press, December 27, 2002

As two men were visiting urinals at a suburban Boca Raton steak house at about 3:00 a.m., they struck up a conversation. It turned out that one man was Turkish, the other Greek. The two nations have clashed for years, especially over ownership of the island of Cyprus. Soon the two men "became involved in an argument over nationality," a police report said. The Turk said he got a wine glass to the head and lost $400 and his Gucci watch. He refused treatment. The other man fled.

Palm Beach *Post*, November 11, 1998

A Virginia man who befriended a police officer as he investigated a crash at a West Palm Beach hotel was arrested on charges that he stole the officer's cellular phone. When the officer realized his phone was missing, he called the phone number and heard it ringing in the man's motel room.

Palm Beach *Post*, July 27, 1998

Two robbers found themselves having a very bad day. They attacked a service station manager with a stun gun as she stopped at a bank to deposit $20,000 in weekend receipts. A roofer atop the bank saw the men and called 911. His colleague on the ground gave chase. A contractor taking snapshots of the work photographed the robbers. The roofer chasing the men caught one. The other robber threw money in the air to distract his pursuer, but that only caught the attention of an off-duty police officer driving home in his cruiser. He caught the second man.

Palm Beach *Post*, July 30, 1996

A Bonita Springs man trying to shoot the button off the top of a baseball cap missed his target and instead struck his friend in the forehead, critically injuring him, authorities said. The men had played the shooting game before and were drinking at the time of the shooting, police said.

Associated Press, August 17, 1998

A 9-year-Port Salerno girl suffered serious burns when a home remedy for head lice set her hair afire. The fourth-grader's mother said she was dabbing rubbing alcohol on the girl's scalp, and then burning the lice with a candle, but it ignited fumes from the alcohol.

Palm Beach *Post*, January 22, 1998

The makers of Busch beer took down a billboard in Jacksonville that read, "Busch Beer and the Okefenokee: two Florida greats." The problem was that only 5 percent of the Okefenokee Swamp is in Florida, and it's not accessible without driving into Georgia, where ninety percent of the swamp lies.

Florida Times-Union, September 24, 2001

A 78-year-old retiree who falsely believed he was "already a winner" when he got his American Family Publishers sweepstakes mailer flew from Hawaii to Tampa to collect his winnings. He said he made the flight after several failed attempts to reach the company by letter and phone. He was so certain he had won, he had oversized checks printed for each of his five children. He turned out to be one of at least 20 people who made the trip in 1998 to Tampa, where the entries are processed, because they thought they had won. Later, the company agreed to a four million dollar settlement in a suit by Florida Attorney General Bob Butterworth.

St. Petersburg *Times,* April 1, 1998;
South Florida Sun-Sentinel, May 29, 1999

A man who worked undercover to help Florida Atlantic University police in Boca Raton break up a phony ID ring for underage students was a phony himself. That's because he wasn't a man. He was the 19-year-old daughter of a local philanthropist. The ruse was revealed when the woman, who wore men's clothes, shaved her head and reportedly hid her gender on dates, was arrested by Palm Beach County Sheriff's deputies for shoplifting.

Palm Beach *Post*, February 2, 2005

TO PROTECT AND SERVE

Two Palm Beach County Sheriff's deputies were fired after photographs of them having sex with their wives appeared on a pornographic web site operated by the wife of a third deputy. One photo showed a nude woman leaning against the third deputy's patrol car. He later resigned after someone complained to the sheriff's office.

The deputies later sued to get their jobs back, arguing their off-duty activities were constitutionally protected. But a federal judge turned them down, saying they were guilty of a "hard-core" violation of the department's ethics policy. Judge Daniel Hurley wrote, "No one would suggest that the First Amendment protects public fornication" and said the department's need for credibility "would unquestionably outweigh the deputies' interest in pursuing a side career in professional sexual performances."

South Florida Sun-Sentinel, May 24, 2003

An Orange County sheriff's deputy was fired after surveillance video showed him urinating in an Orlando-area public elevator. After people complained of a foul order inside a parking garage, the building's manager set up a video camera. It showed the deputy regularly urinating in a corner. The urine caused about $200 worth of damage to the elevator. "It smelled bad," one resident said. "To urinate in a public elevator, that's just wrong."

An Orange County Sheriff's deputy was caught urinating in an elevator. (*WKMG-TV*)

WKMG-TV, December 7, 2004

The police chief in Inverness, north of Tampa, resigned after he had a diner owner arrested in a dispute over a two-hamburger lunch order. Chief Joseph Elizarde had ordered two burgers over the phone, then became upset when he called back 20 minutes later and the meals weren't ready. He came to the restaurant in sweat pants and got into an argument with the owner, who apparently didn't know he was the chief and asked him to leave. Elizarde said the owner then pushed him. The owner said he was guiding him toward the door. A customer backed the owner.

Associated Press/Palm Beach *Post*, January 6, 2002;
St. Petersburg *Times*, September 9, 2004

A 23-year-old candidate for the Boca Raton Police Department was disqualified after he admitted to recruiters during a polygraph exam that he had celebrated his graduation, and later a friend's birthday, by smoking a half cigar at each event. That violated the department's strict ban on any smoking for one year before employment. The man's father, a federal investigator, told city council members, "I've never heard anything so ridiculous." But the city manager said the rule had been negotiated into the police contract and was ironclad.

Palm Beach *Post*, July 23, 1997

A French woman was killed and her sister critically injured when they were run over by a Miami Beach police sports utility vehicle as they sunbathed. The officer said he had been told robbery suspects were on the beach and didn't see the women.

Associated Press/Palm Beach *Post*, February 24, 2003

Some unusual calls made to various city and county authorities in Palm Beach County:

- A woman complained fleas from her neighbor's dogs were coming onto her property.
- A woman called because her light was flickering. The officer found that her bulb was loose.
- A resident complained repeatedly to police that his neighbor was trying to poison him by parking near the air conditioning unit so car fumes could be drawn into his home.
- A woman said her home had been invaded by small people and pointed to what she said were little men hanging from the back of the chair. The officer said he swatted the chair with his nightstick, but the woman said they'd fled to the other side of the room. The officer used his radio to make a buzzing noise and swept it back and forth as if wiping out the creatures. That satisfied the woman.

South Florida Sun-Sentinel, July 10, 1994

A paramedic training himself to be a Sarasota police officer died when a trainer's gun filled with blanks misfired and a plug struck the man in the eye.

158

The 32-year-old paramedic was training for the Sarasota Police Department's SWAT team at the Criminal Justice Academy.

Sarasota *Herald-Tribune*, January 11, 2001

An officer in Greenacres, near West Palm Beach, had stopped at a convenience store for a late night snack when two dogs charged him. He fired at both but missed, instead shattering the store's window and striking a woman in the ankle.

Palm Beach *Post*, February 3, 1999

A Broward County deputy was indicted on charges he ran drugs—even using his patrol car to deal cocaine—and tipped dealers to police activities.

South Florida Sun-Sentinel, May 2, 1999

A Broward County Sheriff's deputy was arrested in a Boynton Beach robbery after the getaway car's license tag was traced to him. Police said they found the lawman still wearing clothing bearing stains from dye packs tellers had hidden with the money.

South Florida Sun-Sentinel, May 2, 1999

Two Altamonte Springs officers were suspended without pay after one exposed himself and the other snapped a picture of him with a fourteen-year-old girl's camera. The girl, who was unable to get close to the stage at the concert, had given the officer the camera in hopes of getting a photo of a popular band. When she got the camera back from the developer a few days later, she saw a close-up of male private parts. The officers said they were fooling around and thought the camera was empty.

Associated Press, August 17, 2000

Delray Beach police fired a dispatcher who they said ignored 911 calls for nearly an hour while she held phone chats with friends. Recordings captured the woman telling a friend during a thirty-three-minute conversation that she wasn't going to answer 911 calls that day. Later that day, she interrupted a forty-eight-minute personal call to send paramedics to treat a man who was in shock after severing a finger, but ignored policy requiring she stay on the phone and give the man medical advice, instead returning to her friend.

Palm Beach *Post*, November 13, 1999

Lake County Sheriff Noel E. Griffin Jr. returned home from vacation to find someone had burglarized his home.

Palm Beach *Post*, December 31, 1987

After a minivan struck the Oldsmobile of off-duty Broward County deputy Cedric Perry, he chased the motorist and, at gunpoint, demanded the driver pay for the damage. The two went to an automated teller machine, where the man withdrew $200. Perry then changed his mind about the money and called Fort Lauderdale city police. The other driver was charged with DUI and Perry with aggravated assault.

South Florida Sun-Sentinel, November 24, 1999

An 80-year-old great-grandmother was frisked and held overnight in a Tampa area jail for writing a bad $145.93 check nineteen years earlier.

Associated Press, January 1, 2005

FLORIDA: LAND OF CRIME

Orlando authorities said a man stole expensive motorized wheelchairs from at least a dozen elderly people. Some of the machines were worth more than $5,000.

Associated Press/*Sun Sentinel*, January 28, 2001

When a man caught two brothers, twelve and fifteen, trying to steal his car in West Palm Beach, he forced them to strip naked, except for their socks, then go home and explain it to their parents. A man saw them run by and called police. The boys were charged in the incident.

Palm Beach *Post*, February 27, 1997

A thief got a surprise after stealing a box from a St. Petersburg woman's car. Among the contents were the woman's mother's ashes.

Associated Press, December 19, 1999

Police said an 88-year-old homeless man who robbed a Pensacola bank unarmed and was caught by customers might be the oldest bank robber in the nation's history.

Chicago *Tribune*, October 20, 1999

A 78-year-old man who had once escaped from California's San Quentin prison in a kayak was charged with robbing a Jupiter bank after he led police on a "slow speed" chase which ended some fifty miles later in Pompano Beach when police forced his car into a palm tree. They found guns, burglary tools, police scanners and a large amount of cash in his vehicle.

Forrest Silva Tucker, a lifelong bank robber and escape artist and once the head of a silver-haired band of South Florida crooks dubbed the "Over-the-Hill Gang," had last made headlines in 1983 when he opened fire on FBI agents and led authorities on a spectacular chase and shootout in West Palm

Beach. Tucker had first been arrested in 1935 as a fifteen-year-old bicycle thief. In 1951, he picked the lock on leg irons holding him in Miami's Jackson Memorial Hospital, then strolled away unnoticed.

Palm Beach *Post,* April 27, 1999

The head of security for the Boca Raton airport, as well as a manager and a maintenance worker, were arrested for firing hundreds of gunshots during what they explained as late-night target practice.

Palm Beach *Post,* November 22, 2002

After a Fort Myers man stole a sixteen-inch, 83-diamond necklace and two loose diamonds from a Boca Raton jewelry store, the owner chased the robber, who was arrested. When he complained of pain to police, a hospital X-ray showed his digestive tract contained the jewelry. Police allowed the robber to return the items in his own way. The owner then put the necklace on eBay, dropping the price from $100,000 to $75,000.

Palm Beach *Post,* August 2, 2002

A man in Stock Island, near Key West, was arrested by undercover detectives after bartering two trays of lasagna for a rock of crack cocaine.

Monroe County Sheriff's Office, April 16, 2002

A Colombian laundry used heroin as starch for shirts and blue jeans and hired a smuggler to bring them into Florida. But customs officials tripped him up when they noticed the clothes were unusually stiff, smelled like vinegar and left a trail of white powder.

Associated Press, December 27, 2002

Authorities in Palm Beach and Broward counties were looking for a robber who ordered coffee at doughnut shops, then threw it in the faces of workers and snatched cash from the register. The man was sought in at least six such robberies. None of the clerks was seriously hurt, authorities said. One shop said it serves its coffee at 196 degrees.

South Florida Sun-Sentinel, November 21, 2001

At least three people were injured when they were attacked by a drive-by crossbow shooter. Two of the victims were schoolboys walking home. The short, powerful bow's mounted crosswise on a stock and dates back to medieval warfare. They are also popular with hunters.

Miami *Herald,* November 23, 1995

Michael Fay, caned in Singapore for vandalizing cars in a case that drew worldwide attention, was arrested in Winter Park, near Orlando, for marijuana possession.

Associated Press, April 2, 1998

When a neighbor's Coconut Grove condominium went up in flames, a Miami nurse, who claims to be a clairvoyant, told police that a firebug had sprayed red paint on a bathroom wall. She credited her "remote perception" and said her Indian statue had told her. Police didn't believe her, especially when they found red paint on her clothes and sneakers and learned she'd bought red paint and gasoline the previous day. She was charged with arson.

Miami *Herald*, September 17, 2000

When workers came to cut down his citrus trees, a 95-year-old man in Tamarac, in Broward County, confronted them with an unloaded rifle. The state had been destroying trees across South Florida to stop the spread of citrus canker and protect Florida's giant citrus industry, and workers had already cut down three of his four backyard trees when he confronted them. He was charged with aggravated assault with a firearm on a law enforcement officer. The crew later cut down the tree.

South Florida Sun-Sentinel, March 28, 2000

In Pensacola, a naked man covered in blood was shot by his neighbor after he threw a flower pot through the man's living room window and crawled inside. The man later died—but not from the shooting, rather from cuts inflicted before the shooting and a drug overdose. A neighbor said the man had been served with divorce papers the previous day.

Pensacola *News Journal*, July 8, 2000

A man held up a Pompano Beach service station/convenience store with a can of oven cleaner, which he used to spray the clerk in the face.

Pompano Beach Police, November 14, 1998

Police in Pompano Beach arrested a 39-year-old man and found on him eight different driver's licenses with his photograph and different names, along with two Brazilian passports, twelve check cards, and numerous checkbooks. The man admitted to obtaining false documents for Brazilian illegal immigrants, including himself.

Pompano Beach Police, September 30, 1998

A former Deerfield Beach resident was arrested in New Jersey and charged with creating the "Melissa" virus, which, in a week, infected computers worldwide. Authorities said David L. Smith named the virus after a topless dancer he knew in Florida.

Associated Press/Palm Beach *Post*, April, 3, 1999

A waiter and restaurant owner who owed more than $15,000 in back taxes hijacked a school bus with thirteen learning-disabled students, sparking a 1-1/2 hour, slow-speed chase across the Miami area. Television news helicopters beamed live images to a transfixed public as the bus driver, on the job only seventeen months, drove at speeds of 15 to 20 miles per hour.

The hijacker finally had the bus stop in front of Joe's Stone Crab, the landmark restaurant in Miami Beach's South Beach neighborhood. When the man stepped off the bus and crouched, authorities feared he had a bomb. A police marksman named Joe Derringer fatally shot him. Police said later he turned out to be unarmed.

Except for one child who got a sliver of glass in his eye, the students were unhurt. They were taken inside Joe's for soft drinks, French fries and vanilla ice cream.

The gunman, a 42-year-old immigrant from the Dominican Republic, was married with two children, one a high school honor student. He owned two Chinese restaurants, which were draining his resources, so he'd also worked for seven years at Joe's, but had quit the night before the hijack.

Miami *Herald*, November 3, 1995

A Largo Burger King customer whose Whopper was served cold attacked and beat the sixteen-year-old cook. The man was later charged with aggravated battery.

Orlando *Sentinel*, November 16, 1987

A man was arrested after he dressed as psychotic *Friday the 13th* killer "Jason," waved a fake ax and chased several people into a restaurant near Florida State University.

Palm Beach *Post*, December 31, 1987

A clerk at a Casselberry convenience store who'd told police a good-hearted robber came back to return the money later admitted she'd made up the story.

Orlando *Sentinel*, January 31, 1993; February 10, 1993

A Fort Lauderdale Christian group set up a "Crime Prevention through Christian Intercession" hotline for criminals with a conscience.

Associated Press, June 8, 1993

DUMB CRIMINALS

A Bay County couple called police and reported someone broke into their home and stole their marijuana. The thief, though, didn't take all traces of the pot and the couple was arrested. A police lieutenant said, "They're America's dumbest criminals."

Associated Press, January 1, 2005

DUMB CRIMINAL DAY

These three stories appeared the same day, August 21, 2004, in South Florida newspapers:

A conspiracy to sell guns to opposing sides in Colombia's civil war was exposed when cardboard boxes stuffed with guns fell from the false ceiling of a storage unit, crashed into a toilet and broke a water pipe. Tenants of adjoining units saw water leaking, broke in, and saw the smashed toilet and the weapons alongside. Miami federal agents seized more than 200 weapons and more than 700,000 rounds of ammunition and later arrested five people.

Associated Press/Palm Beach *Post*

A man, who claimed $75,000 in stuffed bills seized by Port St. Lucie two years earlier was his, fouled himself up in court. The man, who claimed to be the uncle of one two men stopped in the car, said the money was in a bag with a Jaguar emblem on it. Later, in a hearing, a prosecutor showed the man a bag showing the emblem of the Jacksonville Jaguars NFL football team. "Yeah, that's it," the man said. The prosecutor then pulled out the actual bag, with the emblem of the Jaguar luxury car. Police were considering criminal charges.

Palm Beach *Post*

A Port St. Lucie man borrowed an acquaintance's cell phone, then pistol whipped and robbed another man. As he hid in the woods, officers called the phone. Other officers were able to hear it ringing, and the man surrendered.

Port St. Lucie *News/South Florida Sun-Sentinel*

A 61-year-old man who'd written two books about the dumb moves people make was careful when he made a date with a fifteen-year-old girl he'd met over the Internet. James F. Welles told the girl, "We can't be lovey-dovey in public. Bottom line, I'll be committing a crime." He turned out to be right. Undercover officers arrested him at a Lantana Denny's restaurant. The author of two books called *The Story of Stupidity* and *Understanding Stupidity* had really been talking to a forty-year-old male detective.

The man had told his proposed date to call him "Dad" when they met. He first suggested they have sex in his car but nixed that because the window tint wasn't dark enough.

During a three-week courtship, Welles directed his new acquaintance to www.stupidity.com, which touts his *The Story of Stupidity*, subtitled "A History of Western Idiocy From The Days of Greece To The Moment You Saw This Book." A link on that website takes a visitor to the table of contents for the book. Chapters include: Greek Stupidity, Roman Stupidity, Medieval Stupidity, Stupidity Reborn, Stupidity Reformed, Reasonable Stupidity, Enlightened Stupidity, Industrial Stupidity and The Age of Arrogance.

"Unfortunately," a passage in that last chapter ponders, "the arrogance inherent in this 'We can do anything' attitude came to characterize the general stupidity of our age and contributed to the monumental problems we have created for ourselves."

Palm Beach *Post*, November 8, 2002

A lunchtime burglar in Jupiter Farms cut a screen on a window, ransacked the place, and made off with a stereo, TV, VCR and jewelry. But, he left his wallet, authorities said.

Palm Beach *Post*, July 4, 2001

Police said a man from Greenacres, near Lake Worth, robbed a gas station in nearby Lantana, but left his wallet at the scene. He had placed the wallet on the counter when he asked for change for a twenty-dollar bill, then pulled a gun, demanded money and ran off with $200, leaving the wallet. Police used three traffic tickets they found in the billfold to track the man down.

South Florida Sun-Sentinel, January 3, 2003

In 1999, gunmen jumped two jewelers and a security guard in Ocala and stole suitcases the robbers expected to contain $500,000 worth of jewels. But they held only clothes.

Associated Press/Miami *Herald*, December 19, 1999

A man pulled up to the drive-through window of a suburban Delray Beach bank and held up a 3-by-5-inch index card reading, "This is a BOMB. Hand over the cash." When the teller said she had no money at her station, the man asked, "What about her?" pointing to the second teller. When there was no answer, the man drove off.

Palm Beach County Sheriff's Office, August 26, 1998

A Callaway woman accidentally dialed 911 and hung up. Police raced to the house and discovered she was running a methamphetamine lab there.

Associated Press, January 1, 2005

A man who robbed a McDonald's in Okaloosa County left his shoes behind and investigators used them to collected DNA. They matched it to a woman who was already in prison and figured out that her husband borrowed the shoes to commit the crime.

Associated Press, January 1, 2005

In Boynton Beach, two men robbed a Kentucky Fried Chicken restaurant, pistol-whipped several customers and ran off lugging two bulky cash registers containing about $2,000. They made their mistake when they went through a nearby parking lot — the one for the police, who were in the middle of a shift change. The police station is across the street.

Palm Beach *Post*, February 6, 2000

A man wearing a ski mask and brandishing a handgun pulled into a Tallahassee convenience store and ran toward the door. But the place had closed fifteen minutes earlier. The man hit the locked door with such force, he knocked himself out. Clerks called police, who arrested the man.

"Bozo Criminal of the Day" web page, October 18, 1999

A man held up a Naples coin laundry, robbing the attendant of cash and taking her purse. He later called her to say he planned to mail back her automatic teller machine card. The woman checked her caller ID and the man was arrested.

"Bozo Criminal of the Day" web page, October 12, 1999

A man walked into a Palm Beach bar, ordered a drink, and asked the bartender, "Mind if I count my money on the bar?" He then dumped about $10,000 in cash. The bartender called police the next day and the man was charged with robbing two area banks earlier in the week.

Palm Beach *Post*, November 28, 1996

A West Palm Beach man who tried to sell nearly three hundred forged paintings, passing off them off as works of masters, was tripped up when he tried to sell a Picasso "original" for $40,000 and when a dealer noticed a Winslow Homer signature at the bottom of one painting was spelled "Windslow."

Associated Press, December 17, 2001

A sixteen-year-old man who intended to rob a convenience store in Dania Beach, near Fort Lauderdale, pointed the gun at the clerk, then stopped to load it as customers watched. He then realized he'd brought the wrong size bullets. Undaunted, he raised the gun again, but the savvy customers tackled him.

Broward County Sheriff's Office, January 21, 2004

An Englewood woman who got a marijuana cigarette as a birthday present later could not find it and accused her son of stealing it. She called police and explained she couldn't find her joint. They did. She was arrested.

"Bozo Criminal of the Day" web page, October 10, 1999

A man donned a plastic bag to disguise himself before robbing a St. Petersburg Circle K convenience store. But the bag was clear, and clerks gave a good enough description for police to nab the man.

"Bozo Criminal of the Day" web page, October 5, 1999

A man stole a $15,000 set of golf clubs at the 1999 Doral Ryder Cup open in South Florida, then tried to sell them for five dollars each to Senior Tour player Raymond Floyd, who immediately identified them as being worth just a bit more. When police caught the man, he was still out at the course hawking the stolen clubs.

"Bozo Criminal of the Day" web page, September 20, 1999

A man trying to break into a Deerfield Beach pizza restaurant in September 1999 got stuck in the oven vent, where he stayed for twenty-two hours over the Labor Day weekend. When a restaurant manager finally showed up, the man shouted for help. Firefighters greased the vent and pulled the man out.

Broward County Sheriff's Office, September 8, 1999

Police said a Connecticut man flew to Miami three times to hold up the same tellers at the same bank, wearing the same clothes and using the same BB gun.

Orlando *Sentinel*, July 18, 1987

After four men robbed a Boynton Beach bank, one ran to a nearby fruit stand where he posed as a customer buying twenty-cent navel oranges. When he went to pay, he realized he had no money on him, panicked and fled. "I knew something was weird," manager Rob Desjardins said, "but I didn't know what."

Palm Beach *Post*, November 29, 2000

A six-foot man allegedly on the run for four months from Walton County, in the Panhandle, was found curled up inside a television in a mobile home just across the state line in South Georgia.

After receiving a tip from a woman who said the man was hiding under a mattress, Florida and local authorities took a dog inside. They found nothing, but when the dog kept poking around the TV, they unscrewed the back and found the man inside.

He had escaped in handcuffs from two deputies in Florida as they tried to place him in the back of a police car.

Associated Press, January 18, 2005

Anthony Thompson failed to show up for a ninety-day sentence; the thirty-second time he'd done so since 1987. Thompson was later found staying at the Ritz-Carlton near St. Louis.

Palm Beach *Post*, September 7, 1999

Whoever broke into a West Palm Beach home and stole a television, VCR and stereo also scarfed down a bowl of cheese crackers sprinkled with rat poison.

Palm Beach *Post*, September 15, 2000

DEATH

Ghost hunters spent a night at downtown Fort Lauderdale's century-old Stranahan House and concluded Ivy Cromartie Stranahan, who died in her sleep in an upstairs bedroom in 1971, really haunted the place. Her father had died in the same room. Husband Frank Stranahan, a local pioneer, had thrown himself in the New River in 1929 after becoming financially ruined.

The South Florida Ghost Team said it videotaped an ethereal orb of light in the courtyard. They also said they spotted an impression in a cushioned chair in the gift shop and smelled perfume. Both quickly dissipated. One ghost hunter said she felt Ivy brush past her.

But Ivy didn't respond when ghost hunters asked her to tap on glass or otherwise signal her presence.

Over the years, one employee had claimed Ivy talked to her and an events coordinator quit because of the noises. A maintenance man said there was a simple explanation—the floors are at a slight tilt and doors shut when the air conditioner causes a little movement. He said that years earlier, when the alarm kept going off without reason, the source turned out to be a rat. Executive Director Barbara Keith said, "I'm intrigued, yes. I want to say they're nuts. But, at the same time..."

South Florida Sun-Sentinel, May 13, 2003

Does the ghost of pioneer Ivy Stranahan haunt the Stranahan House? (Fort Lauderdale Historical Society)

Organizers planned a one-week Caribbean séance cruise from Miami for more than two hundred bereaved passengers who hoped to contact loved ones from beyond the grave.

South Florida Sun-Sentinel, October 4, 1999

According to the U.S. Bureau of Labor Statistics, thirty-one Americans died in wood chipper accidents from 1992 to 2002. Five were in Florida alone

In April 2004, a Tampa trimmer climbed into a chipper and kicked a large bundle of branches through; the machine pulled half his body in. In March 2003, a Lakeland woman was caught in a chipper and sucked through the 2-by-2-foot opening. In July 2000, a 14-year-old Gainesville boy was pulled in a chipper in front of his father and a crew of trimmers. In January 1999, a Tampa man was using his foot to force a tree into the machine when it grabbed his leg and pulled him in. In 1997, a worker was sucked into a chipper on a job west of Boca Raton; the company was later fined for failing to install safety guards on the chipper.

Palm Beach *Post*, December 31, 2004

A six-year-old whose mother was dying of AIDS leaped in front of a train in Dania and was killed instantly. A deputy said the girl told other children, "I want to become an angel and be with my mother."

Palm Beach *Post*, June 25, 1993

A man severed at the waist by an eighteen-wheeler lived for more than three hours as paramedics rushed his torso by air and lower body by ground. The man was crushed by a truck pulling out of a space at a Pensacola truck stop. Rescue workers presumed him dead, but when the man raised his arms to rescue workers, they raced him to the hospital, where he later died.

Associated Press/Palm Beach *Post*, March 24, 2001

A 75-year-old woman who caught her left arm in a sleeper sofa and was just inches from a telephone and whistle died after being stuck for at least two days, police said. Police in Cape Coral, near Fort Myers, said they found the woman after a worried friend called them.

Associated Press/Palm Beach *Post*, September 6, 2001

A man who cut his thumb apparently bled to death outside a neighbor's home in Cape Coral, near Fort Myers. The man was found dead wearing only a pair of socks. An emergency room doctor said a small artery is just below the thumb and someone could bleed to death from a cut there.

Associated Press/Palm Beach *Post*, July 5, 2003

A South Florida man lost control of his car and struck a tree and utility pole in Miami Beach. The man, unhurt, stepped out of the car. Moments later, another car struck wires dangling from another utility pole, pulling it down. The pole struck the first driver, killing him instantly.

Miami *Herald*, January 18, 1999

A woman visiting her husband's grave in suburban Miami was run over and killed by a tombstone delivery truck.

Associated Press, April 28, 1998

A 62-year-old woman using an oxygen tank to help her breathe lit a cigarette. She burst into flames, ran into a bathroom and collapsed. She was dead when firefighters arrived.

Palm Beach *Post*, February 5, 2005

EVERY BODY LOVES FLORIDA

A group that eventually swelled to more than 1,500 sued two South Florida Menorah Gardens cemeteries and their parent company, Service Corporation International, the world's largest funeral services chain, in what became one of the most far-reaching, and gruesome, cemetery mismanagement cases ever.

The suits alleged managers oversold and misplaced plots in cemeteries near Palm Beach Gardens and Fort Lauderdale.

They claimed, and testimony later showed, that workers buried people head-to-toe or like cordwood, squeezed vaults between two existing plots, crushed vaults and the bodies inside in order to bury people atop them, and even dug up remains and scattered them in nearby woods to make room for a new vault.

SCI said the outrages were the work of rogue local managers who were later fired and that the chain started fixing the problems as soon as it learned of them.

The two-year legal fight was marked by the anguish of relatives wondering where their loved ones were buried and punctuated by grisly images of broken burial vaults, dug-up graves and strewn body parts. The alleged desecration had been especially disturbing to the many loved ones who were observant Jews. Strict Jewish law forbids the disturbing of the dead.

SCI eventually settled for $100 million. About twenty-six million dollars of that went to the families' lawyers.

Another seventy-two families filed a separate suit and opted out of the class action. They also settled; terms were not disclosed.

Palm Beach *Post*, December 3, 2003; November 23, 2004

An errand-runner at a Miami mortuary who hadn't seen his girlfriend in about a week was asked by a co-worker to pick up a body at the county morgue. While there, he saw the body of his girlfriend and identified her for police. The woman had been shot by another boyfriend.

Associated Press/Palm Beach *Post*, May 22, 2000

Two men and a woman ducked into an attic to hide from police, but revealed themselves when they discovered a decomposing body hidden along with them. Police had almost given up their search when they heard a shout, "Get me out of here. There's a body!"

Associated Press, January 1, 2005

In his book, *The Season: Inside Palm Beach and America's Richest Society*, author Ronald Kessler reported that, when the ninety-year-old multimillionaire husband of 57-year-old socialite Gianna Lahainer died in March 1995 in the heart of the island's social season, she had to choose between burying him or attending various parties. She opted to embalm Frank and store him at a local funeral home for forty days, explaining, "My life was going on. Why should I wait? I would miss the whole season."

Parade Magazine, October 31, 1999;
South Florida Sun-Sentinel, November 28, 1999

An apartment manager in St. Augustine Beach found a human brain in a bait bucket in an apartment vacated by a student.

Orlando *Sentinel*, December 31, 1989

Miami-based Eastern Airlines, which filed for bankruptcy after an employee strike, tried to rebuild business by offering half-price fares for shipping bodies and frequent flier miles to funeral directors for shipments.

Orlando *Sentinel*, December 31, 1989

A citrus worker in Lake Placid who injured his finger when another man bit it during a fight later cut it off, cooked it with scrambled eggs and ate it. When deputies arrived, then man came out of his home naked and covered with blood. He had to be subdued by a deputy using a chemical spray after he tried to punch the deputy.

Associated Press, February 23, 1999

After a medical waste truck dropped a human head wrapped in a plastic bag on the way to an incinerator near Lakeland, police later found another head, and enough arms and legs for four other people, inside the truck. The first head was identified as George DeWayne McKown, of Fort Myers, who was fifty-three when he died of a heart attack while cleaning a bar. Polk Medical Examiner Stephen Nelson fumed, "You can't chop a body up and then call it medical waste." He added, "Any reasonable person who knew him would look at it and say, 'This isn't medical waste—it's George.'" The man's family later sued and was awarded $168,000.

Lakeland *Ledger*, November 6, 1998; October 2, 2000

MURDER MOST FOUL

A mother of six, including quadruplets, who had left San Antonio, Texas, for Sarasota during a custody fight with her former husband, was found slain execution style in her new home, her two-year-old quadruplets wearing swimming pool life jackets and crawling in her blood. Police in Mexico later arrested a former Texas high school football star known as "Joey the Bull" in the slaying. Two other men were arrested in Texas and charged with conspiracy in the killing. Later, Sheila Bellush's former husband, Allen Blackthorne, the vice president of a medical equipment firm, was charged with hiring a hit man. The two, divorced in 1988, had been in an ugly custody battle over their two older children.

Los Angeles *Times*, November 28, 1997;
Miami *Herald*, February 24, 2002

A Jacksonville man was charged with shooting another man to death during an argument over a woman that lasted several days, during which the victim said the other man's baby was ugly.

St. Petersburg *Times*, September 5, 1993

An exotic dancer fed up with her rock band drummer stabbed, burned and mulched him, then buried his remains in cement. Police in Sanford, near Orlando, said the woman admitted in secretly-taped conversations that she stabbed the man in her condominium, then contacted relatives who helped her burn it in a field, run the bones through a wood chipper and pour the remains in concrete. She and her relatives then scattered concrete chips up and down Interstate 95. The victim, besides his musical career, also ran a landscaping business and might have been mulched by his own equipment, police said. They had not recovered remains, but found blood in the condo. Said a spokesman, "We feel we have concrete evidence—no pun intended." The woman was later sentenced to seventeen years in prison.

Orlando *Sentinel*, September 23, 1993; November 3, 1994

Lawyers for a Fort Lauderdale-area woman said she strangled her nineteen-month old granddaughter as an act of love, then stuffed her in a freezer with TV dinners to make sure she didn't decay. The Oakland Park woman's lawyers said she believed the child was unloved by relatives so she fed the girl Froot Loops, then decided she would be better off dead and spent ten to fifteen minutes strangling her with a sash. She then wrapped the baby in a poncho and a white department store bag, put her in the freezer, said, "I love you," and went to sleep. She said she called her sister the next day. The woman had been on probation after serving time for killing her boyfriend in a drunken range.

South Florida Sun-Sentinel, August 29, 2002

A man who walked into an all night Naples Wal-Mart, covered in blood, was charged with murder after authorities found a stabbed body in a trash bin. Store workers said the man walked in about 4:00 a.m. and bought clothes, bandages and trash bags, paying with a hundred dollar bill. After the man was arrested, police found the corpse in the bin about two miles from the hotel where authorities found a pickup with blood in it. The man said the victim had attacked him with a knife and he had fought back in self-defense.

Associated Press, June 28, 2004

A Daytona Beach-area undertaker admitted to fatally stabbing his 28-year-old wife as she slept, stashing her body in the funeral home's cooler, and finally placing her in a coffin beneath the body of an eighty-nine-year-old customer. What would seem to be a perfect crime was found out after friends and relatives got suspicious and didn't buy the man's story that his wife had just wandered off and would probably be back.

Orlando *Sentinel*, August 28, 1999

A St. Petersburg man stabbed his ex-girlfriend's new lover to death with a macheté as the man slept in the woman's bed. He then decapitated the man and set the severed head on the hood of the car, lining it up so it could see itself in a side mirror. The man was later ruled incompetent to stand trial on the first-degree murder charge.

St. Petersburg *Times*, February 5, March 28, 2002

When two retirees argued in line at a Broward County movie theater, Seymour Schuss, 68, punched Irving Rosenberg, 74, in the chin. Rosenberg fell backward and struck his head on the pavement. He died two weeks later. Schuss pleaded guilty to manslaughter and was sentenced to six months in prison. Witnesses told police Rosenberg had complained that Schuss was taking too long to buy eight tickets for himself, his wife and three other couples to the film *Never Again.*

Miami *Herald*, December 31, 2002; May 5, 2004

A man who was a perfect blood platelet match for a five-year-old Jacksonville boy was slain in a robbery attempt at a supermarket where he was an assistant manager. The boy suffered a form of cancer that left him unable to make his own blood. Kevin Baker had donated sixty-eight pints of blood and nineteen units of platelets, the component that makes blood clot. After the murder, the boy was forced to use platelets that didn't match as well, leaving him with high fevers and severe headaches.

Associated Press/Miami *Herald*, March 20, 1991

MEDICAL WONDERS

A bogus Miami Beach plastic surgeon gave a body builder fake women's breasts instead of the pectoral implants he wanted. The phony surgeon performed several operations on the 47-year-old champion body builder and at least two women, resulting in gross disfigurement and severe physical and emotional pain.

Detectives said the phony doctor charged patients between $3,000 and $4,000 per surgery. One woman said the man left her breasts uneven and of different sizes. Investigators said some victims might be too embarrassed to come forward. One investigator called a videotape of a surgery "a horror movie," adding, "Amateur doesn't describe what they were doing."

Police said the bodybuilder woke up several times during the procedure because he was given an anesthetic used on animals by veterinarians.

The phony doctor was finally arrested five years later in Belize.

Miami *Herald*, October 6, 1999; October 8, 2004

A 57-year-old Sarasota woman who suffered a stroke suddenly began speaking with a British accent. The woman, who grew up near Philadelphia, had never been to England, but was contemplating moving there. Researchers said the woman's case was one of only twenty since 1919. One of the first victims was a Norwegian woman who suffered a brain injury during World War II and began speaking with a German accent. There's no known cure, but some patients get better with time, as portions of the brain heal.

Sarasota *Herald-Tribune*, November 19, 2003

An Orlando-area meat cutter lost a chunk of a finger while slicing a frozen pig with a band saw at the grocery store where he worked, then underwent leech treatment to save it. A doctor at Disney's Celebration community used the 2,500-year-old remedy. The doctor had spent two hours reattaching the finger, but it turned blue the next day because blood wasn't draining through the veins. So he brought in the creepy creatures to drain the blood.

Orlando *Sentinel*, April 3, 1999

A four-foot-ten-inch tall, 478-pound woman lived on her sofa for most of six years, never moving. Living with a man unable to care for her, she lay in her own waste in the non-air conditioned home. Finally, family members called 911 to say she wasn't breathing. Paramedics, staggered by the smell of stale body waste, donned protective gear and entered the home, but found the woman's skin had grown around the fabric of the couch. They built a make-shift stretcher from plywood and loaded the woman and couch, still connected, on the back of a pickup, then took the woman to a hospital, where she later died.

Family members couldn't explain why the woman was found in such bad shape. One said, she "was a grown woman. She could make her own decisions." A cousin who worked for the state's Department of Children and Families – which has a unit that takes care of helpless adults – said she didn't know her relative's condition.

Palm Beach *Post*, August 14, 2004

OTHER LARGE FLORIDIANS

Francis John Lang, aka Michael Walker, was believed to have reached 1,187 pounds. Born in 1934, he had weighed only 150 lbs. as a soldier in Korea and blamed his weight gain on abuse of prescription drugs. Unable to walk, he had a mobile home built with observation wings and traveled the country displaying himself at carnivals and fairs. Lying nearly nude on an oversize circular bed, he preached about the evils of drugs, using his condition as the moral of the story. He later settled in Gibsonton, a town near Tampa comprised mostly of carnival workers. By 1980, he had reportedly reduced his weight to 369 lbs.

Dimensions Magazine

Carol Haffner of Hollywood reached 1,023 lbs. She said in an interview a week before her death that her parents were heavy and that she weighed two hundred pounds by the time she got out of high school in 1956 and 440 by 1970. For a while, she had a special chair built for her at the Seminole Tribe Bingo Parlor, where she was a regular.

But a few months after the death of her husband, who she described as slim, she broke her hip and became bedridden, and her weight, then around 600 pounds, ballooned.

"I get up about 8:30 a.m. and brush my teeth," she said in the interview. "That takes me about a half hour." She said she would have cereal or a piece of toast, then watch TV talk and game shows until noon. "The afternoon is a bad time. I sleep all afternoon," she said.

She spent her last five years in her mobile home, leaving only once during Hurricane Andrew in 1992.

In 1995, she died at fifty-nine of heart failure at a Hollywood hospital, in two beds welded together to support her body. She had been trying to raise money to attend a $550 program in Boston. On her last trip, it took almost a dozen emergency workers to move her.

"I need help," the Hollywood woman said that night. "I can't do it on my own. I've tried for 45 years. I keep going up and down. I lose 50 pounds, and I gain it back."

South Florida Sun-Sentinel, February 3, 1995;
Miami *Herald,* February 5, 1995

Leonard Brown of Panama City reached 920 lbs. In 1994, when he was forty-one, he publicly appealed for financial help to attend the same Boston program Carol Haffner had sought. But his insurance company refused. Brown had bulked up after a near paralyzing traffic accident in 1973, when he was about twenty years old.

His obesity made him a prisoner in his bedroom, where he read, watched television, listened to the stereo and exercised. He could walk the few feet to the bathroom only with help from his wife, Pam, and a pair of crutches, but the trip left him gasping for breath.

Tests showed Brown's weight problem was mostly genetic. Six of his seven siblings were obese. He had been hospitalized or bedridden by the accident, an epileptic seizure five years earlier and a fall, each time adding pounds. He had tried diet cookies, drinks and pills, grapefruit diets and water diets. He had contemplated suicide until he heard about the Boston program.

"This here gave me something to hope for," Brown said in 1994. "Then, they told us you have to have all this money. It was just like kicking me in the stomach."

Associated Press, October 1, 1994

A Jacksonville man who survived being stabbed in the head with an eight-inch serrated knife entered into the *Guinness Book of World Records* for having the largest foreign object successfully removed from a human brain. The man was visiting his sister when he answered a knock at the door. His sister's neighbor then plunged the knife into his head. The man remained conscious and surgeons were able to remove the knife without severing any major blood vessels. His attacker was later convicted and sentenced to a year in jail. He said the attacker might have mistaken him for his sister's husband, with whom the neighbor had argued.

Associated Press, November 23, 1999

A woman who faked seizures across Florida was arrested some thirty times, including at a Sarasota County hospital where someone recognized her from a photo in the paper after she'd already had a tube pushed down her trachea and into her lung. The worker said, "Hey! Get up," and the woman did. She has been charged repeatedly with making fake 911 calls and fraudulently obtaining medical services. Medical records showed she was being treated for a bipolar affective disorder.

Associated Press, April 9, 2000

A woman admiring a duck in a canal in Oakland Park, near Fort Lauderdale, suddenly sneezed, sending about $3,000 in bridgework into the dark water and oblivion. The woman called a towing operator who specialized in pulling vehicles out of canals. The man donned his scuba gear and, after feeling around, recovered the dentures.

Miami *Herald*, July 3, 1996

In a matter of hours, a doctor at Miami's Jackson Memorial Hospital delivered fifteen babies, including three sets of twins and four quadruplets. The last four came out in three minutes. The likelihood of twins is one in eighty. The likelihood of quadruplets is one in 50,000.

Miami *Herald*, January 29, 1998

A thirteen-year-old Pompano Beach girl, riding in the front passenger seat of her family's van, was impaled by a three-foot steel rod that flew through the windshield and then through her chest and the seat.

The girl, an honor student and top athlete, was on her way home from a school assembly where she'd received a leadership award. Police said the rod probably flew off a truck or had been lying on the roadway and flew up when a big rig drove over it.

The girl's mother, an elderly-care nurse, dialed 911, but an operator would not send help until the family gave an exact location. She stopped at a service station and, within minutes, authorities arrived. They followed the rule in such incidents: leave the object in place, stabilize and transport. They thought about unbolting the seat and placing it in ambulance but finally decided to just drive the van to the hospital and free her in the emergency room parking lot.

The girl was sedated and given oxygen, and doctors and paramedics used a saw to cut the foot-long part of the rod sticking out of the back of the seat. The sawing rocked the rod inside the girl and the friction heated the rod, which had to be cooled down. Paramedics then freed the girl and took her inside, where they slowly and gingerly slid out the rest of the rod.

Doctors said the rod damaged only a small part of her lung and missed her aorta by centimeters. Had it been a little to the left or right she would have been killed.

Miami *Herald*, June 6, 1998

Doctors at Miami Jackson Memorial Hospital removed a football-sized tumor from the face of a 37-year-old Haitian peasant farmer. It took doctors some ten hours to remove the eighteen-inch tumor, which the man said had been growing for up to three years.

Associated Press, August 17, 2000

Moments after an accident victim was declared dead at a Sanford hospital, doctors delivered a healthy baby by emergency Caesarean surgery.

United Press International/Miami *Herald*, September 21, 1990

Five people were charged with diverting corneas intended for a Tampa eye bank and selling them in Saudi Arabia and Argentina. The non-profit facility removed the corneas from cadavers and sold them for $650 each, using the money for operating expenses.

St. Petersburg *Times*, January 10, 1989

Just before surgery, 51-year-old diabetes patient Willie King joked with the staff of a Tampa hospital to be sure they took off the right foot. It didn't work. "Now he'll be without any legs at all. He's very depressed," brother John Hollis said. "It should have been obvious," said his lawyer, Peter J. Brudny. "The right foot was much more visible as a distressed foot."

Associated Press/Orlando *Sentinel*, March 1, 1995

FLORIDA STINKS

The "titan arum" is one of the world's stinkiest plants.

A giant tropical plant which blooms only once in several years drew a small gaggle of plant enthusiasts to the Fairchild Tropical Garden near Miami to admire its bouquet. "Mr. Stinky," the *amorphophallus titanum*, or *Titan Arum*, is a tall plant towering at more than 85 inches high. Experts compared the smell to dead rat, putrid fish and rotting cheese. It comes from heated oily glands at the top of the bloom and the smell is intended to attract flies and carrion beetles. Managers fed the plant kelp meal, chicken manure and gallons of water and it grew as much as a half-foot a day.

Miami *Herald*, May 14, 2003

When maids at a Fort Lauderdale hotel reported a lingering odor in Room 107, police found a corpse under the bed. It was wrapped in plastic, surrounded with deodorant bars and chilled by air conditioning. A German couple had spent at least one night there without noticing anything. A suspect was arrested four months later.

Fort Lauderdale *Sun-Sentinel*, December 31, 1995

Amtrak's *Silver Meteor* slammed into a tanker truck full of sewage near Indiantown, in western Martin County. Nine of the 165 passengers and crew suffered minor injuries and sludge covered the first part of the train.

"You should have seen the conductor and engineer. They were wearing it," said Martin County sheriff's Deputy Glen Zirkle.

Miami *Herald*, May 29, 1990

An area of Florida's Turnpike in rural Central Florida smelled so bad at least two motorists were overcome and had to be treated. One state trooper blamed chicken manure spread on nearby farm land, but a U.S. Department of Agriculture official disputed that. Turnpike authorities set up flashing warning signs near the Yeehaw Junction exit that said, "Strong odor—next four miles—do not stop—keep moving."

Associated Press/Palm Beach *Post*, February 19, 1994

A woman wearing a tan hat, sunglasses and a raincoat walked into the Miami Shores Country Club, sprinkled hundreds of small crystals on the carpeting and furniture and walked out. Within minutes, a rancid smell permeated the clubhouse. The woman was never apprehended and a week later the odor remained.

Palm Beach *Post*, December 31, 1991

Officials in plush Palm Beach used scents in the city's sewers, applying such aromas as vanilla, lilac, cheery and citrus to protect the island residents's fragile noses. To counteract such pungent smells as rotten eggs and grease, town workers placed a gallon of deodorant at the major sanitary sewer pump stations. The scent was then circulated through the system.

Palm Beach *Post*, January 17, 1992

A Jacksonville judge rejected arguments by a paper mill that the city's anti-odor ordinance was unconstitutional. The city passed the ordinance to reduce the city's nationally infamous odor problem.

Orlando *Sentinel*, September 23, 1989

The Boca Raton city council considered an ordinance banning people with offensive hygiene from using the library in an attempt to run off a homeless woman who had sparked numerous complaints that she had powerful body odor. The issue raised such a public outcry from people who considered the ordinance discriminatory that the council dropped the issue.

South Florida Sun-Sentinel, May 7, 1999

SECTION THREE
CHAPTER
21

PLANES, TRAINS AND AUTOMOBILES

Two America West pilots spent hours at a Coconut Grove bar drinking, hugging women and shooting pool from 10:30 p.m. to 4:30 a.m. They then settled their $122 tab—the manager said they were the last to leave—and came six hours later to Miami International Airport to fly 124 passengers to Phoenix. A gate security worker smelled alcohol on their breath and alerted police, who had air traffic controllers order the taxiing plane back to the terminal. The two pilots were arrested and found to have blood-alcohol levels that made them legally drunk.

South Florida Sun-Sentinel, August 6, 2002

Thomas Root found himself in a Hollywood hospital, a gunshot wound in his belly and his plane at the bottom of the sea, at the end of a bizarre day for the Virginia businessman.

While flying from the Washington area to North Carolina in 1989, he radioed air traffic controllers to say he was having chest pains. He put the plane on automatic pilot. When the flight passed through military air space, jets began to tail the Cessna. Pilots said they could see Root slumped in the cockpit as the plane flew some 500 miles by itself. Over the Bahamas, the plane finally ran out of gas and the pilots watched it spiral into the ocean, where it sank in deep water. Root was able to swim from the plane and was pulled into a rescue raft and flown to Florida for treatment.

He was later charged by federal authorities with falsifying radio license applications and was sentenced to thirty-three months in prison. And a North Carolina court sentenced him to fifteen years in prison on other fraud charges. He denied shooting himself even after weapons experts said the gun he kept in the plane could not have fired accidentally.

United Press International, July 13, 1989;
Los Angeles *Times,* May 22, 1992;
South Florida Sun-Sentinel, January 8, 1994

The Tom Hanks character in the film *The Terminal* is loosely based on the experience of an Iranian citizen who spent fourteeen years at a Paris airport after arriving without a passport. Alex Ervasti, a 49-year-old Finnish world traveler and failed businessman, arrived homeless at Miami International Airport on a flight from Colombia and lived at the airport for more than eight weeks.

Ervasti said he left his wallet at a pay phone at the Cali, Colombia, airport, and with it, $2,000 in cash, his U.S. green card, his Social Security card and his phone card. He flew on to Miami, where he called his cousin in Finland to wire more money, but it never came.

Evasti was able to panhandle sympathetic travelers for an average of seven dollars a day, enough to establish a life in the airport.

Every day, awakening at 4:00 a.m., he had a free hot coffee and read free newspapers he got at an airline counter. He then went to a pay phone and waited for his cousin to call from Finland or called his cousin and others collect to ask for money to get out of the airport. Right before 7:00 a.m., he bathed in the sink at a restroom. He then went to the nearby Burger King for his "Cini-mini" - an order of four little round cinnamon rolls for ninety-nine cents. He used his cup for more free coffee. Every day at 10:00 a.m., he exercised on the skywalks, then, at 11:00 a.m., tanned in a tiny park between the terminal and the parking lot.

From 1:00 to 8:00 p.m., he worked international passengers for donations. Dinner was usually a Junior Whopper with lettuce and tomato for ninety-nine cents and a free Coke with his cup from the morning. After dinner, he read his newspapers near the Lufthansa ticket counter. To sleep, he moved rows of hard chairs into a very uncomfortable makeshift bed. It didn't bother him, he said, to sleep in a lighted room. "I grew up in Finland with the midnight sun," he said.

Some days, he went to a nearby coin laundry to wash and dry his clothes. Some days he was treated to a meal, a few beers, even a hotel room by another traveler. He was even able to save money because most days he kept his expenses under three dollars.

Finally, police kicked him out. He left his home for another one — the nearby Fort Lauderdale-Hollywood International Airport. After the Miami *Herald* wrote about him, he got enough money from an appearance on TV's *The Daily Show*, and a winning bet at a dog track, for an $83 one-way ticket to Atlanta. "The airport there is big, which is a plus," he said.

Miami *Herald*, April 6, 1999; July 4, 2004

A passenger on a commuter flight suffered a minor gunshot wound to the head when the plane was fired upon on approach to Fort Lauderdale-Hollywood International Airport. The USAir plane was hit as it arrived from the Bahamas with nineteen passengers and crew. Edward Clark Wright reported hearing a popping noise before feeling a bump on his head.

Associated Press/Orlando *Sentinel*, September 4, 1989

A coffeemaker exploded on a British West Indies Airways flight from Miami to Barbados, ripping a hole through the fire wall of the cockpit and injuring two attendants and forcing the plane to return to Miami. None of the seventy-eight passengers was hurt.

Associated Press, October 4, 1993; October 5, 1993

A psychic's warning that a bomb might be on a plane prompted a search with bomb-sniffing dogs that forced the cancellation of a Dallas-bound American Airlines flight at the Fort Myers airport. Nothing suspicious was found.

Associated Press/*South Florida Sun-Sentinel*, March 28, 2004

A Miami airline passenger created a series of problems as her plane was taxiing for takeoff. Told to turn off her cell phone, she responded, "It is rude to hang up on people." She also tried opening an emergency exit, refused orders to sit down and slapped a federal air marshal. The plane turned around and dropped her off with waiting officers.

Associated Press, January 1, 2005

A U.S. Airways flight from Pittsburgh to Miami landed without one passenger. The flight made an unscheduled landing in Charlotte, North Carolina, after a man tried to open the plane's doors in midair when attendants stopped serving him drinks.

Associated Press, February 10, 2000

Police said a transient on antidepressants got past a six-foot barbed wire fence at the St. Petersburg-Clearwater International Airport, walked onto a runway, climbed up the portable steps of an empty American Trans Air Boeing 737 airliner, and sat down in the tenth row. A mechanic working on the plane about 2:45 a.m. saw the man and called police. Authorities said the man couldn't remember how he got on the plane and told a mechanic he just wanted a plane ride. The airport's manager questioned how the man got onto the property, saying he would have had to scale that fence and another one.

Tampa *Tribune*/St. Petersburg *Times*, January 9, 2003

Police were trying to determine if a woman who fell from the sky to her death jumped from the balcony of a Miami high-rise or fell from a passing airplane. The woman, dressed in black tights and a long black shirt, carried no identification. No one saw her fall before she landed in a planter outside the building. Her body ripped nearly in half. Police later said they were convinced she had jumped from the 27-story apartment tower. They said she had a history of suicide attempts.

On May 23, 1996, a seventeen-year-old boy found the remains of an unidentified man whose body apparently dropped from a plane. Police later concluded that victim was a stowaway who'd fallen from an airplane's wheel well. Police said the man was probably falling at 120 miles per hour when he struck the pavement.

In June 1993, a seventeen-year-old Colombian found in the wheel well of a cargo jet at Miami International Airport told authorities he hid there as the plane flew for three hours to Florida. U.S. officials nevertheless deported him. Two weeks later, workers at the Bogota airport found him in a cargo jet. He said he'd snuck into the wheel well at Cali and endured five takeoffs and landings before being exposed at Bogota. This time he was wearing three layers of clothes. The first time, authorities doubted Juan Carlos Guzman's story. Aviation and medical experts said it was virtually impossible for him to have survived for that long in a wheel well because of lack of oxygen and because at cruising altitudes of 30,000 feet, temperatures drop to at least forty degrees below zero.

Associated Press, July 26, 1993;
Miami *Herald*, May 24, 1996; December 3, December 5, 1997

A chunk of ice the size of a car battery that might have fallen from an airplane flying into Miami International Airport crashed through the roof of a home and landed in an infant's crib. The fifteen-month-old's father said a neighbor had just lifted the girl from the crib when the chunk crashed onto her pillow. Federal Aviation Administration officials said water sometimes leaks from bathroom holding tanks, freezes at high altitudes, then comes off as planes descend.

St. Petersburg *Times*, October 8, 1990

Authorities theorized a Northwest Airlines jet lost an engine over North Florida because of leaking toilet fluid. The jet, which was carrying 139 passengers and a crew of six, made an emergency landing at Tampa International Airport. There were no injuries. Investigators said leaking fluid may have frozen, gotten into the turbine blades and caused vibrations that ripped the engine free of the plane. The 3,500-pound engine was later found in a pasture.

Miami *Herald*, January 10, 1990

A June 20, 1980, Delta flight from Atlanta to Tampa International Airport landed eight miles south at MacDill Air Force Base instead. A passenger who was watching the approach leaped to his feet to alert the crew but was ordered back down. After an hour at the military base, the plane got back to the real airport.

Tampa *Tribune*, January 1, 1989

An Altamonte Springs man opted, at the last minute, not to fly with his buddies to see the Florida Gators in the 1992 Southeastern Conference championship game in Birmingham, Alabama. Lance Wall said he was bothered by a dream two nights earlier that he was in a falling airplane. The small plane crashed, killing all six aboard.

St. Petersburg *Times*, December 8, 1992

Three motorists and two fliers were hurt when a small plane lost control and smashed onto the hood and windshield of a car beside the New Smyrna Beach Municipal Airport. "I just thank God I am alive," said Eddie Cornett said. "It is not very often you get hit by a plane."

Orlando *Sentinel*, March 9, 1987

A small plane made an emergency landing on top of a moving pickup in Edgewater, near Daytona Beach, leaving the truck driver wondering if he should have checked his blind spot in the sky. No one was seriously hurt.

Chicago *Tribune*, March 15, 2004

A former bank robber turned stunt pilot was arrested in 1995 for playing "chicken" with a northbound Amtrak train in northern Palm Beach County. James Ray Hugus, known as the "bicycle bandit" for the getaway bike he used to flee his heists, allegedly flew his red pinstriped plane at tree level directly at the Miami-to-Los Angeles Sunset Limited, traveling 79 miles per hour. One state attorney said the incident was "like one of those old math problems" about two trains approaching each other, except this time it was a train and a plane. It dropped to within thirty feet of the track before pulling up less than 100 yards away. Hugus later pleaded guilty; he was sentenced to ninety days in jail and eighteen months probation and banned from flying.

South Florida Sun-Sentinel, February 13, 1998

An upstate New York couple, Rick and Karen Dobbertin, who planned to travel the world in a floating milk tanker left North Miami Beach but never made it to Bimini after the transmission failed and the U.S. Coast Guard had to tow them back to South Florida. The couple had spent 13,000 hours, over five years, converting the 1959 stainless-steel tanker to travel 70 miles per hour on land and six to eight miles per hour on water. They used $150,000 in donated parts from various sponsors and about $30,000 in cash contributions. They had planned to travel 30,000 milis on land and 5,000 miles across water. They abandoned the project after two and a half years when they ran out of money after traveling 27,300 miles on land and 3,000 miles in the water.

South Florida Sun-Sentinel, February 25, 1994;
Stuart *News*, February 7, 1999

An 82-year-old Palm Bay woman who refused to leave a Greyhound bus in Fort Lauderdale after arguing with the driver was convicted of trespassing but spared jail time. The woman, who uses a walker, was ordered to pay $152 in court costs and undergo a stress management plan.

South Florida Sun-Sentinel, August 24, 2002

As 83-year-old Tillie Tooter drove to the Fort Lauderdale-Hollywood Airport early one morning to pick up a granddaughter, a 23-year-old driver who later admitted being drowsy behind the wheel struck her in the rear on Interstate 595, shoving the car off a bridge. It flew through the air and landed atop a tangle of trees that left Tooter and her car suspended forty feet below the bridge and just inches above a swamp.

The other motorist called 911 but did not tell anyone a car had gone over a wall. A 911 caller reported seeing a car go over. Authorities made a cursory search, then left.

As commuters drove within feet of her, Tooter lay trapped in the car, unseen. She survived on a cough drop, a peppermint and a piece of gum. She soaked up rainwater with golf socks and sucked on them. She was finally spotted by a teen picking up trash along the highway. Tooter recovered.

The motorist pleaded guilty to leaving the scene of an injury accident and making a false police report. He was sentenced to four years in prison for violating parole.

South Florida Sun-Sentinel, August 16, 2000;
Associated Press, April 21, 2004

As two Ford Mustangs drag-raced near Eustis at speeds near 100 miles per hour, one of the cars plowed into the back of a slower-moving car, killing the two women inside. Moments later, the 21-year-old driver learned the victims were his 45-year-old mother and an older friend the woman had been driving around to look at Christmas lights. "It was a one-in-a-trillion thing," a neighbor said.

Associated Press, December 21, 2001

In the Florida Keys, a man followed a high school senior into a parking lot after the two exchanged middle-finger greetings, then rammed the teen's car and bit off a chunk of his ear.

Associated Press. December 19, 1999

After a cabbie took a drunk customer home from a West Palm Beach sports bar, the man became belligerent and wouldn't get out, so the driver zapped his fare with a stun gun and, when that didn't work, pulled out a handgun and shot him dead. The taxi driver was charged with first-degree murder.

Palm Beach *Post*, November 8, 2004

A car caught fire in Winter Haven, then started up and lunged away from firefighters. It traveled 380 feet, went around a curve and eventually crashed into a tree. Firefighters said the blaze caused a short circuit that made the older-model car start.

Associated Press, August 11, 2000

A man driving a stolen SUV led police on a forty-mile high-speed chase through the upper Keys, forcing several motorists off the road. The vehicle reached speeds of 100 miles per hour and sometimes drove on the wrong side of the road. Police later said bystanders threw bricks, rocks and even a bicycle at it. The chase finally ended when authorities put out spikes that punctured the SUV's tires. The driver leaped from the moving vehicle, which then rolled over his leg.

Miami *Herald*, November 6, 2001

A woman who caused a fender bender fled into a Stuart K-Mart and grabbed hair dye, makeup and a change of clothes, then ran into a restroom and tried to change her appearance. Police found her there. Empty boxes and price tags from the stolen items were found in a trash can. The driver of the other car identified her.

Chicago *Tribune*, February 19, 2003

Buckets flew off the back of a truck on Interstate 95 in Boca Raton, sending hundreds of heavy-duty four-inch roofing screws and six-sided tin tabs into traffic. The scattered hardware caused at least one hundred flat tires and closed three lanes of morning rush hour traffic.

Palm Beach *Post*, July 28, 2001

Traffic on Interstate 95 in St. Lucie County was rerouted after an accident scattered more than 250,000 screws on the highway.

Palm Beach *Post*, December 29, 1993

A woman was making a call at a pay phone on the sidewalk of a Miramar shopping center when a car jumped the curb and pinned her against a wall, killing her. The 86-year-old driver said he was parking his car and mistakenly hit the gas pedal instead of the brake.

South Florida Sun-Sentinel, January 29, 1993

Police placed a spike strip on a Boynton Beach road to stop a fleeing bank robbery suspect. It stopped that car, two patrol cars and three other vehicles that happened to come along after that. Police said that was still preferable to a large crash and that they would pay for the damaged tires. No one was hurt.

Palm Beach *Post*, August 12, 1998

A lawyer was struck by a car in Delray Beach and carried nearly 3 miles before being dumped in the road. Kenneth DeLeon, 26, was struck as he walked with his father, burst through the windshield and landed upside down in the passenger seat. The driver repeatedly punched DeLeon and screamed at him to get out of his car before finally stopping and pushing him out, police said. DeLeon suffered several broken bones in his arms and legs.

The driver was later arrested and eventually sentenced to six years in prison.

"He's really laid back. He's chilled," his roommate said at the time of the incident. "He's not crazy like that."

Palm Beach *Post*, August 19, 1998;
South Florida Sun-Sentinel, February 27, 1999

A 71-year-old Miami man with Alzheimer's disease left his wife at a Utah rest stop as she collected rocks and drove off. Although the woman had been gone only a few hours, her husband believed he had waited for three days and decided his wife was dead so he drove off to tell his family. The 63-year-old woman spent the night in cold and snow but eventually got back to the highway. The man was spotted five days later at a convenience store near Fort Worth, Texas.

Associated Press/Palm Beach *Post*, February 6, 1993

A ten-year-veteran Pensacola crossing guard, frustrated by motorists racing through his school zone, began using a hair dryer wrapped in electrical tape to fool them into thinking it was a radar gun and get them to slow down. The ploy worked. Later, six fifth-graders at the school raised about $100 to buy the guard a real radar gun.

Pensacola *News Journal*, February 12, 2002

Three men and an eight-months pregnant woman caught up in road rage on a Panhandle highway fought a melee that include a rake, a baseball bat and a chainsaw that ended with two men in a hospital and two arrests. Lynn Haven Assistant Police Chief Greg Smith said, "People like that shouldn't be driving."

Associated Press/Palm Beach *Post*, October 10, 1999

Authorities said security cameras caught a motorist with a *JST CRZY* vanity license plate running Orlando-area tollbooths 705 times from August 1999 to June 2000. The man claimed someone else stole his plates. But authorities said during two one-week periods, *JST CRZY* wasn't caught once running a toll. During that time, the man was in a Virginia jail for speeding. The driver eventually paid about $7,600 in fines and fees.

Orlando *Sentinel*, November 29, 2000

A Pompano Beach motorist had to make like Evel Kneivel when an Intracoastal Waterway bridge suddenly opened, forcing the driver to leap an eight-foot gap. "I can't believe how close we were to getting killed," said Gary Darras, 34; his car's frame was twisted and he lost his oil pan and exhaust pipe. The sixteen-year-old drawbridge operator did not lower warning gates before raising the bridge; it was the second, and last day on the job for the boy, who had said on his application that he was nineteen and who fled on his bicycle shortly after the incident. It was later reported he had held dance parties with friends inside the tender's cabin.

Orlando *Sentinel*, June 29, 1988; Palm Beach *Post*, December 25, 1988

In two separate Broward County incidents two hours and several miles apart, a tractor trailer overturned on Alligator Alley, spilling some of its cargo of 22-1/2 tons of frozen chicken, and a construction firm's truck dropped a case of inch-long roofing nails.

Associated Press/Orlando *Sentinel*, November 4, 1988

Two boxes of 15-inch-high legless plastic pink flamingos dropped off a truck onto State Road 436 in Casselberry. Police collected most of the seventy-four flamingos, but some were grabbed by motorists or run over by passing cars.

Orlando *Sentinel*, January 16, 1988

A schoolteacher struck four children on a Tampa street, leaving a 13-year-old and his three-year-old brother dead. It would be twenty-eight hours, before she and her family contacted a lawyer and four days after that until she stepped forward in public. During that time, no one suggested calling police. Also, the teacher threatened more than once to commit suicide by overdosing on pills and asked her mother to suffocate her with a pillow. Her father cleaned blood from the car. And every morning, she drove to school and then to teach dance lessons at night.

St. Petersburg *Times*, July 14, 2004

A St. Augustine woman became furious at three teens after their golf ball bounced atop her SUV. She ran both over, leaving one 14-year-old in a coma and fracturing the skull of the other fourteen year old. The third teen escaped. The driver's husband said later that she suffered from paranoid schizophrenia but "has never done anything like this before."

Orlando *Sentinel*, December 8, 2004

The man who ran the "Drive Legal" program for Miami-Dade County courts was arrested on a DUI charge.

Miami *Herald*, February 15, 2003

A 79-year-old woman was taking her afternoon walk across the Hallandale Beach Boulevard Bridge, south of Fort Lauderdale, when the drawbridge began to rise. The woman did not see the flashing light or hear the bell or the grinding of the mechanism. The bridge tender didn't see her. Her walk became more strenuous as the incline grew steeper. Soon she was clinging to the railing. She hung on as the bridge got to the top and came back down, leaping off for the last few feet. She escaped with only scrapes and bruises.

Miami *Herald*, January 31, 2005

SECTION THREE
CHAPTER
22

GOOD SPORTS

Baseball legend Ted Williams' family fought over his frozen remains. (Major League Baseball)

When Ted Williams died in July 2002 at the age of eighty-three in his home in Citrus County, north of Tampa, what had been the story of a fabled baseball star became a bizarre and gory saga of family squabbles and frozen body parts. Williams, a Hall of Famer and the last man to bat .400, is considered one of the greatest players of all time. The body of the Boston Red Sox slugger known as "the Splendid Splinter" was later reportedly taken to an Arizona cryonics lab for freezing. He reportedly was suspended upside down in a solitary stainless steel tube filled with liquid nitrogen. Williams' children fought in court with a half-sister who wanted to retrieve her father's body, cremate it and sprinkle the ashes in the Florida Keys, as dictated in Williams' will. But a lawyer later produced a soiled note he said proved Williams wanted to be frozen. The half-sister later dropped her objections.

Palm Beach *Post*, July 26, August 28, 2002

When racing legend Dale Earnhardt was killed at age forty-nine on the last lap of the 2001 Daytona 500, NASCAR racing's premier event, newspapers, fans, and lawyers would argue over pictures not of the crash, but of Earnhardt's autopsy.

The driver known as "the Intimidator" was killed when his car, emblazoned with the famous number 3, struck the outside wall on the final turn. The track's director of emergency medical services said the likely cause of death was a fracture at the base of the skull, an injury that had previously killed three other drivers. NASCAR had

Access to racing legend Dale Earnhardt's autopsy photos created a furor. (NASCAR)

199

recently allowed changes in car designs to produce more passing and excitement. But the racing league was under pressure to include head restraints after the three deaths.

NASCAR, Daytona International Speedway and the Daytona Beach police came under fire for the secretive manner in which Earnhardt's death was investigated. Newspapers wanted to see for themselves. So they cited a part of the state's "Government in the Sunshine Law," a national model for its sweeping openness of government meetings and records. The package of rules—known in the business as "119" for the chapter in the state statutes—included a provision that made autopsy photos public. It had been around for decades.

The press said it didn't necessarily trust doctors, track officials and authorities to be objective in a county in which car racing is a top industry. Newspaper lawyers argued those people had a lot to lose if Earnhardt's death was ruled preventable.

The public, led by Earnhardt's widow, lobbied to close the exemption, saying it was an invasion of privacy. They said they feared unscrupulous journalists would put the graphic photos on television or on the front pages of tabloids. Newspaper lawyers agreed to only view the photos, not copy them. And they pointed out that a photo stolen under these circumstances could be stolen and published even under tougher rules.

Earnhardt's widow and the Orlando *Sentinel* finally agreed to have an independent expert view the photos. The expert later concluded Earnhardt died because of the sudden, violent whipping forward of his head and neck upon impact. NASCAR eventually approved changes in the size of the driver's side window to better accommodate HANS (Head and Neck System) safety devices.

Three days after the medical expert and Earnhardt's widow had viewed the autopsy photos, Governor Jeb Bush signed a bill eliminating the photos portion from the public records law. Newspapers challenged that in court, but it was eventually upheld.

About a year after Earnhardt's death, fans of the racing great flocked to a North Florida farm to see a brown Nubian goat named Lil' Dale that was born with a distinctive white three on her right side.

Palm Beach *Post*, July 6, 2001;
Associated Press, December 27, 2002;
South Florida Sun-Sentinel, April 13, 2004

Visiting Tampa in January 2001 to cover the Super Bowl, Chicago *Tribune* columnist Rick Morrissey noted the long list of sports stars who have had run-ins with the law in the area:

Tennis star Jennifer Capriati was charged with petty theft. Pitchers Dave Stewart and Todd Stottlemyre were charged with battery on a police officer after arguing over a three dollar cover charge at a local nightclub. At least seven Tampa Bay Buccaneers had been arrested since 1991 on various charges.

Football star Lawrence Taylor was arrested in his St. Pete Beach hotel room in 1995 after allegedly buying crack cocaine. He later pleaded no contest.

Baseball star Darryl Strawberry reportedly solicited a prostitute in April 1999 who turned out to be an undercover Tampa police officer. Strawberry later violated his probation three times. In November 2000, Strawberry told a judge he had stopped his cancer-fighting chemotherapy while in jail and left a drug treatment center for a drug binge he hoped would end his life. The eight-time All Star and father of five told the judge, "Life hasn't been worth living for me, that's the honest truth, and I'm not afraid of death."

Baseball player Darryl Strawberry was charged with soliciting a prostitute (Hillsborough County Sheriff's Office)

Pitcher Dwight Gooden and his nephew, slugger Gary Sheffield, were arrested in December 1986 after Tampa police pulled over Gooden's silver Mercedes and he either punched two policemen or was attacked by a group of white officers. The two players were later sentenced to probation and the officers were cleared of wrongdoing. Gooden said later: "If I go to Tampa during the day, I'm fine. But...after the sun goes down, it's like I'm a vampire." In October 1995, a man ran up to Sheffield's white Mercedes at a stoplight in Tampa and fired into the car. Sheffield was slightly injured. No arrests were made.

Associated Press/*Bergen County* (NJ) *Record*,
December 1, 1999, November 4, 2000; Chicago *Tribune*, January 25, 2001

Bob Probert, a former National Hockey League "enforcer," was arrested in Delray Beach after scuffling with police who had to shock him with a Taser gun. Police said Probert fought with officers and refused their orders to drop to the ground. Probert played seventeen seasons in the NHL. He was arrested six times for driving under the influence and convicted of smuggling cocaine across the Canadian border.

Associated Press, June 4, 2004

Bermuda's Olympic soccer team was suspended from play after seven players were arrested at Miami International Airport when a drug-sniffing dog picked up the scent of marijuana. Authorities said the players hid the pot, about a pound apiece, in the hollowed soles of their tennis shoes. They were on their way back to Bermuda from Jamaica.

Philadelphia *Daily News*, December 16, 1994

For more than forty years, Kenny Bethel lived at the Palmetto Golf Course near Miami, reselling stray golf balls, using the club's showers and toilets at night and sleeping in a sheltered area. The staff finally chased him off and locked the restrooms at night. A spokesman said complaints increased from female golfers who said they were nervous about using restrooms when he was nearby.

Former hockey "enforcer" Bob Probert was arrested in Delray Beach. (Palm Beach County Sheriff's Office)

Chicago *Tribune*, January 13, 2004

Florida State University's two Waterford crystal national championship trophies were stolen from their locked wood and glass cases. The school offered a $2,500 reward. The trophies, for the 1993 and 1999 national titles, were not insured, a school athletic official said. **UPDATE:** The trophies were recovered, and two men arrested, in November 2005.

Associated Press/Palm Beach *Post*, June 25, 2004, November 17, 2005

Los Angeles Dodgers baseball manager Tommy Lasorda wrote a letter-to-the editor to explain his appearance at a Stuart museum. Attendees complained Lasorda showed up late and left without signing autographs. Lasorda said he filled in for the unpaid visit at the last minute when another speaker canceled and had told officials he couldn't leave Dodgertown in Vero Beach for the one-hour ride until 10:00 a.m. and had to be back by 1:00 p.m. He said he later learned the crowd had been told he'd show up at 10:00 and sign autographs. "Nobody felt worse than I did" about the misunderstanding, Lasorda wrote. The Palm Beach *Post* also wrote a clarification. It said that while the newspaper had originally reported Lasorda told "mostly unprintable" jokes, "Lasorda did not use profanity or tell jokes with sexual content, but did tell jokes based on ethnic stereotypes involving Jews, Cubans and Haitians."

Tommy LaSorda had a bad day at a gathering of baseball fans (Major League Baseball)

Palm Beach *Post*, March 21, 23, 26, 2004

It was revealed that the 19-year-old woman who alleged basketball star Kobe Bryant sexually assaulted her in a Colorado hotel room sought treatment for substance abuse at rehab centers in Arizona and Florida and, during a stay in Delray Beach, found a part- time job as a hostess at a Lucille's Bad to the Bone barbecue restaurant. The restaurant's manager said he recognized her name from the application, even though it had been mostly kept secret.

The woman who alleged basketball star Kobe Bryant sexually assaulted her sought substance abuse treatment in South Florida. (Eagle County (Colo.) Sheriff's Department)

Boca Raton *News,* New York *Daily News,* March 29, 2004

A coach was banned from a youth baseball league when he "mooned" other parents during a confrontation after an argument-marred game. Parents said the coach, who was 6-foot-3 and weighed 275 pounds, dropped his pants not once, but twice, after his team of ten-year-olds lost at a game in Boca Raton. The coach later said his pants fell down by accident.

Palm Beach *Post,* August 5, August 6, 1998

A lawyer fired as coach of a girls' softball team sued the village of Wellington in Palm Beach County Circuit Court, saying his dismissal violated his free speech rights. A village liaison said she tried to talk to the man about his opposition to pitching machines when he began shouting at her.

Palm Beach *Post,* April 20, 2004

An 89-year-old golfer in Holiday, north of Tampa, went searching for lost balls in swampy woods bordering a golf course, then got stuck in the muck and had to spend the night before being rescued by a search party. A Pasco County Sheriff's helicopter found him two hundred yards from the sixth green.

Associated Press, April 11, 2002

Three homeless men arrested for drinking in a Jacksonville park put on an inspired defense. The park was scheduled to be a designated party zone for the 2005 Super Bowl. If the rich and powerful were permitted to drink there, the men's lawyer argued, why couldn't they? A judge overturned the ban, saying it was a double standard.

Florida Times-Union, June 15, October 7, 2004; January 13, 2005

A Pop Warner League football game of fourteen and fifteen-year-olds in Port Orange, near Daytona Beach, ended with an overtime touchdown for the home team and a brawl involving more than one hundred parents, coaches and players; police said one youth slugged an officer. One fifteen-year was arrested and a thirty-three-year-old woman criminally charged with resisting arrest in a scuffle in the parking lot that followed the initial brawl. The league later booted one player out of the league, suspended two for two games each and put the coaches on probation. And every player, parent and coach connected to both teams had to attend a two-hour seminar on sportsmanship.

Orlando *Sentinel*, September 30, 2000

Nearly 2,000 Honduran soccer fans, apparently angered by poor officiating in a game against Peru, stormed the field at Miami's Orange Bowl and wound up fighting with more than one hundred police officers. Thirty-four were arrested.

Miami *Herald*, February 20, 2000

A rider for a polo team in Wellington, near West Palm Beach, was suspended for fourteen months after he hit his horse in the head with his mallet during a match. Agustin Merlos was also fined $5,000 plus $3,000 administrative costs. "I overreacted," Merlos said in a letter of apology. The suspension was believed the longest in the history of the polo league.

Palm Beach *Post*, February 19, 2000

The American Airlines arena in Miami brought in children from a recreation center to flush every toilet to test plumbing at the arena before its grand opening on New Year's Eve, 1999.

South Florida Sun-Sentinel, December 28, 1999.

A seventeen-year-old Cystic Fibrosis patient from Auburndale who got to meet Walter Payton at a Chicago Bears-Tampa Bay Buccaneers game said later she didn't know any of the Bears players and just wanted free tickets.

Palm Beach *Post*, December 31, 1987

Malaprops by former Florida State football coach Bill Peterson: On his induction into the Florida Sports Hall of Fame, "I want to thank everyone here who helped me get indicted." After a loss, "Don't you think for a minute that I'm going to take this loss standing down." On the Dale Carnegie course, "I used to have this slight speech implement, and I couldn't remember things before I took the Sam Carnegie course."

The 365 Stupidest Things Ever Said, 2000 Calendar, Workman Publishing

Sent to cover basketball's 2000 NBA All-Star game in Oakland, Calif., Guy Rawlings, a sportscaster for Miami's *WTVJ-TV*, was lost for hours across the bay in San Francisco, unable to find the Oakland arena. He later explained his station flew him to San Francisco and "I go where I'm told."

Palm Beach *Post*, March 5, 2000

The first 20,000 fans at the July 9, 1999, Florida Marlins baseball game got commemorative pins featuring star pitcher Matt Mantei — *but Mantei had been traded to Arizona that afternoon.*

Palm Beach *Post*, July 10, 1999

YOUR GOVERNMENT AT WORK

A barge carrying more than 14,000 tons of incinerated Philadelphia trash went on a 15-year odyssey that led to places as far apart as Singapore and Haiti. In 2001, Florida officials approved a plan to dump the ash, now down to 2,000 tons, at a landfill near Fort Lauderdale. But by 2002, the trash had still not been dumped and had been sitting in the St. Lucie Canal in Stuart for two years. Finally, in the summer of 2002, the material was trucked back to Pennsylvania.

Port St. Lucie *News*, July 17, 2002

A pregnant mother of two spent a day in jail for allegedly failing to appear in court on seven counts of failing to return overdue library materials to the Clearwater Public Library.

The 24-year-old woman said she had changed addresses and never got any notices from the library or courts until two detectives showed up at her door. Fines totaled $40 for the materials, valued at $127.86, which were mostly for her small children and included books titled *War and Peas* and *Midnight Fridge* and videotapes of *Peter Pan* and *Starring Chip 'n Dale*. Relatives agreed to pay for them. The library said it waited sixteen months before turning the case over to the courts.

The woman was the second person in a week to be jailed for overdue library books at the same library. A nineteen-year-old Fort Myers man was jailed overnight when he was stopped on a traffic violation and a check revealed a warrant for failing to return reference materials. The man said he had wanted to learn Spanish. The materials, worth about $80, included Spanish language books and a tape of the film *Terminal Velocity*. The man said he had tried to return them, but each time the library was closed and there was no drop box.

Fort Myers *News Press*, January 11, 2000;
Tampa *Tribune*, January 14, 2000

The Florida Comptroller's office's annual list of people with unclaimed property the office had been unable to find included some seemingly findable people.

The list, totaling $725 million, included actor Sylvester Stallone ($5), former president Ronald Reagan ($133), Miami music icon Gloria Estefan ($972), and the man who signs the checks at the Comptroller's office. John Ellis Bush, known locally as "Jeb" and "Governor of Florida," was owed $85, part of a health insurance reimbursement. The comptroller's office said the system had a lot of John Bushes, so no special effort was made to track down the one who worked down the hall.

Reagan's money had never got to him because it was addressed to 1700 Pennsylvania Avenue, not 1600.

Florida Times-Union, February 17, 2001

In 2000, planners in West Palm Beach proposed placing a fifteen-foot troll under the middle of the three bridges to Palm Beach. The figure from Scandinavian folklore would clutch a Rolls Royce, an homage to the ritzy resort island. Ideas included having its eyes light up and having it growl when people on a pedestrian walkway under the bridge fed it a quarter.

The Florida Department of Transportation okayed the project and the National Endowment for the Arts hinted at a grant. But West Palm Beach Mayor Lois Frankel was cool to the idea, especially the $250,000 price tag, and she asked planners when she saw a drawing, "This would scare kids, wouldn't it?"

Later, Bill Meyer, a hotel chain mogul for whom a local amphitheater is named, offered to pay for not one troll but a family of four — mother, father and two kid trolls.

"Most of the Meyer family contributions have been of a more serious nature," Meyer said. But, "There's no reason to we can't do something with a little more levity."

Palm Beach *Post*, June 29, July 11, 2004

Paychecks for about 150 Pensacola-area U.S. Postal Service workers got lost in the mail. A local supervisor said employees who were not on direct deposit or could not wait until the paychecks arrived from Minneapolis would receive advances.

Pensacola *News Journal*, March 22, 2000

Fort Pierce postal workers heard a humming noise coming from a package and called the bomb squad. Deputies blasted the package with a water cannon, killing the *Furby* doll inside.

Associated Press, December 19, 1999

Some 155 judges, prosecutors and co-workers signed a petition after a supervisor at a Brevard County justice center transferred a court security guard for being too nice. "Due to your caring and giving nature, you are compromising your position as a security officer by trying to be everyone's friend," 68-year-old Elsie Holdren's supervisor wrote. "This is not a job requirement, nor is it what you are paid to do."

Associated Press, August 6, 2000

Thousands of trees planted along Interstate 95 in Broward and Palm Beach counties died when workers, hired by the state, forgot to water them.

South Florida Sun-Sentinel, December 30, 1995

Florida Atlantic University paid $620 to have a twelve-foot Cuban raft bathed in a chlorine solution before putting it on display. "The FAU maintenance department could have cleaned the raft," Associate Vice President Al Bielen explained, "but it makes life a lot simpler for me to go from A to Z with one person."

Palm Beach *Post,* December 31, 1994

DISGRUNTLED EMPLOYEES

When Robert Rose, a Tampa salesman of concrete repair products, won $2.4 million in the Florida lottery, he called his boss and played Johnny Paycheck's *Take This Job and Shove It*.

Palm Beach *Post*, May 25, 1995

The Palm Beach County Office of Equal Opportunity was sued by a white employee who said black supervisors fostered a hostile work environment.

South Florida Sun-Sentinel, December 29, 1996

A 64-year-old white South Florida woman, Ruth Jandrucko, won $200,000 in workers compensation in 1991. She said her mugging by a black man five years earlier left her with an irrational fear of black people that made it impossible to function in an integrated workplace. An attorney for her employer appealed. "If we are to award Ruth Jandrucko money, then every Ku Klux Klansman should be awarded money," Jonathan L. Alpert said.

Associated Press/Palm Beach *Post*, October 5, 1991

A 38-year-old Tampa woman sued a co-worker she claimed hypnotized her to help her kick smoking but instead uncovered as many as two hundred personalities.

Palm Beach *Post*, April 10, 1993

Vendor Sean Ostman, who gained fame for tossing peanuts to fans at Port St. Lucie's Thomas J. White Stadium, lost his job when an errant throw struck a Connecticut woman at a New York Mets spring training home opener in March 1993. Helen Thomas, 62, later demanded the city's insurance company pay her medical costs. Ostman had become a fan favorite for tossing the bags up to two hundred feet. Later, baseball maverick Mike Veeck offered Ostman a job with the Fort Myers Miracle, but Ostman said he had lost his driver's license.

Palm Beach *Post*, May 9, 1993

Two former Tampa television news executives apologized publicly and were sentenced to probation after pleading no contest to breaking into the computer news files of a competing station. Prosecutors said the two *WTSP-TV* employees broke into the computers of *WTVT-TV*, where one had helped set up computer security, and accessed stories, budgets, contracts and plans of news operations.

Associated Press/Miami *Herald*, May 20, 1989

The manager of a Coral Gables Publix supermarket was reassigned after he suspended a cashier, reportedly for asking a fellow worker in Spanish, "Where is Jorge?"

Palm Beach *Post*, December 25, 1988

A waffle maker at Boca Raton's Rascal House restaurant, on learning the place was out of waffle mix, attacked a co-worker with a frying pan full of raw eggs. A month later, the eatery got into a spat with rival deli Flakowitz, accusing that diner of stealing their trade secrets.

Boca Raton Magazine

MONEY! MONEY! MONEY! MONEY!

A Miami man driving a tractor-trailer from a Federal Reserve Bank in New Jersey to one in New Orleans vanished with his load, $180,000 in currency. Actually, it was in coins. Nickels. About $3.6 million, weighing 22-1/2 tons, in 900 fifty-pound bags.

The missing eighteen-wheeler was found empty and abandoned, with the keys in the ignition and the doors locked, in the parking lot of a truck stop in Fort Pierce on December 23, 2004.

The man was hauling the coins for a private outfit that contracted with the U.S. Mint. A supervisor said he last called on December 20, the day he was supposed to be in New Orleans, to say he was driving through Tallahassee and would be a few hours late. The company's last record was of a fill up on the 19th in a town near Tallahassee.

The nickels were found six weeks later, buried in a four-foot hole in the backyard of a suburban Miami home, still stored in their Federal Reserve bags and lying in a wooden box covered under a plastic tarp. Police said the driver might have left the country.

A supervisor said, "What would someone do with 45,000 pounds of nickels, anyway?"

Miami *Herald*, January 8, 2005;
Associated Press, February 8, 2005

An armored truck overturned on an Interstate 95 overpass, sending $800,000 cascading down to a street in downtown Miami's impoverished Overtown neighborhood. Hundreds of residents and motorists scrambled to scoop up the cash. Two weeks later, only $300 had been recovered. The incident came 9-1/2 years after $40,000 in bills fell out of the back of another armored car on the same expressway in Miami.

Palm Beach *Post*, January 24, 1997, December 31, 1987

In Miramar, a box of Cheer detergent fell out of an SUV, split open and scattered $340,000 on the road.

Associated Press, December 19, 1999

St. Lucie County school bus driver Janet Dersam was driving her empty bus near Mets Stadium in Port St. Lucie when she spotted one hundred-dollar bills fluttering in the breeze. Dersam stopped the bus and chased down $1,650, which was later returned to a woman who said she'd left her purse on top of a car and driven away from Mets Stadium.

Palm Beach *Post*, December 29, 1993

Palm Beach National Bank & Trust Co., on the island's tony Worth Avenue, announced it would open a money store, where shoppers could buy sheets of money to use as gift wrapping, as well as bags of $150 in shredded money.

Palm Beach *Post*, December 29, 1993

A New Jersey man named Michael Schwartz, who ran a business stocking 160 automatic teller machines, stole five million dollars in twenty-dollar bills and fled to Florida. He contacted a real estate agent and eventually gave her boyfriend, Christopher Lacroix, $10,000 to stay in a room in Lacroix's apartment for three months.

On Christmas Day, Lacroix, a West Palm Beach carpenter, found Schwartz dead on his couch. Lacroix also found the money. He moved it from a van to a storage locker and eventually to an abandoned home in nearby Boynton Beach. Authorities found three million dollars there and Lacroix was eventually arrested for theft, convicted and sentenced to seven years in prison. But prosecutors said about $1.3 million was still unaccounted for.

At one point, police learned from a jail snitch that Lacroix had told him he had spiked Schwartz' drink with drugs in order to look for the cash. But that investigation stalled when police could not rule out that Schwartz took the pills voluntarily.

Palm Beach *Post*, August 30, 2002

A troop of Junior Girl Scouts in Port St. Lucie learned a hard lesson when thieves used two counterfeit twenty-dollar bills to pay for Girl Scout cookies. Police Chief John Skinner said he was so angry he offered to cover the loss out of his own pocket. The crooks made off with fifteen dollars' worth of cookies and twenty-five dollars in change.

Palm Beach *Post*, January 23, 2002

A Port St. Lucie man hauled 105,000 pennies, in 2,100 rolls inside seventeen sacks, into the courthouse to pay his $1,050 fine. The man had been handcuffed during the traffic stop and given two tickets, for doing 53 miles per hour in a 35 mph zone and for having an expired tag. The man was incensed and felt "abused by the system" when a judge fined him the maximum on each count: $525. The local sheriff said the man had a long history of violations and could have been taken to jail after the stop rather than just ticketed.

Port St. Lucie *News*, November 14, 2001

Robin Hewitt of West Palm Beach, who had argued with Dr. Michael Belloti after she paid sixty dollars for treatment and later found that workers' compensation covered it, finally got her refund two months later. A bag carrying 6,000 pennies was dropped off at her office.

Palm Beach *Post*, February 2, 1993

Upset by a speeding ticket and a $150 fine, Dirk Papania paid with seventy-five pounds of pennies.

Palm Beach *Post*, December 31, 1991

A Fort Lauderdale man decided to pay his ten dollar parking ticket with 1,000 pennies. Six weeks later the city told him the payment was unacceptable. A parking clerk said the city was considering billing the man for the time it would take to count the pennies.

St. Petersburg *Times*, May 17, 1991

After a mobile home fire killed a 75-year-old Fruitland Park man, Lake County investigators found thousands of coins, enough to fill six garbage cans. The coins included mint sets and old gold and silver pieces from around the world. Neighbors said the retiree lived like a pauper.

Orlando *Sentinel*, July 12, 1988

An Aventura travel agent whose accountant lost his $235,000 in an investment took out a life insurance policy on the man, hoping to recoup some of his losses sooner rather than later. "I'm praying for his death," Harvey Rosenthal, 65, said. The man was among scores of investors who said they lost money to the Boca Raton accountant. He said Donald Bunsis agreed to the policy. Rosenthal said a federal agent told him there was no law against wishing someone dead "as long as you don't do anything about it."

South Florida Sun-Sentinel, December 29, 1994

THE HALLS OF POWER

Jeb Bush, son and brother to presidents, was elected governor of Florida partly on a tough law-and-order platform. Bush had to show a lot of tough love in his own family. His daughter struggled with drug addiction and his wife was caught slipping $19,000 worth of contraband through Customs.

Noelle Bush began her very public eighteen-month odyssey through drug court in January 2002 when she was arrested in the early hours of the morning at a Tallahassee Walgreens drive-through trying to buy the anti-anxiety drug Xanax with a bogus prescription. Before her arrest, the Bush family had acknowledged that one of their children had a drug problem.

Governor Jeb Bush had family problems. (Florida Governor's Office)

Noelle graduated from drug court in August 2003 and the charges were cleared.

In a statement, Bush said his family was "pleased that our daughter, Noelle, has completed this step, and grateful for the treatment she's received. She has worked hard to get here. We are proud of her efforts and love her very much."

Noelle had gone to jail twice for violating the rules during rehab. She was jailed for three days in July 2002 after being caught with prescription pills and served ten days in October after being accused of having a small rock of crack cocaine in her shoe.

Noelle was sent to the drug court program because she was a first-time offender. If she had gone through the regular criminal justice system, she could have faced a maximum penalty of five years in prison and a $5,000 fine.

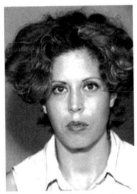

Gov. Jeb Bush's daughter Noelle was arrested on drug charges. (Orange County Sheriff's Office)

In June 1999, First Lady Columba Bush was briefly detained by Customs agents at the Atlanta airport as she returned home from Paris. She declared $500 worth of merchandise on a form. But during a random check, agents found receipts indicating she was toting about $19,000 worth of clothing and jewelry.

Columba wrote a personal check for $4,100 to cover fines and duties and was allowed to continue. A Customs spokesman said the agents did not realize she was the wife of Florida's governor until after she had left.

Bush said his wife didn't declare all of the merchandise because she didn't want him to find out how much money she had spent in Paris.

"I can assure you it was a difficult weekend at our house," the governor said. "She knew that what she did was wrong and made a mistake."

Family fame hasn't always been negative. In 2000, *People* magazine named his son George P. one of the 100 "sexiest men alive."

George P., a lawyer living in Dallas, told a Hispanic rally during the 2004 Republican convention in New York that he hoped to someday enter public service. Some in the crowd chanted, "Bush 2020."

Gov. Jeb Bush's wife failed to report purchases from a trip to Paris. (Florida Governor's Office)

South Florida Sun Sentinel, August 16, 2000,
Orlando *Sentinel*, June 22, 1999,
Miami *Herald*, August 9, 2003,
Dallas Morning News, September 1, 2004

The former mayor of Hialeah Gardens, near Miami, was sentenced to nearly five years in prison for plotting her ex-husband's murder. The slaying didn't happen. She was also convicted of forcing city workers to change addresses on voter registration forms so they could vote in the town.

Associated Press, August 31, 2000

Gulfport City Councilman Kirby Rohrer was arrested for selling 150 grams of cocaine stashed in a Girl Scout cookie box.

Associated Press, March 1, 1989

State Representative Dick Locke, D-Inverness, was stunned to learn that a bill he'd introduced on behalf of a hotel owner would have wiped out a law requiring hotels over three stories to have smoke detectors and sprinklers. When a reporter explained the bill to him, he withdrew it.

Orlando *Sentinel*, January 1, 1989

A member of the state House of Representatives gave a twenty-five pound box of cow manure to a lobbyist who had entered the legislator's empty office, reclined on a couch and put her feet up to watch a televised debate on a bill the two had battled over. The legislator was later admonished and lost leadership of an important committee, but colleagues gave her big hugs for her spunk.

Associated Press, December 17, 2001

A Pompano Beach city commissioner was robbed at gunpoint by a seventeen-year-old-man who took the commissioner's pants.

Associated Press, December 27, 2002

VOTING IRREGULARITIES

Jon Larsen Shudlick turned "hot loins" into a campaign platform.

In 1988, Shudlick, then mayor of Ocean Ridge, a coastal town south of Palm Beach, filed to run for the U.S. Congress. Reporters made their usual background checks and discovered that, two years earlier, he'd pleaded guilty and paid a $55 fine for soliciting a lewd act from an undercover deputy in Orlando for twenty dollars. Shudlick, who'd spent ten years on the Ocean Ridge commission, the last three as mayor, then made the mistake of opening his mouth.

"I was going down the street. There was a pretty little blonde in shorts. We had a little talk. I asked her to get in the car and I was apprehended," Shudlick said.

"I did it," he said. "I'm not crying about it. I had hot loins and there was a little blonde on the corner. Unfortunately, I fell for it. Stick a blonde out in front of me and, hey, that's my soft spot."

Shudlick admitted he had paid a lawyer $500 to have the court record purged. He said the crime did not reflect on his character and should not affect how voters feel about him.

In the race, Shudlick campaigned as an "Americanist" and said he opposed sanctions against South Africa for its racist *apartheid* policy.

Congressional candidate Jon Larsen Shudlick was arrested for soliciting a prostitute.

After he was defeated in the August Republican primary, the Ocean Ridge Town Commission voted to urge his resignation, saying he embarrassed the town by his description of his sex encounter. Shudlick, who had planned to resign when his term ended in January anyway, refused.

When he had run for office in 1986, he had complained that the local press ignored his campaign. This time around, his complaint was the opposite. He attacked the local newspaper for running the "hot loins" story, saying, "I was picked not because of the transgression—it was relatively minor, a misdemeanor—but because I am a spokesman for the conservative ideology. It's a tragedy that with all the problems today the focus has to be on a two-year-old incident of me being involved with a pretty blonde."

A year later, Shudlick, recently divorced, put a personal ad in the same paper for "A woman who can clean, cook fish, dig worms, sew and who owns a good fishing boat and motor. Please enclose photo of boat and motor."

"I was never shy for publicity," he said.

And in 1990, when he ran unsuccessfully for a state House of Representatives seat, he welcomed the endorsement of the Independent Populist party, a minor party with a "pro white" platform and links to the Ku Klux Klan.

"I am white, and I think basically the white people have been taking it on the chin as far as affirmative action and quota systems, which are the most grotesque form of racism," Shudlick said. "It's a very patriotic and God-fearing group of people, and their heart is in the right place."

Shudlick didn't exactly crawl back into the shadows. In January 1993, he and ex-wife Pamela went on the national Oprah Winfrey show to debate their alimony. Shudlick said he could not afford the $660 a week in alimony and child support; she disagreed. Shudlick had been jailed five times for not making payments. The gregarious Oprah was rendered speechless while the former couple argued over the value of one of their properties,

Shudlick eventually moved to the Gulf Coast. In 2004, he sought a congressional seat being vacated by retiring U.S. Representative Porter Goss, who was later named chief of the CIA.

But he ruffled Republican feathers when, at a speech, he said things had gone downhill in the country since Ronald Reagan was president and criticized the Patriot Act as an attack on the Constitution and the Iraq War as having been started under false pretenses. He also said the September 11 terrorist attacks were "the largest hoax the world has ever seen," arguing Osama bin Laden could not have possibly pulled it off and that only two countries benefited from it: Israel and the United States.

He eventually ran for a spot on the North Fort Myers Fire Board. He was defeated by a margin of almost three to one.

Palm Beach *Post,* August 12, August 18, 1988;
August 9, 1989; July 22, 1990;
South Florida Sun-Sentinel, January 5, 1993;
Fort Myers *News-Press,* February 14, November 3, 2004

The Bilirakis political family, out of the Tampa Bay area, seems to draw unusual opponents.

When Gus Bilirakis ran for State Representative in 2000, his Democratic opponent alleged he was actually dead and his father, U.S. Representative Mike Bilirakis, had hired an imposter. Candidate Diane Ellis, who described herself as a self-employed legal assistant, said a private investigator had told her the real Gus Bilirakis died three years earlier and her opponent was a man named Danny Divito—apparently no relation to comedic actor Danny DeVito. The head of the local Democratic Party said the woman "is not going to win any intelligence contests. This does not give me confidence in her candidacy." Bilirakis won by a three-to-one margin.

When Chuck Kalogianis ran for State Representative, he admitted he was once a male stripper. (Pinellas County Democratic Party)

U.S. Rep. Mike Bilirakis' (U.S. House of Representatives)

Two years later, Mike Bilirakis ran for reelection against Chuck Kalogianis. The 39-year-old attorney acknowledged his two-year stint as a stripper a decade earlier when he was a struggling Boston law student. In his act, he said he had worn a Big Bird suit that masked his face but exposed his legs. It ended with him doing a chicken dance, tearing off the costume to reveal a French bikini thong. Kalogianis insisted his act was tasteful and didn't go "the full Monty." Mike Bilirakis was reelected by more than a three-to-one margin.

St. Petersburg *Times*, October 2, 1998, November 8, 2000; February 16, 2001; November 6, 2002

Radio "shock jock" Bubba "the Love Sponge" Clem, fired by radio giant Clear Channel Communications in a crackdown on raunchy radio following the 2004 Janet Jackson Super Bowl debacle, filed as the lone Democrat to challenge two Republicans for sheriff of St. Petersburg's Pinellas County. His sexually explicit show, which aired in four Florida markets, prompted a $755,000 fine

Radio job Bubba the Love Sponge Clem ran for Pinellas County Sheriff. (thehotfm.net)

from the Federal Communications Commission. His name appeared on the ballot as "Bubba Clem." Bubba didn't win.

Associated Press/Palm Beach *Post*, July 18, 2004;
St. Petersburg *Times*, November 3, 2004

As Broward County elections officials wrapped up after a long day of canvassing votes in the 2004 election, something unusual caught their eye. Tallies should go up as more votes are counted. That's simple math. But in some races, the numbers had gone down. Officials found that, because of a glitch in computer logic, the software used in Broward can handle only 32,000 votes per precinct. After that, the system starts counting backward. But bad numbers showed up only in running tallies through the day, not the final one. Final tallies were reached by cross-checking machine totals, and officials were confident they were accurate.

Palm Beach *Post*, November 5, 2004

Just before the 2004 presidential election, a pro-Bush Marine recruit in Lake Worth allegedly beat and threatened his girlfriend, a Kerry supporter. Police had to zap the man with a Taser to get him to release the girlfriend. He later was sentenced to 90 days in jail and had to apologize.

Palm Beach *Post*, November 2, 2004; April 1, 2005

A Democrat walking by the Alachua County Republican headquarters stopped in and punched a cardboard cutout of President Bush. When the county GOP chairman angrily followed him out, the man punched him too and was arrested.

Associated Press, January 1, 2005

The mayor of South Miami lost his re-election bid by 130 votes after being arrested the night before and charged with accepting illegal campaign contributions. He was later found innocent.

Associated Press, January 1, 2005

In Groveland, a city council race was decided by a coin flip after two candidates each received 689 votes.

Associated Press, January 1, 2005

In Broward County, a candidate for the state House and his campaign manager surrendered to a SWAT team after barricading themselves in an apartment a week after losing the election. The candidate had run on an anti-gay platform, telling *The Daily Show with Jon Stewart* that "the gays have made it difficult for me to shoot pool in Fort Lauderdale."

Associated Press, January 1, 2005

When Volusia County Sheriff Bob Vogel, investigated for alleged racial profiling of motorists, was up for reelection in 2000, his parents donated money to his opponent, saying it was time for a change. Vogel eventually chose not to seek a new term.

Associated Press/Palm Beach *Post*, January 29, 2000;
Orlando *Sentinel*, May 3, 2001

Maude Ford Lee, chair of the Palm Beach County Commission, called a Saturday news conference to say she would not seek the endorsement of the Palm Beach *Post*, accusing the newspaper of unbalanced reporting for a decade. Only one news outlet sent a reporter — the Palm Beach *Post*.

Palm Beach *Post*, August 13, 2000

A candidate for Baker County sheriff went missing after complaining he was being harassed by the sheriff's office. Julian Pendleton, 35, was last seen heading for a candidate's forum. Incumbent Joey Dobson had alleged Pendleton spread sugar to draw ants and disrupt a Dobson rally and circulated fliers alleging Dobson impregnated a 19-year-old. Investigators said they did not suspect foul play in Pendleton's disappearance. He later resurfaced but lost to Dobson by a landslide.

Associated Press/Palm Beach *Post*, August 23, 2000;
Florida Times-Union, November 8, 2000

SECTION TWO
CHAPTER
28

TOURIST SEASON

Miami International Airport managers banned sales of the June 1999 issue of *Cigar Aficionado* magazine at its 18 privately run concession stands after airport managers decided the edition flattered Fidel Castro, encouraged people to visit Cuba, and urged an end to a decades-long embargo of the Communist island nation. After the American Civil Liberties Union threatened to sue the airport, Miami-Dade County Mayor Alex Penelas ordered airport officials to lift their ban. Later, the fiercely anti-Castro Cuban American National Foundation bought a $26,000 full-page ad in the magazine's October 1999 edition, titled, "Lift the smoke screen, not the embargo." It complained the magazine romanticized Cuba.

Miami *Herald*, July 14, 1999

One of the major draws at the 2005 South Florida Fair was a walk-through colon. The 22-foot-long, eight-foot-high, inflatable, walk-through colon was displayed at a building completely devoted to different types of cancer. It included authentic-looking, but larger-than-life, polyps and interior sections of healthy and diseased tissue. Organizers expected some 30,000 people a day to pass through. The arrival of the colon was delayed when it sprang a leak.

Palm Beach *Post*, January 12, 2005

Protestors at Walt Disney world staged a "toad in" to protest replacing Mr. Toad's Wild Ride with a Winnie the Pooh ride.

Associated Press, June 19, 1999

A Pennsylvania man bobbed in the ocean for nearly two hours after a dive boat mistakenly left him four miles out at sea. The boat captain said she forgot the passenger count. A passing yacht eventually picked up the diver.

Palm Beach *Post*, December 31, 1992

A model sued a Tampa theme park for forcing her to get on a roller coaster she couldn't get off. The woman appeared at Busch Gardens to play the role of wife and mother in a promotional film. She claimed that after one trip on the "Scorpion" roller coaster, she began complaining of neck pain and a headache, but the park officials threatened to withhold her $1,000 fee and blackball her and, in fact, made her ride another attraction called "The Python."

Palm Beach *Post*, December 18, 1994

When Donald Trump built a golf course, he said, in his magazine, that it was in "Palm Beach, Florida." That's where his *Mar-a-Lago* mansion is, but the course is across the waterway on the mainland in West Palm Beach, within jet wash distance of Palm Beach International Airport. It's also across the street from the Palm Beach County jail, which Trump officials reportedly described as a courthouse.

A New York man playing Trump's course killed one of four black swans given to the millionaire developer by a friend. The golfer told investigators he killed the bird with a titanium driver after it attacked him and two children on the 17th hole. Trump later said the man was not welcome on any of his properties, including his Atlantic City casino.

Donald Trump built a golf course near the Palm Beach County Jail. (Trump Enterprises)

Palm Beach *Post*, January 10, January 14, 2001

A Long Island couple sued a Clermont motel, claiming they felt someone was watching them through a peephole in their room.

Orlando *Sentinel*, October 19, 1993

Three straight couples said they were turned away from a Key West hotel because they weren't gay. The six were vacationing with a gay couple and had reservations at the hotel, but the manager said no.

Chicago *Tribune*, April 17, 2004

The Saks Fifth Avenue department store chain sued a Saudi prince who charged more than three million dollars to his charge account at a South Florida Saks store in a year. The suit said crown prince Abdulla Bin Faisal, heir to the Saudi throne, had an outstanding balance of $720,673 for purchases between 1997 and 1999. Documents showed he charged $1.5 million in a single day, May 2, 1998. Lawyers later dropped the charges because they could never serve papers on the prince.

Palm Beach *Post*, May 24, 2000;
interview with attorney Scott Chapman, December 16, 2004

BE TRUE TO YOUR SCHOOL

A teacher was charged with clandestinely renting out Lake Worth High School's swimming pool and pocketing the $60,000 he collected for lessons. The school district later said it knew he had a criminal record when it hired him. The man had seven convictions for falsifying bank checks, two counts of theft by deception and two counts of going AWOL from the Army.

Investigators said the man established a club called Trojan Aquatics and, for two years, collected money for pool use or lessons. He allegedly told parents the money was going to the school but directed then to make checks out to him or Trojan Athletics. He was caught only after he transferred to another school and the principal of a nearby elementary school called Lake Worth High about renting the pool for a second year.

Palm Beach *Post*, December 16, 2004

The yearbook staff at Lake Region High School in Eagle Lake thought it would be cute to have the cover show their school's initials turned into an imaginary web page: www.LR2000.com. But it was a real web page—for a French adult web site. Staffers said they'd checked for the web page the previous spring and come up with nothing. The yearbooks sold out for the first time in the Polk County school's five-year history. Principal Stephen White said, "It was all a horrible coincidence. This is a principal's nightmare."

Associated Press, August 31, 2000

Palm Beach County School District secretary Dianne Auster was charged with running a prostitution ring out of the district's headquarters. Auster was charged with running her Mardi Gras Models escort service from her desk. She pleaded guilty to a misdemeanor and received six months probation.

Palm Beach *Post*, March 1, 2000

Police say a Lakeland seventh-grader attacked a teacher who tried to take away his *Pokémon* trading cards in class. The twelve-year-old reportedly pushed and choked his Sleepy Hill Middle School teacher after he caught the boy violating a ban on the popular cartoon characters.

Associated Press/Palm Beach *Post,* November 13, 1999.

Soon after the deadly Columbine High School shootings in Colorado, a teacher at Palm Harbor High School in Brevard County lectured his students on how to create a pipe bomb and where to place it to hurt the most people. And two Ocala teachers were suspended after one pretended to shoot the other with a toy gun "to lessen the tension" after the shootings.

Associated Press/Miami *Herald,* December 19, 1999

A Panama City teacher seized a fourth-grader's magazine, calling it "pornography" and ripping it to pieces. It was a *National Geographic,* open to an article on evolution that included drawings of naked humans.

Associated Press/Miami *Herald,* December 19, 1999

A gay high school senior in Pierson, near Daytona Beach, was allowed to attend his prom in a red floor-length evening gown.

Associated Press/Miami *Herald,* December 19, 1999

A gay teenager at a Tampa school tried, and failed, to run for homecoming queen.

Associated Press/Miami *Herald,* December 19, 1999

A 12-year-old Inverness boy was arrested after stomping his foot in a puddle, spraying classmates and a school resource officer.

Associated Press, December 19, 1999

A 12-year-old Pensacola middle school student had to serve a three-day suspension because she came to school with a small diamond stud in her nose. The principal said it was distracting.

Associated Press/*South Florida Sun-Sentinel,* March 28, 2004

An arbitrator ruled that a Pensacola middle school teacher was wrongly fired for showing up at work in a cocaine-distracted state later measured at fifty times the level to prompt a "positive" reading. The arbitrator said the school's "zero tolerance" drug policy applied only to students.

Associated Press/Miami *Herald,* August 11, 2002

A man who wore fingernail polish and his mother's scarves to work was ordered to seek psychiatric help and barred from working with children. The man's occupation: psychologist at a Punta Gorda school. He later filed a discrimination complaint, saying if female employees were permitted to dress this way, so should he.

St. Petersburg *Times*, March 12, 2001

A Sarasota elementary school teacher ate a sandwich of ten earthworms rolled in cornmeal, deep fried to a golden brown, and loaded onto a hoagie bun with mustard, ketchup, hot peppers, hot sauce and a "secret worm sauce." Teacher Tom Desjardins said the concoction "tasted a little like dirt and cow manure." His feast was the payoff of a challenge to his fourth-grade class to read 230 books.

Houston *Chronicle*, December 26, 1993

SECTION THREE
CHAPTER
30

OH, THOSE KIDS!

Nathaniel Brazill, a 13-year student at a Lake Worth middle school who'd been sent home early on the last day of school for his part in a water balloon fight, returned to the school later with a gun he'd retrieved from the dresser of a family friend. When Barry Grunow, a popular English teacher at the school, refused to let him say goodbye to two girls in his classroom, he pointed the gun. Grunow said, "Don't point that thing at me." Brazill fired, striking Grunow in the face. Brazill was later convicted and sentenced to 28 years in prison.

Nathaniel Brazill fatally shot his schoolteacher. (Florida Department of Corrections)

Palm Beach *Post*, May 27, 2000

Lionel Tate was the youngest person ever sentenced to life in prison without parole. (Florida Department of Corrections)

Lionel Tate became the youngest person ever sentenced to life in prison without the possibility of parole. He was fourteen when he was convicted of first-degree murder in the death of six-year-old playmate Tiffany Eunick. Tate said he was just emulating wrestling moves he saw on television when he body-slammed, stomped and kicked the girl at her home in Pembroke Pines, near Fort Lauderdale. The life sentence was mandatory under tough Florida criminal laws.

Tate's case stirred national debate over the state's aggressive prosecution of juveniles as adults. After an appeals court overturned his conviction, ruling the teen deserved a new trial because his competency to stand trial wasn't measured, Tate agreed in January 2004 to plead guilty to second-degree murder and was sentenced to time served, allowing him to go free after three years in prison.

Palm Beach *Post*, January 30, 2004

A fourteen-year-old boy stabbed a classmate to death in the restroom of a Miami-Dade County middle school. Michael Hernandez confessed to stabbing Jaime Gough, whom classmates said was one of his best friends, more than forty times but gave no explanation. According to police, he packed a serrated knife and a latex glove in his book bag before heading off to school.

Hernandez compiled exhaustive lists of violent video games and movies, kept instructions for making Molotov cocktails and explosives, doodled crosses on some pages, and wrote "White Power" under a swastika on ruled school paper, even though he was Hispanic.

A psychology professor later testified Hernandez is a delusional schizophrenic who has no concept of the judicial system or the seriousness of the charges. Documents seized by investigators showed the straight-A student fixated on cults or murder.

South Florida Sun-Sentinel, February 6, March 20, December 9, 2004

A twelve-year-old boy charged with his 57th crime got a second chance when a Lauderdale Lakes church promised to reform him. The church sent "Crime Boy" to a charm academy, where he learned table manners and polite conversation, and set up a fund for him.

The boy's mother was in prison for murder and he didn't know where his father was. He lived with his grandmother, who worked. He was left alone and got into trouble. "He's not a criminal," said Broward Circuit Judge Robert Collins. "This boy is a victim of society."

"Crime Boy" Percy Campbell was arrested nearly 60 times. (Florida Department of Corrections)

The boy eventually went to a camp called the Last Chance Ranch. He stayed there for four years, got out, got into trouble again and went to prison.

Associated Press/Palm Beach Post, April 8, 1993;
South Florida Sun-Sentinel, March 7, 2001

A teenager who painted his face white, dyed his hair black and believed drinking blood would make him live forever abruptly ended his murder trial when he asked for his mother and then pleaded guilty. Roderick Ferrell, 17, admitted bludgeoning his ex-girlfriend's parents in 1996 in Eustis, north of Orlando, as part of a bizarre vampire fantasy, perhaps to avoid the electric chair. "He wants to live," his public defender said. But his mother said, "We live forever." Ferrell was sentenced to life in prison. The girlfriend had told friends she was a demon in past lives. It later turned out she was the granddaughter of a retired lawyer for evangelist Billy Graham.

Palm Beach Post, February 6, 1998;
Orlando *Sentinel*, March 25, 2003

Self-professed vampire Roderick Ferrell killed his girlfriend's mother. (Lake County Sheriff's Office)

Two girls, ages 12 and 13, were charged with plotting to lure three classmates behind a North Lauderdale classroom and murder them with homemade "kill kits" which included batteries and knives. Classmates said the girls were angry over a stolen pager. They packed a clear plastic purse full of batteries to knock their victims unconscious and two "kill kits," plastic pencil boxes containing knives and razor blades, to slash their throats. They also packed latex gloves to make sure they didn't leave fingerprints. The mother of one girl said they never intended to carry out their plot and were just fantasizing.

Miami *Herald*, April 15, 2000

Miami-Dade police who confronted a six-year-old boy in an assistant principal's office, who was out of control and had already cut his face and hand with glass, used a 50,000-volt Taser gun to subdue him. Police say they followed their Taser guidelines, the child wasn't injured by the shock and he might have hurt himself seriously if they hadn't shocked him. But child advocates called it excessive. One retired judge said that if officers were unable to subdue the boy through more traditional means, "he must have been a pretty big kid." Police said the boy, who had a history of behavioral problems, had broken a picture frame and said officers called a supervisor who approved the use of the stun gun.

The day after that story broke, police admitted an officer had used a Taser two weeks after the first incident, on an unarmed, 12-year-old girl who was running away after being caught playing hooky and was probably drunk. The police chief said while he defended the first incident, the second one was wrong and the officer would be disciplined.

Miami *Herald*, November 12, November 13, 2004

Two boys who thought it would be funny to e-mail a death threat to President Clinton on the White House's web site got a visit by U.S. Secret Agents and 10-day suspensions from school. After one had written, "Mr. President, I'm going to kill you," he got ready to delete it. "But before he could do it, his friend hit the 'send' button, and it was gone," Palm Beach Gardens High principal Paul Houlihan said.

Palm Beach *Post*, November 2, 1999

A teenager won a two-dollar bet by pelting two police officers with eggs. He was fined $750, sentenced to twenty-five hours of community service and ordered to write an apology to the officer. The 18-year-old and a six other teens were riding in a convertible when they spotted the officers. The eggs landed on an officer's gun and radio and caused $230 in damage.

Associated Press, June 15, 1999

Police were trying to figure out how a 15-year-old Port Charlotte boy used the Internet to buy a $15,000 car, which he drove through a fence and over a stop sign. The boy had electronically sent a check drawn on an account belong to a state agency that issues child support payments. The Internet check service said the boy sent out an additional $105,000 in checks, but only the car dealer delivered. "If Terrance was such a criminal mastermind," his mother said, "I guarantee you he wouldn't have brought home no car. He would have brought home clothes."

Associated Press/Palm Beach *Post*, September 20, 2000

Two boys were arrested and charged with a felony after allegedly making pencil-and-crayon stick figure drawings showing a ten-year-old classmate being stabbed and hanged. The boys' parents said they should be punished by the school and families, not the legal system.

Associated Press, January 26, 2005

SECTION IV:

ACKNOWLEDGEMENTS

THANKS!

Some portions of *Weird Florida II: In a State of Shock* appeared originally in the Palm Beach *Post*, which has graciously granted permission for their adaptation and republication. *Post* archives have provided many of the photographs.

As always, special thanks go to the management and staff of the *Post*, including Publisher Tom Giuffrida, Executive Editor emeritus Edward Sears, Executive Editor John Bartosek, Managing Editor Bill Rose, Associate Editor Jan Tuckwood, Metro Editor Carolyn DiPaolo, bureau chiefs Price Patton, Gary Kane and Glenn Henderson, fellow reporters who submitted many of the entries and often covered them, and the talented staff of the *Post* library.

And, of course, my wife and sons, who continue to put up with my addiction.

Eliot Kleinberg
Casa Floridiana
Boca Raton, Fla.
January 20056

About Eliot Kleinberg

Eliot Kleinberg, a Florida native, has written seven previous books and contributed to two others, all of them focusing on Florida. He is a member of the Florida, South Florida and Palm Beach County historical societies. He was born in Coral Gables in 1956, was graduated from the Miami-area public schools, and received two degrees from the University of Florida. His career as a radio and television reporter and editor, from 1979 to 1984, included work in Miami and at the Cable News Network. He was a reporter for the Dallas *Morning News* from 1984 until 1987, when he returned to Florida. Since then, he has been a news and features writer for the Palm Beach *Post*. He lives at Casa Floridiana in Boca Raton with his wife and sons, Robert and Henry.

Books by Eliot Kleinberg

Black Cloud: The Deadly Florida Hurricane of 1928 (2003)
Our Century (2000) (key writer)
War in Paradise: Stories About World War II in Florida (1999/2005)
Weird Florida (1998)
Historical Traveler's Guide to Florida (1996)
Florida Fun Facts (1995; 2004)
Pioneers in Paradise: West Palm Beach, the First 100 Years (1994, 2004)
    (with Jan Tuckwood)
Mean Season: Florida's Hurricanes of 2004 (2004) (contributor)
The Great Hurricane and Disaster, 1926 & 1992 (1993) (contributor)

CHAPIN HOUSE BOOKS

The Popular Book Division of
The Florida Historical Society Press

From Ron McFarland, the director of the Creative Writing Program at the University of Idaho, is *Confessions of a Night Librarian and Other Embrassments*—a delightful collection of humorous essays about growing up in a small southern town during the tumultuous 1960s.

ISBN 0-9771079-0-6   Paper, 166 pp $17.95

Southern Cooking: A Man's Domain by Nick Wynne is a humorous trip through the kitchens of the South, featuring proven recipes and containing the author's commentary about Southern society, exquisite cuisine and the social mores of a fast disappearing region. "An unusual cookbook that acknowledges the rightful roles of lard, okra and conversation in Southern cooking," comments author Don David Argo, an Arkansas native. "It ranks right up there with Lewis Grizzard and Justin Wilson!"

ISBN 0-9771079-1-4   Paper, 117 pp $16.95

For individual orders of books, call (321) 690-0099, Extension 211. Shop via the internet at www.floridabooks.net VISA, MasterCard and Discover cards accepted. E-mail orders can be placed at tebeaulib@aol.com

PRESS

A ONE OF A KIND EXPERIENCE!

The Sage of Cross Creek is at it again with *Guardian Angel 911* (ISBN 1-886104-19-0, Paper, 165 pp, $17.95). J. T. Glisson, the rustic raconteur from Cross Creek, provides a captivating look at how growing up in Florida and surviving all that Fate hurls at you just might be the product of having the supernatural help of *Lucille*, a desperately overworked guardian angel!

Guardian Angel 911 is not only an autobiography, it is a guide for "how-not-to-live you life." Told as only J. T. can, this entertaining book is an automatic entry for the category of "Best of Southern Humor."

Guardian Angel 911

A Series of Interconnected True Stories

Author of The Creek

J.T. Glisson

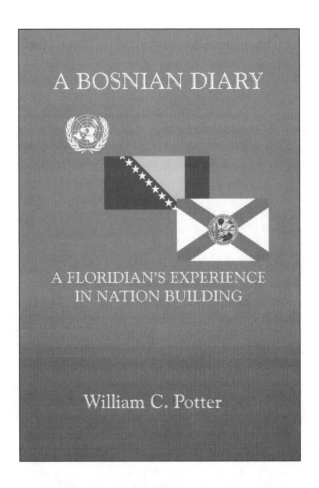

A BOSNIAN DIARY

A FLORIDIAN'S EXPERIENCE
IN NATION BUILDING

William C. Potter

William C. Potter, *A Bosnian Diary: A Floridian's Experience in Nation Building* (ISBN 1-886104-22-0, Paper, 584 pp., $23.95). "Bill" Potter, an attorney, retired Air Force colonel and the legal representative of the United Nations High Representative in Bosnia-Herzegovina from 2002 until 2005, reveals his reactions to the personalities, issues and events in the U-N effort to rebuild war torn Bosnia after the bloody "ethnic cleansing" upheavals of the 1990s. This book contains copies of e-mails that he sent regularly to his friends around the world and which include candid commentary and documentary evidence of the successes and failures of this international effort. This book is a "must have" for any student of international affairs, public administration or urban planning. In addition, this book is simply a "good read" for anyone.